P9-DGU-777

Themes in Old Testament Theology

William Dyrness

InterVarsity Press
Downers Grove
Illinois 60515

aternoster
ress
EXETER U.K.

InterVarsity Press
P.O. Box 1400
Downers Grove, Illinois 60515, U.S.A.

The Paternoster Press, Ltd.
Paternoster House
3 Mount Radford Crescent
Exeter, U.K. EX2 4JWP

InterVarsity Press is the book-publishing division of InterVarsity Christian Fellowship, a student movement active on campus at hundreds of universities, colleges and schools of nursing. For information about local and regional activities, write Public Relations Dept., InterVarsity Christian Fellowship, 6400 Schroeder Rd., P.O. Box 7895, Madison, WI 53707-7895.

Distributed in Canada through InterVarsity Press, 860 Denison St., Unit 3, Markham, Ontario L3R 4H1, Canada.

ISBN 0-87784-726-6
Library of Congress Catalog Card Number: 79-2380

Printed in the United States of America

20	19	18	17	16	15	14	13	12	11	10	9	8	7
99	98	97	96	95	94	93	92	91	90	89	88	87	

To my parents
Enock and Grace Dyrness
"In the house of the righteous
there is much treasure." Proverbs 15:6

1 The Self-Revelation of God   *25*
Self-Revelation: Basis of OT Revelation   *25*
Major Instances of God's Self-Revelation   *27*
   1. Genesis 12   *27*
   2. Genesis 15 and 17   *27*
   3. Genesis 28:13   *28*
   4. Exodus 3   *30*
   5. Exodus 6:1-2   *32*
   6. Exodus 19:3 and 20:1-2   *33*
   7. Exodus 33:18-23   *34*
   8. Exodus 34:5-10   *35*
   9. Further Self-Revelations   *35*
Summary   *36*

2 The Nature of God   *41*
Media of Revelation   *41*
   1. The Angel of the Lord   *41*
   2. The Face of God   *42*
   3. The Glory of God   *42*
   4. Anthropomorphisms   *43*
The Nature of God   *44*
   1. God Is Personal   *45*
     a. El   *45*
     b. Jahweh   *46*
     c. Lord Sabaoth   *46*
     d. *Melek* (King)   *47*
   2. God Is Spirit   *47*
   3. God Is One: Monotheism   *48*
The Character and Activity of God   *49*
   1. The Power of God   *50*
   2. The Holiness of God   *51*
   3. The Righteousness of God   *53*
   4. The Mercy and Love of God   *57*

3 Creation and Providence   *63*
Creation   *63*
   1. By Word and Work   *65*
   2. Ex Nihilo   *65*
   3. Note on the Two Accounts of Creation   *66*
   4. Summary: The Character of Creation   *67*
Myth and History in the OT   *68*
Providence: God's Continuing Relationship to Creation   *73*
   1. Completion of Creation   *73*
   2. Continuing Care   *74*
   3. Levels of God's Care   *75*

4 Man and Woman   *79*
The Creation of Man and Woman   *79*

   1. A Special Relationship to Creation   *79*
   2. The Special Relationship among Persons   *81*
   3. A Special Relationship to God   *83*
The Nature of Humankind   *84*
   1. Soul *(nep̄eš)*   *85*
   2. Spirit *(rûah)*   *86*
   3. Flesh *(bāśār)*   *87*
   4. Heart *(lēḇ)*   *89*
   5. Blood *(dām)*   *91*
   6. Members of the Body   *92*
Summary   *94*

---

5 Sin   *99*
The Origin of Sin: The Fall   *99*
   1. The Boundary of Fellowship   *99*
   2. The Breaking of Fellowship   *101*
   3. The Protection of Fellowship   *102*
The Vocabulary and Definition of Sin   *105*
   1. Deviation   *105*
   2. Guilt   *106*
   3. Rebellion   *106*
The Character of Sin in the OT   *107*
   1. Its Theological Character   *107*
   2. Its Objective Character   *108*
   3. Its Personal and Conscious Character   *108*
   4. Its Universal Character   *109*
   5. Its Fixed Character   *109*
The Results of Sin   *110*
   1. Guilt   *110*
   2. Punishment   *110*

---

6 The Covenant   *113*
Background of the Covenant Idea   *113*
Development of the OT Covenant   *116*
   1. The Covenant with Noah   *116*
   2. The Covenant with Abraham   *117*
   3. The Mosaic Covenant   *118*
   4. The Covenant with David   *120*
Theological Implications of the Covenant   *124*

---

7 The Law   *129*
Background and Development of the Concept   *129*
   1. Development of the Law   *130*
   2. Some Basic Legal Sections   *131*
   3. OT Law and the Law of Neighboring Peoples   *133*
The Law in the Community   *135*
   1. Priority of the Covenant   *135*
   2. The Law in the Prophets   *136*

  3. Postexilic Developments   *136*
The Character of the Law   *138*
  1. Comprehensive Scope   *138*
  2. Personal Appeal   *139*
  3. Unconditional Force   *139*
  4. Universal Application   *140*

---

8 Worship   *143*
The Need for Form   *143*
  1. Form and Worship   *143*
  2. The Place of the Cult in OT Religion   *145*
Sacred Places   *146*
Sacred Times   *148*
  1. The Feast of Unleavened Bread   *148*
  2. The Feast of Weeks   *149*
  3. The Feast of Booths   *150*
  4. The Day of Atonement   *150*
  5. The Sabbath   *150*
  6. A Covenant Renewal Ceremony   *151*
Sacred Actions   *151*
  1. Purification Rites   *152*
  2. Sacrificial Worship   *153*
    a. The burnt offering *('olâh)*   *154*
    b. The meal or meat offering *(minhâh)*   *155*
    c. The peace offering *(zebah* or *šelāmîm)*   *155*
    d. The guilt or sin offering *('āšām* or *hattā't)*   *155*
The Theology of the Cult   *156*

---

9 Piety   *161*
Theological Character of Piety   *161*
  1. The Fear of the Lord   *161*
  2. Faith in God   *162*
  3. Love for God   *163*
Characteristic Expressions of Piety   *164*
  1. Praise to God   *164*
  2. Prayer   *165*
  3. Glorifying God   *167*

---

10 Ethics   *171*
The Basis of OT Ethics   *171*
  1. The Character of God   *172*
  2. Creation in the Image of God   *173*
Development of the Principles of OT Ethics   *175*
  1. Instructions and Ordinances Associated with Creation   *175*
  2. Institutions and Instructions for God's Covenant People   *176*
    a. The Ten Commandments   *177*
    b. Problem areas   *180*
The Teaching of the Prophets   *184*

11 Wisdom   *189*
The Development of the Idea of Wisdom   *189*
  1. The Wisdom Idea   *189*
  2. On Learning to Be Wise   *192*
The Theological Character of Wisdom   *193*
  1. Wisdom Comes from God   *193*
  2. Religion for the Common Man   *194*
  3. The Two Paths: Wisdom and Folly   *195*
The Future of Wisdom   *198*
  1. The Limitation of Wisdom   *198*
  2. The Promise of Wisdom   *198*

12 The Spirit of God   *201*
Vocabulary and Basic Meaning   *201*
Theological Development   *203*
  1. Early Period   *203*
  2. Judges and the Monarchy   *204*
  3. The Prophetic Period   *205*
    a. Ethical import of the Spirit   *206*
    b. Personal presence of the Spirit   *207*
    c. The universal work of the Spirit   *208*

13 Prophecy   *211*
The Origin of OT Prophecy   *211*
  1. Moses as the First Prophet   *212*
  2. The Prophetic Tradition   *214*
  3. The Monarchy   *216*
The Classical Prophets   *217*
  1. Their Character   *217*
  2. Their Message and Philosophy of History   *219*

14 The Hope of Israel   *227*
The Vision of the Kingdom   *227*
  1. The Prophetic Picture of God's Final Kingdom   *230*
    a. Based absolutely on God's decision   *230*
    b. A new creation   *230*
    c. A mediator   *231*
    d. The goal of God's redemptive work   *234*
  2. The Idea of Judgment   *235*
Death and the Afterlife   *237*
  1. Death and Sheol   *237*
  2. The Resurrection of the Body and the Hope of
  Eternal Life   *239*
    a. Theological foundation   *240*
    b. Ethical foundation   *241*
    c. Historical/eschatological foundation   *241*
Basic Bibliography for Old Testament Theology   *243*
Scripture Index

Preface

The impetus for writing this book came from the experience of teaching Old Testament theology at the Asian Theological Seminary in Manila. As I taught I became aware, on the one hand, of the immediate relevance of this material for my Asian students, and, on the other hand, the lack of an adequate, recent theological survey to put in their hands. This little book is more an acknowledgment of that gap than an attempt to fill it.

My own primary teaching area is systematic theology, and it was only the faculty limitations at our seminary and my own curiosity that made this extended excursion into the Old Testament possible. Clearly my own theological reflection has been profoundly affected and my whole approach to theology altered. It occurs to me that all theologians ought to serve an apprenticeship in the Old Testament. Still a lack of expertise will no doubt be evident in the pages that follow. Despite every effort to remain true to the data of the text, I have at times fallen into the trap of "systematization." No doubt difficulties have been passed over and important questions neglected.

But without significant assistance the results would have been even more meagre than they are, and I should like here to record these debts. Three former teachers in Old Testament will recognize their influence at various points: Professors Ludwig Dewitz, F. W. Bush and Walter Kaiser, Jr. (who also read the manuscript and made helpful suggestions). Beyond this Professor Robert Hubbard, Jr., of Denver Seminary read the manuscript and made several suggestions, and Professor Douglas Stuart of Gordon-Conwell Seminary was generous with his time and wisdom. It is from the pen of these scholars that we look for more substantial contributions in this field. Finally, I would like to thank Mr. James Hoover of Inter-Varsity Press for his warm encouragement and friendly prodding.

The Old Testament and the Third World—it is not by accident that these together should furnish the occasion for this book. The result is sent forth with the confidence that as more is heard from the vital and growing Third World churches we will all understand more of God's marvelous revelation of himself, especially that part we call the Old Testament.

Manila, Philippines
June 1979

Abbreviations

ANET	*Ancient Near Eastern Texts*
DOTT	*Documents from Old Testament Times*
IDB	*Interpreter's Dictionary of the Bible*
LXX	*Septuagint*
NBD	*The New Bible Dictionary*
NT	New Testament
OT	Old Testament
TDNT	*Theological Dictionary of the New Testament*

Introduction

A book about the Old Testament (OT) would not be an obvious candidate for a best seller today. Even among those who eagerly study the Bible and continue to make Scripture the runaway best seller of all time, conferences on the OT do not turn people away. The reason for this is not hard to find. All too often Christians spend most of their study time in the New Testament (NT), only occasionally making forays into the Psalms and Proverbs, or now and then into the Prophets. The result is that many Christians fail to understand the whole scope of God's revelation of himself—they have an incomplete picture of God's purposes. Indeed in many languages of the world there is not even an OT translation. It is understandable, of course, why the NT is the first part of the Scripture translated when funds and manpower are limited, but when missionaries and pastors base their entire instruction on the NT they cannot give the Word of God its full power. This is particularly serious in evangelistic situations where there is often a natural bridge between the OT and the common people, especially those of non-Western cultures. The OT is set in the home and marketplace and communicates God's love and mercy in concrete terms. The truth is, the NT simply cannot stand by itself.

Illustrations of this are not hard to uncover in missionary literature. In China, for example, missionaries in the early days often used only the NT for their preaching. In discussing the weakness of missions in China, Arthur Glasser notes:

> The real flaw in the missionary movement was its inadequate use of the word of God. It took seriously only part of the Bible, the New Testament and the Psalms. . . . The Bible not only contains the Evangelistic mandate of the New Testament it also contains God's call to the cultural task: a stream of obligation that courses throughout both Old Testament and New Testament. Whereas the New Testament focuses largely on the individual before God, the Old Testament stresses his corporate relationship (family, community and state). At Sinai, God gave his people a style of life that was both egalitarian and humane. . . . In short the Old Testament teaches a way of life in which the rights of man are safeguarded. (*New Forces in Missions,* ed. David Cho, Seoul, 1976, pp. 194-95)

This book then is written with the intention of opening up the OT for the Christian. Properly speaking this is a book of OT theology, and it is important that we understand what this means. All good theology is biblical to a greater or lesser extent, but biblical theology is that special discipline that seeks to study biblical themes on their own terms. In distinction from systematic theology, which seeks to understand the interrelationship of biblical themes and their historical and philosophical implications, biblical theology studies the leitmotivs of Scripture as they develop in the course of God's dealings with people in the biblical period. It is historical and progressive. It centers on God's saving self-revelation as it takes the shape of certain events in which God calls to himself a people who will reflect his character and further his loving purposes. It sees these developments against the background of a world which God created as a vehicle of his purposes and values. Finally, it sees how God refuses to abandon his purposes despite the unfaithfulness of his own people and works even in their unbelief to create a people more perfectly and completely his own.

If we can hold these ideas in mind and read the NT (and all of history for that matter) in the light of them, we are making an important start in thinking theologically—dare we say, in the way that God himself has thought about the world. What is certain is that these central ideas find their characteristic expression in the OT.

It is perfectly true, however, that we read the OT in light of the appearing of Jesus Christ and the NT elaboration of his work. In other words we read the OT as Christians, and we must ask ourselves what this means. What is the relationship between the two testaments for the Christian? Some, especially those in the Lutheran tradition, have stressed the distinction between the OT and NT and the general superiority of the NT. The law of the OT has been superseded by the gospel of the NT. I prefer to see both OT and NT as equally Christian.

This is not to deny the differences between the two testaments. God's purposes are seen with a greater clarity in the NT. The covenant is sealed once and for all with Christ's death rather than many times as in the OT sacrifices. The OT deals primarily with the nation of Israel while the NT displays a greater concern for the whole world. But the similarities between the two testaments are more important than these differences. The two testaments together record the one history of God's progressive dealings with humankind. The work of Christ is a culmination rather than a denial of OT truth. Though the NT presents something new, it is not altogether new. There is an important continuity that links the two testaments together, both in the manner and substance of God's revelation and in the way people respond to that revelation. As John Calvin put it: "I freely admit the differences in Scripture . . . but in such a way as not to detract from its established unity. . . . All these pertain to the manner of dispensation rather than to the substance" (*Institutes,* II, 11, 1).

An approach to the study of Scripture that has proved fruitful in illustrating this overall unity is typology, or the study of correspondences between elements of the two testaments. While this has often been subject to abuse and has led to the fanciful interpretation of details, understood properly it helps underline the consistent, historical development of God's revelation. A type is "a biblical event, person or institution which serves as an example or pattern for other events, persons or institutions" and is based on the consistency of God's character and activity (Baker 1977, 267). That is, the OT event or object, while retaining its full import in the whole biblical context, finds its meaning enlarged through the appearing of the NT correspondence (and fulfillment), in what we might call its NT context. This line of thinking lies behind much of the discussion in this book when reference is made to the NT.

One way of clarifying this relationship between the testaments is to liken the Bible to a symphony. All the basic themes of the symphony are presented in the OT and can be seen and enjoyed on their own terms. All the reality of God's self-revelation in creation and redemption comes to expression in these themes. There is a real movement of God toward humankind and a real fellowship between them—not just the promise of such movement and fellowship. The NT then takes these themes, develops them and, while adding melody lines of its own, transposes the whole into a higher key, weaving everything together in a rich and beautiful way. What was a simple melody line in the OT—say, for example, the discouragement and provision of the wilderness wanderings—is picked up in another setting and made to enhance the NT revelation—as in Paul's warnings and encouragement to the Corinthian Church (1 Cor. 10). If we do not listen carefully to the OT we may miss some of the most moving melodies of the NT. So rather than seeing the OT as temporary or partial—something to be outgrown and discarded—we see its incompleteness more as chords calling for resolution, or, to change the metaphor, as plots calling for dénouement. What the NT gives us then does not leave the OT behind so much as bring out its deepest reality. One has the feeling that in going ever more deeply into the reality of the OT one comes to the truth of the NT. The NT and OT call for each other for their full self-expression. For a more complete discussion of the relationship between the testaments see D. L. Baker, *Two Testaments: One Bible,* listed in the bibliography.

This may help us answer the perennial question: what is the central element of the OT? We can answer this question with another question: where does one find the central point of a symphony or a play? Of course there are central themes, but no single point can be taken as the center, unless it be the unity of the whole. So the themes that we will discuss are all overlapping and interrelated. The nature of God leads him to relate himself to men and women in the covenant; the law fills out the covenant; the cult (formal worship) and piety grow together out of the covenant relationship that is defined in the law; all of this expresses itself in the moral life of the community (ethics and wisdom), which leads in the prophets to a vision of the final covenant which Christ will seal with his death. Perhaps the unity of the whole is best expressed as God's creative-redemptive self-revelation, or in simpler words, his bending down to be a father to his people.

I have chosen to develop all of this in a topical way. This risks misconceptions. Any form of division of the material must be somewhat arbitrary and may suggest separation where there is none. So it must be remembered that the ideas and institutions discussed in individual chapters are organically related and underwent historical development in the life of Israel. God's revelation has a progressive and cumulative character. This is the reason that some scholars (such as Gerhard von Rad) prefer a historical approach to the OT. But if one bears in mind the historical character of revelation, the

topical method helps us understand the coherence of God's
program. The historical background, incidentally, can best be
kept in mind by consulting standard OT histories, such as
that of John Bright or Leon Wood, listed in the bibliography.

In most chapters the method has been the same. Beginning
with a brief statement of the material, I have described
briefly the development that took place in the OT (where
possible in its Near Eastern setting) and closed with a summary of the theological principles that are present. In some
cases—notably the discussion of man and woman and of sin—
I have made extensive use of word and concept studies to
complement the other approach. It should be recognized that
no single method can lay claim to more than a partial perspective and that where possible different methods should
be employed together.

The use of word studies is a common method of Bible study,
and it is fitting to say a word about this approach to OT
studies. Basically there are two kinds of word studies: etymological and semantical. The former gives attention to the root,
origin and development of words; the latter deals with the
meanings of words as they are used in their contexts. Although etymological studies have traditionally been more
widely used by Bible students, it has recently been recognized that the context of a word is more important than its
origin (which may in fact be quite forgotten). In NT Greek,
therefore, scholars tend now to give more attention to the OT
(or Aramaic) backgrounds of the Greek words than to their
etymological history in classical Greek (though this should
not be ignored). The best solution, of course, is both to understand something of the origin of the word (and perhaps its
meaning in cognate or related languages) and to note carefully how the word is used in its biblical contexts. In these
studies I will make use of both emphases. In the chapter on
God and man and woman I make more reference to etymological similarities, while in the chapter on sin I devote more
attention to semantic relationships which bear no etymological relation. Interested students may consult James Barr,

The Semantics of Biblical Language, listed in the bibliography, for a complete discussion of these things.

The intrinsic excitement of the OT has been underlined in recent years by the wealth of scholarship made available through research in comparative religion, history and archaeology. Several OT theologies have been written which make use of these materials. I have sought to make use of this material within the limits of my purpose and capabilities. Part of this purpose is defined by the fact that this book is written from an evangelical perspective, that is, one that accepts the entire Bible as the Word of God. While not all of the sources I have used reflect this point of view—and they may not be happy with some of the use I have made of their conclusions—they all have much to teach us about the OT. When the biblical text is allowed to be the final court of appeal, the Bible student need not shrink from learning from the wealth of available contemporary critical scholarship. (R. K. Harrison's *Introduction to the OT* is a most useful survey of the critical views and the evangelical response.) I have listed some of the most important of these studies in the bibliography at the end of the book. Because data can be found there, I have limited my references to these books in the text to the author, date (if needed for clarity) and page number.

All biblical quotes are from the Revised Standard Version, except where noted (when *Heb.* appears after a reference, it means the word in question appears in the original Hebrew but not in the English version). I have limited Hebrew transliteration wherever possible, as these are usually unsatisfactory both to the beginning and advanced student. When necessary I have used the following system:

א = ʼ	ד = $\underline{d}$	י = y	ס = s	ר = r
ב = b	ה = h	כ = k	ע = ʻ	שׂ = ś
ב = $\underline{b}$	ו = w	כ = $\underline{k}$	פ = p	שׁ = š
ג = g	ז = z	ל = l	פ = p̄	ת = t
ג = ḡ	ח = ḥ	מ = m	צ = ṣ	ת = $\underline{t}$
ד = d	ט = ṭ	נ = n	ק = q	

Long Vowels		Short Vowels	Very Short Vowels
(ה)ָ = â (h)	ָ = ā	ַ = a	ֲ = ^{a}
◌ֵי = ê	◌ֶ = ē	◌ֶ = e	◌ֱ = ^{e}
◌ִי = î		◌ִ = i	◌ְ = ^{e} (*if vocal*)
וֹ = ô	◌ֹ = ō	◌ָ = o	◌ֳ = ^{o}
וּ = û		◌ֻ = u	

It goes without saying that this book has as its primary goal getting the student into the OT. For this reason I have put Scripture references in almost every paragraph. These are not to support what I say; they are rather the source of my observations. And they are intended to be read and pondered. If some who read this begin to see the OT as the exciting and moving document that it is, if it can lead us all to deepen our faith and strengthen our praise, this book will have achieved its purpose.

All men have the general knowledge, namely, that God is, that He has created heaven and earth, that He is just, that He punishes the wicked, etc. But what God thinks of us, what He wants to give and to do to deliver us from sin and death and to save us–which is the particular and the true knowledge of God–this men do not know. Thus it can happen that someone's face may be familiar to me but I do not really know him, because I do not know what he has in his mind. So it is that men know naturally that there is a God, but they do not know what he wants and what he does not want.

Martin Luther, *Epistle to Galatians*

1

The
Self-Revelation
of God

Self-Revelation: Basis of OT Revelation

The focal point of God's revelation in the OT is surely his self-revelation to his people; the revelation of his person and character precedes and explains the revelation of his purposes. In recent years OT scholars have emphasized God's revelation in his mighty works, no doubt giving us a deeper insight into the actual character of OT revelation. God has not revealed himself by propositions alone, but in and through events which he interprets through his prophets. Recently Wolfhart Pannenberg and his circle have emphasized this historical character of revelation. Rolf Rendtorff writes: "Jahweh (the Hebrew name for God) himself becomes visible in his powerful acts of salvation. He becomes revealed in them" (Pannenberg, 32). Pannenberg avers: "Faithful trust was effected by the evidence of historical facts that brought about salvation and revealed Jahweh's deity and power" (Pannenberg, 126).

All of this is helpful. But it is surely not—as they argue—

because God's self-revelation in Genesis is an inappropriate
vehicle of revelation. Rather it is on the basis of his self-
revelation to the fathers that it was possible for Israel to understand God's mighty acts as revelation. As reference to "my
father's God" (Ex. 15:2) shows, it was in the light of God's past
appearances that the exodus was understood. We must remember as well that revelation in the OT always leads to a
personal relationship between God and his people. If communion is to be possible, we must know the character of God
through his personal self-disclosure. We shall not have a full
understanding of revelation in the OT unless we have an eye
for the many-sided disclosure in word and event. But we will
understand nothing at all if we do not see God's self-revelation as the basic revelation. Let us look at the record to see
why this is so.

In a sense the creation of the world is a manifestation of
the character of God. He shaped it with an intimacy that expressed his concern and pronounced it a worthy expression by
calling it "very good" (Gen. 1:31). Then, as recorded in Genesis 2, God personally gave Adam instructions for living in
the garden. But it was not until the harmony of the original
creation had been broken by disobedience that a fresh self-
revelation of God became necessary. Revelation had from this
point on to take on its special character of restoring this broken relationship. It had to become redemptive.

In Genesis 3:9 God comes to the man with the question:
"Where are you?" Adam had pathetically tried to hide from
the presence of God and had experienced a new sensation,
that of shame, that was surely rooted in his estrangement
from God. From here on men and women must be afraid before
God. They are aware of their nakedness before their maker, a
spiritual state which becomes manifested in their awareness
of physical nakedness. (Later in Israel it was an abomination
to appear naked before the Lord—Ex. 20:26.) God's question
is obviously not a request for information but an attempt to
draw Adam and Eve to himself, to show mercy to them. The
same purpose lies behind the questions to Cain in Genesis

4:6, 9, 10: Why are you cast down? Where is your brother? What have you done? God knows what has been done, and he wishes Cain to acknowledge it and turn back to him. From the beginning God's response to human sin expresses his mercy. His desire is not the death of the sinner but his life.

Major Instances of God's Self-Revelation
1. Genesis 12. The discussion of God's self-revelation properly begins with Genesis 12 where God calls Abraham to leave his country and his people and go to a land that he would show him. Verse 1 begins straight-away with the command; God does not make any identification of himself. He says simply: Leave your country and go to a place I will show you. It is clear, however, as with all the appearances of God in the OT, that there was no doubt as to his identity or his authority. With modern skepticism we wonder how Abraham might have known this was God, whether he doubted even for a moment, but we are not told. The command is simple and straightforward. As von Rad comments: "Jahweh is the subject of the first verb at the beginning of the first statement and thus the subject of the entire subsequent sacred history. The divine address begins with the command to abandon radically all natural roots" (von Rad 1961, 154). A promise follows immediately (v. 2): "I will make of you a great nation, and I will bless you." God's concern is all the nations, as the succeeding phrase shows, but it begins with the establishment of a relationship with Abraham and his seed. Here is the core of OT religion: the intimate bond between God and his people. It was through such a people and such a bond that God would bless all the nations.
2. Genesis 15 and 17. In these chapters God appears again to Abraham to formally establish his covenant with him. In 15:1 he promises to be a shield for Abraham and in 17:1 he identifies himself with the name El Shaddai. There has been no general agreement as to the source or root meaning of this name. The meaning, however, probably focuses on the might of God over against the frailty of humanity. Implied is the suffi-

ciency of God for them. Following this self-identification God gives these instructions: "Walk before me, and be blameless" (17:1). The response God requires is a moral one; from the start the relationship between God and his people has a moral dimension. There is particular behavior that is appropriate to a relationship with God. Then God promises to make a covenant with Abraham, implying that he wishes this communion to be not a temporary or occasional affair, but permanent. This permanence is to be sealed by the physical sign of circumcision down through the generations (v. 10).

God's disclosing his name to Abraham is of such significance that it calls for comment. For the Hebrews, as for the Chinese among many other peoples, the name is of great significance. It is to reveal something of the character of the person involved. Adam's importance as God's image bearer is reflected in his naming of creation. In naming creation he made it his own, even while he expressed his freedom over the material world. But the name was also the means of his relationship to it. In the case of a person, where the name is revealed there the person is actively present. The name and the person were bound up in the closest possible way. So true is this that a change in the person's condition necessitates a change in his name. Thus in Genesis 17:4-6 Abram becomes Abraham, that is, "exalted father" becomes "father of a multitude." Consequently, when Christ says that he has come in his Father's name, he is to be heard as the Father (Jn. 5:43). John in fact concludes his gospel with the statement that all he has written has as its purpose "that believing you may have life in his [Jesus'] name" (Jn. 20:31). So when God reveals his name to Abraham the significance is very great. Though he is great and exalted, he has seen fit to allow himself to be known by men and women, to give himself over to them as it were. Now that humankind have the name of God the way is open to call upon him, to ask for his presence and, of course, to blaspheme.

3. **Genesis 28:13.** The significance of the name is seen in the next reference to God's self-revelation in Genesis 28. Here Jacob has a dream of a ladder extending up to heaven and the

Lord standing above saying: "I am the LORD, the God of Abraham your father and the God of Isaac." Added to his name here is the statement of his relationship with Abraham. He is the God that identified himself with the father and grandfather of Jacob. Then God gives a promise which was a kind of repetition of the covenant promise: I will give you this land. It is interesting that pagan and primitive gods were often identified with a particular place, but the God of Israel identified himself with persons and events (Ex. 20:1-2) and promised—with a grand freedom of ownership—to give the land to his people. All the earth was his, but in this particular place they were to call upon his name. The response of Jacob was very human. He was afraid. He was in awe of the place because he felt God was there. In a further encounter (Gen. 32:29) Jacob asks urgently for the name of the one wrestling with him. Who is this strange person? "Thus embedded in this most urgent of all human questions, this question about the name, is all man's need, all his boldness before God" (von Rad 1961, 317). God does not answer him, but rather blesses him. Perhaps God knew the question implied a desire to have the name as a weapon to use against this unknown assailant. In any case God withheld it in his freedom.

These events are not the only significant ones in Genesis, but they are clearly the foundation upon which the whole patriarchal history rests. Take them away and the whole account makes no sense. The history of the patriarchs as a history takes its starting point and finds its explanation in these disclosures. Secure in the knowledge that God had appeared to them and called them for a special mission, their lives took on significance far above that of their neighbors. Contrary then to some modern scholars, I hold this period of Israel's history to be the true germinal period. The pattern is set in which all subsequent religious thought is to develop. God wishes this people to be his unique possession. He has chosen them as an object and vehicle of his blessing and presence in the world. He has given them his word of promise, seen in the physical sign of circumcision. Moreover, this promise has an earthly future: this people was to have a land which God would give them.

Though revelation is progressive throughout Scripture, it should not be thought that faith goes from a primitive, simple notion to a higher, more sophisticated level. Hebrews 11:8-12 indicates that the response of Abraham to God is a normative example for the person of faith. Abraham could stand throughout Scripture as one who "looked forward to the city which has foundations, whose builder and maker is God" (Heb. 11:10).

4. Exodus 3. Here we come to one of the most striking and decisive moments in God's self-revelation. In 3:2 God appears as the "angel of the LORD." We will see below that God sometimes appears through an intermediary and sometimes rather more directly, though because of sin perfect face-to-face encounter is impossible in this life (Ex. 33:20). But whatever the medium it is a real revelation that is involved. Again, verse 6 gives the self-introductory formula. As Theo. Vriezen notes, this authoritative introduction "dominates the theological conception of revelation in the Old Testament" (Vriezen 1970, 177). God says, "I am the God of your father, the God of Abraham, the God of Isaac, and the God of Jacob," and then promises to deliver the people from Egypt. Moses—the shepherd become leader—is to be the chosen instrument. Then Moses asks (v. 13) what name he is to give to the children of Israel. It is clear the people will want to know who this is. What sort of person promises to deliver them? He has been the God of their fathers. What will he be to them now? God's answer is: I AM WHAT I AM, or I WILL BE WHAT I WILL BE (the Hebrew is in the imperfect or uncompleted tense). What kind of an answer is God giving to Moses?

There are those who say that God is evading Moses' question and refusing to commit himself. This is the view of Karl Barth who quotes Judges 13:18: "Why do you ask my name ... ?" Says Barth: "A delivering over of God to man, as awareness of his peculiar name would imply, is not to take place even in revelation, but revelation itself is to be regarded as the revelation of the free loving-kindness of God" (*Church Dogmatics*, 1/1, 369-70). Barth is concerned that God's transcendence be preserved even in his self-revelation. God is hidden even as he is revealed. Granted that there is some imprecision of language, is this to be taken as an expression of God's freedom, of an evasion? In the previous verse (Ex. 3: 12) God had already promised his presence. It would seem strange to imply now that he would not commit himself.

Another view is based on the LXX (Greek) reading of this verse, which is best translated "I am the One who is." This view sees God giving here the basic meaning of his personhood. God is being itself. Theologians in the Catholic tradition, such as Etienne Gilson and E. L. Mascall, believe this is the philosophical key to understanding God: one whose existence is identical with his essence. The one who completely "is." This concept Mascall sees as the "fertile soil of all the fulness of Catholic devotion" (*He Who Is,* 1966, 13). Quite apart from the questionable rendering in the LXX, it is hard to imagine that God intended to communicate such a highly abstract idea to the unsophisticated, agricultural Hebrews.

A more interesting suggestion comes from W. F. Albright and his disciples. On the basis of etymology Albright suggests that the best translation is "He who causes to be" growing out of the basic idea of God as creator (Albright, 259-60).

But the view most consistent with the context would appear to be that of Vriezen, who insists this is not an evasion but a clear assurance of his (continued) presence. The best translation in this case would be: "I will be there, as I am here" or "I am here for you." "Revelation in the Scriptural sense could be defined as God himself coming to man, revealing himself as the One who is there for man, anyhow. When God reveals himself he introduces himself in the first person singular, and his words point to his deeds" (Vriezen, 180).

In support of this view scholars have pointed out that this grammatical expression, where a second verb functions as a predicate for the first, in its very redundancy can emphasize verbal action, just as in many languages a word may be repeated for emphasis. F. W. Bush gives two illustrations of this usage. First, Ezekiel 12:24-25: "For there shall be no more any false vision or flattering divination within the house of Israel. But I the LORD will speak the word which I will speak." Since it is the Lord who will speak—the verb is repeated for emphasis—there will be no doubt about it. Then, Exodus 33:19 ("I will be gracious to whom I will be gracious") need not be thought of as an expression of God's freedom to bless or not, but rather as an expression of the certainty of his grace, in which case the verse would read: "I am indeed the one who is gracious and merciful" (Bush, 11).

From the context of this verse in Exodus 3 it is clear that God wishes to emphasize his presence. As he was the God of the fathers, so his presence will continue to be the (only) guarantee of his promises. True, there is an indefiniteness to God's response, but this is because his intentions will (and must) be revealed in his future acts which he refuses now to explain. Meanwhile his name alone will be the primary means of his relationship to them and the "medium of continous worship" (Childs 1974, 77).

5. Exodus 6:1-2. When Pharaoh does not respond to Moses' request God again assures him of his deliverance, and, as if to support his promises, identifies himself: "I am the LORD [Jahweh]. I appeared to Abraham, to Isaac, and to Jacob, as God Almighty [El Shaddai], but by my name the LORD [Jahweh] I did not make myself known to them." This verse has been consistently used by critical scholars as one of the bases for dividing up the Pentateuch into various sources. Those places in Genesis where *El Shaddai* appears belong to the so-called P (Priestly) source which is thought to be later, and those places where Jahweh appears belong to the so-called J (Jahwist) source. But is it really to be imagined that the patriarchs had not heard the name *Jahweh* at all? This may be doubted quite apart from the critics' supposition of the later editing of the Pentateuch.

It is possible, for example, that this verse should be read in the form of a question: "Did I not let myself be known to them by my name Jahweh?" Robert Dick Wilson suggested this back in 1924 (in Kaiser, 1972, 29-40) and other scholars have found further evidence to support this view in recent years.

But perhaps the best way to understand the verse is to see that God is not insisting on a completely new name, but a new understanding of his presence that will come to be associated with this name. The name *Jahweh* means the covenanting God, the God sustaining faithful relations with his people. Now they are to experience the reality of this name in a way their fathers could not have dreamed. This suggestion fits better with the dynamic understanding of names that we noted earlier. This verse would then be interpreted: "In the character of my name Jahweh did I not make myself known to them." As he had promised earlier to do, the Lord is saying that he is now making himself known as the God who remembers his covenant and brings it to fulfillment. This verse then is related to the patriarchal accounts as a fulfillment of those promises. As Brevard Childs puts it: "The name of Jahweh functions as a guarantee that the reality of God stands behind the promise and will execute its fulfillment" (Childs 1974, 115).

6. Exodus 19:3 and 20:1-2. God says to Moses: "You have seen what I did" (19:4). This emphasis has led some scholars to see a change in the way God appears from a direct communication—a person-to-person encounter—to revelation through his works. But rather than a change, perhaps we should see an advance. God's direct appearances do not cease, but now it is possible for him to refer to his works as confirmations of what he promised to do. The exodus would have no meaning apart from his appearances to Moses and the patriarchs. Deeds in the OT are proofs, tokens and elaborations of God's presence and cannot be understood apart from this background. Earlier, Israel had been confronted with the person of God, now this experience has been filled out, but certainly not superseded by the revelations of his mighty works. Now the law would be added to confirm and describe the relationship God had established with his people.

7. Exodus 33:18-23. In these verses Moses asks that God show him his glory. Moses is at another point of decision and wishes a more complete vision of God. God refuses a more complete manifestation, not because God must be invisible, but because man in his sinful condition cannot see him and live (v. 20). But he does promise to make his *goodness* pass before him (v. 19) and proclaims his name Jahweh. He wishes to show himself "in terms of his attributes rather than his appearances" (Childs 1974, 596). God does not refuse absolutely to reveal himself but wishes to make known his character, his goodness. Notice that this was precisely the revelation that Moses and the people needed at that time, specifically, to know his mercy. The work they needed from God was a redemptive work. God had to take them in their sinful condition and in his mercy lead them on. As if to illustrate this need he passes by Moses and covers him with his hand (v. 22) to protect him from his immediate presence, which Moses in his sin would have had to experience as wrath. In this very covering, then, God is not hiding his glory but showing it in a form that his sinful people can appreciate.

This idea of the revelation of God's glory is also present in the NT where Christ claims to glorify his father precisely in his death, that is, in the redemptive cover of human sin and protection from the wrath of God (see Jn. 13:31; 17:1, 4). God's revelation is never arbitrary but always fits his redemptive purposes. Throughout the history of OT revelation it becomes progressively clearer that revelation in a fallen world must have a redemptive character. God must reveal himself in terms of humanity's sinful condition for the purpose of dealing with that condition and restoring them to fellowship.

To emphasize his character further God uses the construction which we discussed in connection with Exodus 3:14: "I will be gracious to whom I will be gracious" or "I am indeed the one who is gracious" (33:19). This is certainly no expression of God's arbitrary election as is sometimes thought—such a meaning makes little sense in the context—it is precisely the assurance of his mercy.

8. Exodus 34:5-10. Here God descends in a cloud and stands before Moses to proclaim his name: the Lord, the Lord. Now this name is given additional content: merciful, gracious, loving and faithful (v. 6). But notice the purpose of this revelation was to give surety to the promises of the covenant (v. 10). He is a God who keeps steadfast love, but who, at the same time, will judge those who are guilty. His presence and love are unconditional, but they will mean judgment as well as blessing. Again, as in Genesis 17:1, the moral response that God's character demands is made clear. It is this dimension that is made explicit in the law.

In these passages in Exodus it is clear that Moses enjoyed a unique relationship with God. In Exodus 33:12 Moses acknowledges that God knows him by name. God explains this further in Numbers 12:7-8. Speaking of Moses he says: "He is entrusted with all my house. With him I speak mouth to mouth, clearly, and not in dark speech; and he beholds the form of the LORD." Edward Young states: "Moses occupied a unique position in the Divine economy and stood in unparalleled relationship to God" (Young 1952, 51). We will see that this position makes him the archetype of the prophet to arise later. At the same time, these verses in Exodus 33 imply that there is an intrinsic limitation placed even on the relationship of Moses. God allowed his form to be seen, but not his face. That experience is reserved for the vision of God in heaven, even for Moses. "Now we see through a glass, darkly; but then face to face," Paul says in 1 Corinthians 13:12 (AV). But with the coming of Christ even the final vision is anticipated by life in the Spirit as Paul explains in 2 Corinthians 3:18: "We all, with unveiled face, beholding the glory of the Lord, are being changed into his likeness from one degree of glory to another; for this comes from the Lord who is the Spirit."

9. Further Self-Revelations. There are of course continuing self-disclosures of God throughout the OT especially to the prophets. As von Rad puts it, these "received their call through God's direct and very personal address to them, and this created a totally new situation for the man concerned" (von Rad 1962, II, 57). As recorded in 1 Samuel 3:10-14 God calls Samuel and without introducing himself announces that he is about to do a new thing in Israel: he will judge the house of Eli. Here again the word of explanation precedes the event and gives it meaning. As Amos explains (3:7) God does nothing without revealing it to his prophets. In Is. 6:1-5 it is the revelation of the person and character of God that precedes Isaiah's call as a prophet. Ezekiel is given a view of the likeness of the glory of the Lord (1:28) that is accompanied with an elaborate vision. In every case there is an element of surprise, sometimes fear, certainly shock. These were extraordinary experiences no more easily understood then than they would be today. Because sinners are restless in the presence of God, these appearances needed to be protective, comforting and reassuring. In a word, they had to be promissory. The psalmist yearns for the day when "I shall behold thy face in righteousness; when I awake, I shall be satisfied with beholding thy form" (Ps. 17:15).

Summary
In all these appearances one is struck by the fact that while God appears to people he is at the same time transcendent, having his person above the limits of the world. Though this would seem contradictory to us—that God could be present and distant at the same time—it is no problem to God. On the one hand, we never have the feeling that God does not belong in this world order, that his appearances are out of place. Nor is there any difficulty in "coming down from heaven" as other Near Eastern myths suggest. He walks with a person as naturally as any human companion. On the other hand, he is high and lifted up in his character and his being; the world itself cannot contain him. Here lies the significance of the media (to which we turn in the next chapter): his face, glory and name. These express God's real nearness, at the same time they imply his otherness.

Then we notice the thoroughly concrete character of God's

appearances. Over sixty times the verb for seeing is used in connection with God's presence. "And God appeared...." "And Moses saw...." Often other faculties are involved: hearing, even smelling. Here is no vague spiritual awareness, but a tangible experience that threatens to overwhelm. In a day when religious experience has been reduced to the scope of our jaded feelings, it is well to remember this biblical truth: God is the absolutely real one; when he enters a person's life, it is we who are suddenly aware of our tentative and fragile existence. At the same time, an encounter with God calls for a fully human response. In fact, in their response to God people realize their true nature and freedom. Brevard Childs notes of the man of God: "Exodus 3 offers a classic description of the office as one which even though initiated by God, incorporates a genuine human personality" (Childs 1974, 73). Notice as well the character of God's revelation to a person as a summons to do, follow, obey. The emphasis is on command rather than the giving of information, although the latter is not lacking. One would do well to think of this core idea to fully appreciate OT revelation: God is calling a people to himself. There is a great deal to be known about God and his purposes, but this knowledge is always relevant to relationship, either with God or with his people.

We have noticed already that God never needed to prove his existence when he appeared. It is not God who must prove himself, but man. We have seen often enough in modern thought how radically a person's life and meaning are called into question when God is ignored. The existence of God is a challenge and not a question. In his self-revelation God merely announces that since he is God he will do what he plans. We noted as well that the complex of OT revelation includes personal encounter, the giving of information and interpretation of events, and God's mighty works. All together make up what is properly called revelation. But the most important element remains God's personal revelation of himself. It is to his person that the truth of revelation leads. As Israel responded in faith to his person it understood more of the words and works of God. Knowledge in the OT is always personal and intimate, it leads to relationship as well as to objective understanding. So God's revelation of himself demands ultimately not assent, but a concrete life of obedience. God not only calls us to understand his words, but he summons us to obey his voice.

Of course people do not want to hear God's voice and obey him. They are still—like Adam and Eve—busy running away from God. So God's revelation of himself had to take on the character of making provision to cover his people's sin and to allow them to stand in his presence. This is why the law must follow the covenant, as that which facilitates relationship. In a word, revelation must be redemptive.

*Am I a God at hand, says the L*ORD*,*
  and not a God afar off?
Can a man hide himself in secret places
  *so that I cannot see him? says the L*ORD*.*
*Do I not fill heaven and earth? says the L*ORD*.*

Jeremiah 23:23-24

2
The
Nature
Of God

Media of Revelation

As we have seen there is never a tension in the OT between God's nearness and his distance; rather it was a part of the character of his transcendence that one could not escape his presence. In Hebrew thought God was at home in heaven and on earth. Of course this was more perfectly understood only later in the OT. But throughout there was the belief that God could appear at any time in any place, even though he was not permanently identified with any particular place. While no spot could hold him, it was a condition of his freedom that he could make some visible object the means of his presence. Let us look at some of these media of his revelation.

1. The Angel of the Lord. In the OT the angel of the Lord might be only a messenger of God (the Hebrew word itself means messenger), distinct from God himself (2 Sam. 24:16), or he might be identified with the Lord himself speaking in the first person (Gen. 16:7-14; Judg. 2:1, 4; 6:20-23 et al.). He could be a bringer of blessing (Ex. 32:34) or of judgment

(2 Sam. 24:16). When the angel of the Lord is present, God's protecting or fearful presence can be felt, while his transcendence is not questioned. It is typical of OT theophanies that the line between a representative and an actual appearance of God cannot be sharply drawn. This is seen even in the prophets where the identification with God and his word was so close that the prophet could lapse into the first person, seemingly without realizing it. God is free to make his presence known, even while humans must be protected from his immediate presence.

2. The Face of God. In the account of Moses' request to see the glory of God, the face of God appears as the presence of God without restriction (Ex. 33:20). Human beings cannot see God's face and live (though Jacob claims to have seen the face of God, in Gen. 32:30). More common is the use of God's face in a metaphoric way for his presence in general. To have his face shine upon one is to experience God's blessing (Num. 6:25), to have his face hidden from one is to experience pain and sorrow (Ps. 13:1). When Adam fled from God in the garden, the Hebrew has it "he hid himself from the face of God" (Gen. 3:8). But the later understanding is that the face of God is his immediate presence, the experience of which is not to be known in this life (Ps. 17:15). As with *angel,* usage of this word is on a line from a metaphoric to a more literal understanding.

3. The Glory of God. The fundamental notion of glory in the OT is that of weight or visible substance. The glory of a man consisted in his possessions, a man of "glory" was a man of substance (see Gen. 31:1 where the word translated "wealth" is the Hebrew word for glory). The idea of glory is used in the double sense of showing respect (or glorifying) and of that which inspires such respect. When applied to God the word implies (the usually visible) manifestation of his divine potency. Johann Bengel called it "discovered sanctity." In Exodus 16:7 when God promises to show his glory, the meaning is that Moses and the people will see his care. His glory accompanied his presence on Mount Sinai (Ex. 24:16). It filled the tent of meeting so that Moses was not able to enter it (Ex.

40:34-35). Here again is a rich symbol of God's presence, often interchangeable with that presence itself and usually associated with visible (even luminous) phenomena. But it rested in particular where God was to be worshiped, in the temple (1 Kings 8:11). The inescapable limitation of OT worship is apparent here, for where the glory of the Lord filled the house the priests could not minister. Nevertheless, glory called out to be manifest, not only in the house of the Lord, but over the whole earth, as the waters cover the sea (Num. 14:21; 1 Chron. 16:24 and Is. 6:3). For this, glory needed radical reinterpretation in the mission of Christ who in his death fully revealed God's redemptive glory (Jn. 17:1).

4. Anthropomorphisms. While not a medium of God's presence, this is perhaps the place to consider the use of anthropomorphisms in the OT. Often God is spoken of (and refers to himself) in human terms. God speaks (Gen. 1:3), converses (Lev. 4:1), hears (Ex. 16:12), sees (Gen. 1:4), smells (1 Sam. 26:19, Heb.), has a face (Num. 6:25), a back (Ex. 33:23), hands (Is. 14:27) and so forth. Beginning with Ludwig Feuerbach in the last century, it has been popular to see this as evidence of the entirely human composition of the Bible. God is simply a projection of human ideals, "man" spoken with a loud voice. But a closer reading of the OT shows the impossibility of such ideas. Indeed this phenomenon clarifies in important ways the OT view of God. It is an instance of God's loving attempts to reach down, not of human desire to reach up.

In the first place, speaking of himself in human terms emphasizes that God in his unique way shares our world. We have noted before that God nowhere exhibits frustration with the physical world. He created it and pronounced it good and seems effortlessly to work out his purposes in it. By speaking of himself anthropomorphically, God comes to us in a human and earthly way. Of course these expressions have their limitations but tend in these very limitations to point beyond these imperfect appearances to the final appearance of the God-man. In this sense all revelation points to incarnation.

Secondly, anthropomorphisms speak of our creation in the
image of God and of God's desire for communion and relationship with us. If this is to be possible, God must come to us and
speak our language. So he makes a point of contact for us (note
well: *he* makes it—as we shall note in OT worship—on his
terms not ours). He speaks of himself in personal terms so
that communion is possible. John Calvin has expressed this
well: "As nurses commonly do with infants, God is wont to
'lisp' in speaking to us. Thus such forms of speaking do not so
much express clearly what God is like as accommodate the
knowledge of him to our slight capacity. To do this he must
descend far beneath his loftiness" (*Institutes* I, 13, 1).

The result is that these expressions give a great richness
to our conception of God, for they make him accessible while
preserving his greatness. For, as we shall see in a moment, no
one imagined for a moment that God was simply like us. He
was high and lifted up, filling heaven and earth. Yet his
greatness and love is shown in such a way that he comes to us
in a way that we can appreciate. As one student commented
to me while discussing these things, this is a beautiful model
for our contextualization of the Christian message.

The Nature of God

Theoretical atheism (the actual denial of God's existence) is
unknown in the OT. Even the fool who says there is no God
(Ps. 14:1) is a practical atheist, one who denies God's relevance to his life (Jer. 5:12). Nor does the OT attempt to prove
God's existence. One has the feeling the OT believer would
have regarded all such attempts as completely unnecessary.
For God's existence is announced in all the world (Ps. 19:1-3).
Further, there are no definitions of God (such as "God is love"
or "God is Spirit" that we have in the NT). The nearest we
come to this is Isaiah 31:3: "The Egyptians are men, and not
God; and their horses are flesh, and not spirit." Or Numbers
23:19: "God is not man, that he should lie." Or Malachi 3:6:
"I the LORD do not change." These emphasize the distinction
between God and human beings without denying his relation-

ship with them. In fact, this last passage implies that it is because he is God that the relationship can be preserved. If he were a man, he would have long since tired of Israel's unfaithfulness. Thus the OT is concerned to elaborate the concrete reality of God in his activity, rather than to present a systematic elaboration of a doctrine about God (Vriezen, 156). Yet it is possible for us to understand certain aspects of his character from the account of his dealings with his people.

1. God Is Personal. God is personal in that he is the God who gives himself a name. The proclamation of his name is the act whereby "God himself came forth from his secret place and offered himself in fellowship" (Eichrodt, I, 206). We have discussed above the importance of a name. To know a name is to have a relationship with that person. Though God's name is not to be taken in vain (Ex. 20:7), there is no magic associated with it as in pagan religions. God's giving himself names serves to emphasize three things. First, a name stresses God's presence among his people apart from any material or visible aspect to this presence. God's majesty and love are manifest clearly in his names, but his people are given no exhaustive knowledge of his essence. Second, the use of various names reflects his dynamic intervention in the life of Israel. His is a restless activity (Vriezen, 318). One name does not exhaust the character of God or the possibility of his care. Finally, all the names have to do with God's relation with his people. They do not identify God with any part of nature (as so often with Israel's neighbors), but reflect the history of his dealings with Israel. He is actively involved in the life of his people in various ways.

a. El. El (often appearing in compound names) is the general and perhaps the oldest Semitic designation for God (the Semites were the racial family to which Israel belonged). The basic meaning is a mighty leader or governor and stresses the distance between God and man, as well as his power over nature. It is commonly used with individual leaders (God of Abraham, Gen. 31:53, Ex. 3:6; God of Isaac, Gen. 28:13).

It is used often in the compound names: *El Shaddai,* stress-

ing the exalted and mighty character of God (Gen. 17:1 and
forty times in Job); *El Alion,* the Most High God (Gen. 14:18-
19; at times *Alion,* "Most High," appears alone as in Ps. 50:
14); *El Olam,* God of ancient of Days, Everlasting God, which
is the earliest indication of the eternity of God (Gen. 21:33;
Is. 40:28); *El Roeh,* God of seeing (Gen. 16:13) and of course
the common *Elohim* (Gen. 1:1 et al.). The latter, which is
plural in form in Hebrew, probably is to be understood as an
abstract plural of intensity or of majesty. It is not the result
of the unification of all deities but rather the "summing up of
the whole divine power in a personal unity" (Eichrodt, I, 185).
While a reference to the Trinity is probably not specified by
the plural, one cannot rule out this association.

b. Jahweh. This name is connected with the verb "to be" (see
Ex. 3:14 and the play on words in Hos. 1:9) and is the specifically Israelite designation for God (though from recent find-
ings in Tell Mardikh there may be some reason to think it
existed before the time of Israel). After the time of Moses (Ex.
6:3), this becomes the name by which the worship of Israel is
marked off from all the other nations. It is the particular
name of the covenant relationship and thus speaks of God's
nearness and concern for his people (Deut. 3:24 et al.). The
implications of this nearness will one day be fully seen when
God will be immediately present (Ezek. 37:26-28).

c. Lord Sabaoth (Lord of Hosts). The idea of this name is
probably connected with God as a warrior as explained in
1 Samuel 17:45. At an earlier period it was likely connected
with the ark. Some believe that more than armies may be involved in *hosts,* perhaps hosts of heavens, the stars and all
the creatures that are instruments of his will. The name
may have been originally associated with God as a leader and
deliverer of his people in battle (*the living God* seems to be
used in this connection as well, 1 Sam. 17:26, 36). But later it
outgrew this association and became (especially in the prophets) simply a designation for God's exaltedness and omnipotence (Is. 23:9; 24:23; Zech. 3:10). For this reason Eichrodt
translates this name as "Lord of all that exists in heaven

and earth" (Eichrodt I, 193; Vriezen agrees, 298).

d. Melek *(King)*. Exodus 15:18 speaks of the Lord reigning forever. We will see in our discussion of the covenant below that God's kingship is implicit in the covenant form of the early books of the OT. There seems to be some reticence, however, to speak of God simply as king (Num. 23:21 shows how it is used indirectly). Perhaps the political life of Canaan with its pagan kings seemed alien to Israel in the beginning. With the monarchy of course the term becomes more commonly referred to God (Ps. 24:7-10 is a good example). The prophets of the eighth century avoid it with the exception of Isaiah (6:5; 41:21; 44:6; 52:7). Perhaps they avoided it because of the false worship of the *melek* cult in seventh-and-eighth-century Jerusalem. In postexilic thought the title of king is associated with God's salvation at the last day (see Zech. 14:16). As so often in the OT one notes a clear development of thought. In 1 Samuel 8 the idea of a king is clearly a concession, but the idea is taken up as the OT proceeds, and finally purged of its bad connotations, it is put in the service of God's rule of his people to which they look. As Eichrodt puts it: "Something new has been made of the old concept of God as king, the inherent defects of which have been overcome now that it has been removed from the sphere of the cultus and linked inseparably with the idea of universal religion" (Eichrodt, I, 199).

2. God Is Spirit. This definition of God which becomes so important in the NT (Jn. 4:24) is for the most part absent from the OT. Why is this so? We have noted already that the characteristic revelation of God lends itself to anthropomorphisms and focuses on the giving of his name. All of this stresses the personal nature of God. This leads Eichrodt to see "personhood," rather than spirituality, as basic to OT religion. Similarly Vriezen believes life, rather than love or spirit, is the key category in which to understand God in the OT (Vriezen, 319). This is not to deny God the qualities that later came to be identified with his spirituality. But it is important to note that *spirit,* whose basic meaning is wind or breath, had a concrete connotation in the OT. Perhaps it took a Greek vocabulary and way of thinking to develop the idea of spirituality so common to us today. Quite simply *spirit* in the OT was not suited to express the immediacy of OT religion and communion. Nevertheless, the same intimacy and nearness that is later expressed by spirituality is certainly prominent in the OT view of God. He is the source of life (Ps. 36:9); he does not sleep (Ps. 121:4); he is the searcher of hearts (1 Sam. 16:7) and there can be no limiting, materialistic expressions of him (Ex. 20:4). He is supreme over all creatures (Is. 31:3), quite distinct from man (Hos. 11:9).

3. God Is One: Monotheism. At the beginning of Israel's history there is apparently no clear understanding of monotheism. As J. B. Payne remarks: "Historically this truth was only progressively revealed by God and grasped by fallen man" (1962, 125). Obviously the patriarchs worshiped only the Lord (Gen. 35:2-4), but technically this is monolatry. Abraham understood that God was the possessor of heaven and earth, the Most High God (Gen. 14:22), which is an expression of virtual monotheism. The patriarchs' practical experience was of God as supreme and alone, but we have no indication of their denial of the existence of other gods.

By the time of Moses the uniqueness of God is recognized. Moses tells the people that they have seen that the Lord is God and there is no other (Deut. 4:35, 39). It is clear from this that such a statement is the result, not of philosophical speculation, but of the close experience of God's activity (Eichrodt, I, 227). That this was an expression of a living faith is seen most clearly in the psalms. God's greatness is such that it simply excludes competitors. He ruled out all rival deities by his power and wisdom (Ps. 66:6-7). David realized that the presence of God went beyond the practice of worship (Ps. 139). The people's experience of God's deliverance extended to all the periods of their history so they could say: "The eternal God is your dwelling place, and underneath are the everlasting arms" (Deut. 33:27). The highest expression of this uniqueness is the so-called *shema* which begins with Deuteronomy 6:4: "Hear, O Israel: The LORD our God is one LORD." This can be understood as saying God is one, so that there is only one proper way of worshiping him (which is explained in subsequent verses), or it can be understood that God is alone over all. The latter seems to best fit the context.

Whether or not the belief in monotheism suffered a decline during the period of the judges, it reaches a unique expression in Elijah and is assumed by the major prophets. In 1 Kings 18 Elijah is not afraid to put the Lord to stand against the "gods" of the false prophets. His charge to the false prophets implies an evident monotheism: "If the LORD is God, follow him; but if Baal, then follow him" (v. 21).

The highest statement of pure monotheism comes with the major prophets. For them other gods are all as nothing (Is. 44:10; Jer 2:5). But even here the stress is on their worthlessness rather than on their nonexistence: they cannot hear or answer prayer; therefore, they are no gods at all. Among all the wise ones there is none like the Lord; all others are stupid and foolish (Jer. 10:8); they are impotent (Jer. 14:22). The classic defense of monotheism is found in Isaiah 44—46. There all the idols are contrasted with the Lord who made heaven and earth: "I am the LORD, and there is no other" (Is. 45:18). The gods of the nations composed a capricious and confusing pantheon. But it is a function of the vigor of the faith of Israel that none of these were seen to offer the slightest competition to the Lord God of Israel, before whom all supposed gods were considered an empty fetish.

The Character and Activity of God

It is clear by now that the nature of God was first seen in his self-revelation and then illustrated by his concrete acts in the life of the people. Even in the highest expressions of praise in the psalms there is a surprising absence of statements about God's essence as one might elaborate it philosophically. Rather than an abstract reflection on God's nature, there is a grateful acknowledgment of his working and the familiar refrain: "Let them thank the LORD for his steadfast love, for his wonderful works to the sons of men!" (as in Ps. 107:8, 15, 21, 31).

But from his works we can really understand his character. We are not left to wonder what God is like; we can see it clearly. So we have learned to speak of God's attributes. But while we do so, we must remember that they are not separable ideas but "symbolical, partially overlapping indications" (Vriezen, 312). They are different ways of looking at the single living reality which is God.

1. The Power of God. All the works of God display his power, but it is never a naked or arbitrary power. The concrete experiences of Israel could lead the psalmist to testify: "Our God is in the heavens; he does whatever he pleases" (Ps. 115:3). But this confession was born of particular instances of his deliverance. It was the specific promise of the birth of Isaac that led the Lord to ask: "Is anything too hard for the LORD?" (Gen. 18:14). It was the memory of the exodus that led God's people to sing: "The LORD is my strength and my song. . . . Thy right hand, O LORD, glorious in power . . . shatters the enemy" (Ex. 15:2, 6). This awareness of God's power expressed on behalf of his people was enriched by the belief in his power as creator. Perhaps they came more easily to believe in his power as creator after they had undergone his miraculous deliverance and guidance. In any case, along with his lordship in history, they believed fully in his intimate care of nature (Ps. 89:9 and 104).

Associated with his power is the idea of God as *terrible*. God's power was experienced in judgment as well as blessing. That is to say, God's power is always expressed within a moral context. Jacob after his nighttime encounter with God could say how dreadful that place was because God was there (Gen. 28:17). God will show his judgment with "terrifying power" (Is. 10:33). The enemies of Israel knew the Lord as a "dread warrior" who protects his own (Jer. 20:11). Just as he is mighty in his faithfulness toward those who love him (Ps. 89:8), so his wrath is terrible to those who have turned against him (Ps. 59:13 and Deut. 29:28).

The concept of God's *jealousy* is another closely allied idea (Ex. 20:5 and 34:14 where his "name" is jealous). The basic idea of this word, which can mean "jealous" or "zealous," is the self-assertion which is the prerogative of God, the inevitable maintenance of his rights. "The zeal of Jahweh is a conception necessary to him" (Vriezen, 302). This is because of the unique strength of his character which cannot be shared with any creature (Is. 42:8). This has little to do with God's "pride" as we understand pride; it is simply a necessary reflection of the actual state of affairs. This is why his zeal is provoked by idolatry: it is sheer illusion (Deut. 32:16). It is also provoked by the willful departure from the covenant (Deut. 29:20). But this same jealousy can also be the assurance of God's protection of his people (2 Kings 19:31 and Is. 26:11) without ceasing to be a threat of his righteous judgment (Num. 25:11). This leads Ludwig Koehler to suggest that the fear of the Lord is obedience (Koehler, 56).

2. The Holiness of God. Closely allied to the idea of power is that of God's holiness. This is perhaps the central characteristic of God. The etymology of the Hebrew word is "to cut off" or "mark off." It was used to denote that which is separated from regular, everyday use for sacred service. For example, in Genesis 2:3 the seventh day is "marked off" or "holy" unto the Lord.

In the Near Eastern setting there was often a fearful *mysterium* associated with places and objects (and less frequently with persons) that were holy in the sense of being removed from common life. Significantly, it is applied only rarely to deities (Eichrodt, I, 271). Very often the thought of holiness was tied to *mana*, or the elemental forces of nature, believed to be resident in particular objects or persons, which must be appeased by rites very carefully and faithfully performed. Fear and awe are the common feelings associated with such a concept.

Quite a different conception comes to light in the OT revelation of holiness. In the first place, holiness is primarily associated with God himself and only secondarily (and by his in-

struction) with objects and places (Ex. 15:11 and Is. 40:25). He
delights in goodness and truth (Jer. 9:24) and hates what is
evil, which is said to profane his holy name (Lev. 20:3). Objects and places are marked off by God as holy, not because
they are places of fear or terror, but because he himself is present or has identified himself with that place. Moses was told
he was standing on holy ground because God was there (Ex. 3:
5). The ark became holy and unapproachable because God's
presence was associated with it (1 Sam. 6:19-20; Ex. 29: 43).
Significantly, the awareness of holiness, what we think of
as awe, came later. The fact of holiness preceded, rather than
followed, the human experience of it. God had to tell Moses
that he was standing on holy ground, he never would have
known otherwise. The feelings would come later.

Very early the idea of holiness was associated with moral
purity. It is a misreading of the record to make this connection
a later one. When God punished the sin of Nadab and Abihu
by devouring them with fire he said: "I will show myself holy
among those who are near me, and before all the people I will
be glorified" (Lev. 10:3). It is true that holiness is ordinarily
employed in the religious sense of places, objects and people
that are holy unto the Lord, but, as Eichrodt puts it, "the
whole system of tabu is pressed into the service of a loftier
idea of God" (I, 274). The system of worship was to be a symbol
of God's unique ownership of his people, a grand object lesson
to illustrate his purity, as well as a means of maintaining the
relationship established in the covenant. As Paul was to put it
later, the law was a schoolmaster to bring people to Christ
(Gal. 3:24).

By extension, the holiness of the Lord had also to do with
the people he had called to himself; the covenant is a unique
expression of God's holiness. Israel was to be a people holy
unto the Lord (Ex. 22:31). Because he is holy, they are to be
holy as well (Lev. 11:44). In his acts on their behalf he shows
himself holy (Num. 20:13). For this reason God is called the
Holy One of Israel (30 times in Isaiah; Ps. 71:22; Jer. 50:29
et al.). God is the holy one, and Israel is not holy in herself but

because she is consecrated to God. As Edmond Jacob puts it: "God is holy and that is why he chooses to enter into the covenant; man, on the contrary, can become holy only by entering into the covenant" (Jacob, 90). Though even within the covenant Israel could experience God's holiness as judgment (Is. 10:17) or as salvation (Is. 43:3, 14).

Holiness throughout the OT maintains an underlying sense of plenitude of power and life exercised in a personal and moral context. Though God alone is uniquely holy, holiness shines forth from him and bursts forth onto the earth (Ex. 15:11), seeking to show itself until it be true, as the prophets imply, that the whole earth knows that it is full of the glory of the Lord (Is. 6:1-3). Gustave Oehler explains: "All demonstrations of the divine covenant of grace are the issues of the divine holiness. Outside of the theocratic relations it is closed to the world; but as soon as the world comes into connection with the divine kingdom, it receives manifestations of the divine" (Oehler, I, 157). The nature of the world as God's handiwork is such that God's character may be reflected on this earth, in a distinctly earthly way.

3. The Righteousness of God. Closely related to holiness is righteousness. The root of the Hebrew is lost, but its usage denotes right behavior or right disposition: straightness, conformity to a norm. The forensic element is often present, that is, having to do with courts or legal decisions. But by extension it comes to mean the genuine or the natural. Paths of righteousness are simply walkable paths (Ps. 23:3); trees of righteousness are lovely trees (Is. 61:3).

It is first used of God in the Song of Moses in Deut. 32:4: "Just and right is he." In Judges God's deliverances of his people are called "righteous acts" (Judg. 5:11, Heb.). Basic to such references is the idea that God's works express his sovereignty in the moral realm. Righteousness is holiness in action, the bringing it to pass, creating it out of nothing. There is no abstract norm of righteousness to which God must submit. Rather his will and character are moral in themselves, and his activities surely express his moral nature.

This attribute lies behind the metaphor of the potter and the clay (Is. 45:9-12; Jer. 18:1-12). A. B. Davidson comments on this metaphor: "This figure means that it is God that does shape the history and destinies of mankind, particularly of his people; but it says nothing of the principles according to which he shapes them" (Davidson, 131). But it could be added that since God is righteous, he will be righteous in all his works. We are not left without a clue as to his moral nature, for it is clearly expressed in the law given at Sinai. The psalmist declares: "Righteous art thou, O LORD, and right are thy judgments" (Ps. 119:137). The gods of the nations were capricious and could not be counted on, but God's judgment was dependable, just and strong (Ps. 36:6). Everything that God did necessarily became a manifestation of his righteousness (Ps. 50:6; Is. 5:16).

Earlier in the OT God's righteousness is shown especially in his intervention on behalf of his people and in the maintenance of the rights of the covenant people (Ex. 32:10; Num. 14:12). The unique relationship between God and his people is then the context for the revelation of God's righteousness. The acts of God's deliverance are themselves called righteousness (1 Sam. 12:7, Heb.; Mic. 6:5, Heb.). Recent OT theologians, following H. Cremer (von Rad, I, 370-76 and Eichrodt, I, 240-44), have recovered the importance of this idea of relationship in the OT. This means that righteousness is a concept of relationship that implies responsibilities growing out of the claims of that relationship. The controlling factor is the character of God, but loyalty and righteousness must be manifested in the concrete interchange of the community. It is a righteousness of the household and the market. It leads in the way of righteousness, doing justice rather than only being just. Of course each has his or her own justice to render: the king, the parent, the child, the tradesman. The task of righteousness is to display the qualities that each particular relationship calls forth. The standard of it all, however, is the righteous character of God especially as this is revealed in the law and understood in the wisdom movement. The foundation of it all is God's act of righteousness in placing his people in the covenant.

By the time of the classical prophets the idea of God's righteousness becomes more explicitly tied to a visible kingdom of righteousness, which according to Isaiah 9:7 is to be established "with righteousness . . . for evermore." Israel is to be betrothed in righteousness when that kingdom comes (Hos. 2:19). More than anything else—even the correct formulas of worship—God desires this righteousness to characterize his people (Amos 5:24). This goal John sees on Patmos, where the fine linen that will clothe the Bride of Christ for the marriage supper of the Lamb is the righteous deeds of the saints (Rev. 19:8). The righteousness of God as it is progressively revealed seeks embodiment, reflection in God's people, so that they will be like him (Is. 51:6, "deliverance" here is the Hebrew word meaning righteousness). Well has A. B. Davidson said that righteousness is more than attribute; it is also an effect of God's work. "It is something produced in the world by God, a condition called his . . . because when it is produced men and the world will be in attribute what he is" (Davidson, 143). As with holiness, we come again to the principle of the imitation of God, which we will note is a basic principle of OT ethics.

Note too that the righteousness to be revealed has a concrete and visible character. It is outward transformation as well as inward spiritual change. Justification has in the OT an outer side of prosperity and restoration as well as an inward renewal (Davidson, 139). As the NT expresses this same principle, faith without corresponding works is dead (Jas. 2:17).

So the righteousness of God through the course of the OT has been extended from its narrower context in the covenant to express God's will for the entire created order. Here the concept spills over the idea of conformity to a norm to an active making right, to a "rightwising" as the old Anglo-Saxon puts it. "The maintenance of fellowship now becomes justification of the ungodly" (Eichrodt, I, 274). David already knew of course that God's deliverance is a result of his righteousness (Ps. 51:14, "salvation" is a translation of the Hebrew "righteousness"). In Isaiah's vision God is raining down righteousness (45:8), which comes in the form of vindication (54:17). Once again God's revelation of himself is redemptive in purpose and leads to a final and universal embodiment of his glory.

During the intertestamental period the idea of righteousness underwent an important change. The vision of the prophets seems to have been lost and replaced by an almost mechanical obedience. Justice became distributive justice: to each his due according to the standard of the law. Justification became the verdict of the righteous judge at the last Day. Meanwhile, human righteousness came to be identified with keeping the law—giving alms, not eating with unwashed hands and so forth. This is apparent already in Daniel 4:27 where Daniel instructs the king to break from his sins by practicing righteousness, that is, doing good works. Against this narrowing of righteousness Christ spoke vigorously in Matthew 5:20: "For I tell you, unless your righteousness exceeds that of the scribes and Pharisees, you will never enter the kingdom of heaven."

Before leaving this let us note two associated concepts. The first is that of the *judgment* of God. This concept is very closely related to the idea of "rightwising" that we noted above. Judgment in the OT is much broader than our modern idea of verdict. It is the total activity of judging even to the point of making right the wrong in vindication or redemption. The judge not only passes sentence, he collects the evidence and works creatively to carry out his judgments. As ruler God is also judge who will surely do right (Gen. 18:25), whose will is the basis of all judging. This will was revealed at Sinai, and the law became the basis of all legal decisions. But there was a broader sense in which even the victories of Israel in battle were seen as the outworking of the judicial decisions of God: the Lord, the Judge, will decide (Judg. 11:27; 2 Sam. 18:31). Later the prophets use the image of God pleading his case before Israel. On a minimum standard of justice God's people were guilty (Jer. 2 and Hos. 6), but God could not forget his people. So his judgments become redemptive; judgment partakes of mercy and grace (Is. 30:18).

The second allied concept is that of God's *wrath*. Here the central focus is on God's consistent attitude of opposition, as one who is holy and just, when confronted by sin and evil (Deut. 29:23-25 and especially Nahum 1:2-6). God's wrath is neither an inevitable process nor a spontaneous feeling, but the personal response to evil appropriate to his holy character. At times it is necessary to express this in human terms (as will be seen in the case of love), but this is simply to affirm the reality of God's personal presence, not to liken his reactions to ours. Even God's wrath is tempered with mercy, illustrating again the inseparability of God's attributes (Hos. 11:8-9; Jer. 18:20).

In this connection we must call attention to God's use of evil for the accomplishing of his purposes. Closely following a description of God's wrath in Psalm 76 is the amazing statement: "Surely the wrath of man shall praise thee; the residue of wrath thou wilt gird upon thee" (v. 10). I take this to be much more than a casual reference that describes God's sovereignty, rather it is a fundamental expression of the course that sovereignty must take in a fallen world. God in Scripture time and again takes the very rejection of men and women and makes use of it in his redemptive plan. People turn from God; God uses the very turning to encourage and bring about salvation, and that without violating their freedom. The meanness of Joseph's brothers is made into a way of saving God's people from famine and preserving them (Gen. 45:5); the hardness of Pharaoh's heart becomes a means of displaying God's salvation in the exodus (Ex. 6:1); the institution of the king, as we have seen, Israel wanted for the wrong reasons (1 Sam. 8: 5, 7), yet God used it as a sign of and a means to his own future reign (2 Sam. 7:12). Finally, of course, in the NT it is the very rejection of Christ which caused his death that God used to work for our salvation (1 Cor. 2:8-9).

4. The Mercy and Love of God. Here we are reminded

again that these conceptions, which we struggle to define, overlap. Distinctions blur and meanings spill over into neighboring ideas. We are faced with the perennial problem we have in speaking of God: the vessels we bring to this font cannot hold all that is there. But what often happens is that, like the widow's cruse that did not run dry, God takes our simple words, uses them and expands their meaning far beyond their original scope. (Further on we will see how this often happens with Israel's institutions as well.) They become bearers of larger meanings than we could have imagined at the start.

We have noticed already that the ideas of the power and the holiness of God tended in the direction of mercy. Israel experienced God not only as high and lifted up, as awful in holiness, but also as turning toward them in loving-kindness.

The word variously translated as "mercy" (Heb., *ḥeseḏ*), "loving kindness" (ASV), "covenant love" (Berkeley) or "steadfast love" (often in the RSV) lies at the heart of the biblical revelation of God. The fundamental idea of the word is that of strength (preserved in Ps. 144:2, where "my mercy" is paired with "my fortress"; RSV "my rock and my fortress"). This background is especially pertinent in the light of the modern tendency to associate mercy with weakness. When used of God it implies grace—favor without regard to merit; when used of man or woman it means piety or devotion (Snaith, 94-95).

The idea is already present in Genesis 3:15 when a promise replaces and tempers the judgment God had threatened (2: 17). To the patriarchs the word indicated God's faithfulness to his covenant promises (Gen. 32:10; 39:21). Mercy in fact is really the prior reality to the covenant—the belonging together of God and his people. That is, because God chose Israel to this "belongingness" with himself, he makes a covenant with them (see Ex. 19:4-6; Deut. 7:9; 7:12; 1 Kings 8:23; 2 Chron. 6:14; Neh. 1:5). As the prior fact of God's revealed character, mercy will outlive the covenant (Ps. 136; Jer. 3:12; 33:11).

Mercy then, in the context of the covenant, developed into

the "mutual liability of those who are relatives, friends, master and servant, or belonging together in any other way; solidarity, joint liability" (Koehler in Payne 1970, 162). By extension the word will often imply loyalty or faithfulness, a firm indissoluble union (Ex. 34:6 and Is. 55:3), while of course God's faithfulness and forebearance to Israel likewise express his mercy (Lam. 3:22-23).

Many ideas gather around the theme of mercy. Mercy and faithfulness, for example, often appear together (Is. 16:5; Hos. 4:1; Mic. 7:20; Is. 55:3). So God is called—on the basis of his mercy—Father (Ex. 4:22; Num. 11:12), which leads to a recognition of his dominion over all natural life as creator. Accordingly he is a father to the fatherless (Ps. 68:5); he punishes his children (Deut. 8:5; Prov. 3:12); he leads as a shepherd (Gen. 48:15; Ps. 23). With Israel's depiction as an unfaithful child the idea of mercy is deepened in Hosea 11:1-3. This same image of Israel as a prodigal son appears in Jeremiah 3:19 and 31:20. The final goal is the universal awareness and reflection of God's mercy (Ps. 33:5 and 119:64).

The love which God shows in his choice of Israel is a deliberate direction of the will and a readiness for action (Eichrodt, I, 252). In the OT it is closely related to the idea of election: God's choice of his people. At the beginning the motive for God's choice is not clear, but by the time of Moses it is explained as God's love (Deut. 4:37; 7:7). Again the revelation of God's character lies at the basis of the covenant which he makes with Israel. Thus the covenant is not limited by any of its institutions, but ultimately only by the will and nature of God himself (Snaith, 95). How distinct and sober-minded a relationship this produced can be seen in the marked contrast of Israel's religion with the flagrant eroticism of the Canaanite religions.

Edmond Jacob observes that the normal usage of the word *love* is of a superior toward an inferior (a notable exception is Deut. 15:16; see Jacob, 108-9). God's love is for all his creatures (Ps. 145:9, 16), but especially for humankind (Ps. 103:17).

In the prophets—especially Hosea—the expression of love reaches its highest expression. There it is shown to be that suprarational choosing power which lies beneath and upholds Israel's covenant with God (Hos. 11:1-4). In Isaiah 49:15 it is likened to a mother's love; in Isaiah 43:3 and 49:26, to that of a redeemer. God's love is everlasting (Jer. 31:3), and throughout it is educative (Jer. 12:7-13 and Hos. 11:7-9).

Associated with his love is the idea of God's longsuffering. His favor outlasts his anger (Ps. 30:5), though this too has its limits (Nahum 1:3; Ex. 34:7). Further, God is merciful in that he expresses his goodness to those in trouble (Ps. 146:7-9; Is. 54:10). Finally, there is God's grace itself, God's love for the undeserving (Gen. 6:8). As Snaith says:

> We find that the word is used, practically without exception, of the attitude of a superior to an inferior. Thus *chesed* [mercy] works both ways, but *chen* [grace] only one way. It therefore tends to carry with it . . . the idea of unmerited favor, or of supreme graciousness and condescension on the part of the giver, who is superior. (Snaith, 128)

The OT revelation of God's redemptive generosity (Ps. 86:5) does much to anticipate that amazing NT conception of agape love which is fully revealed in Jesus Christ (1 Jn. 4:9-10).

*O Atum-Kheprer, thou wast on high on the
(primeval) hill ... thou didst spit out what
was Shu, thou didst sputter out what was Tefnut.
Thou didst put thy arms about them as the arms
of a ka (vital force), for thy ka was in them.*

Egyptian creation myth, 24th century B.C.

*When on high the heaven had not been named,
firm ground below had not been called by name,
naught but primordial Apsu, their begetter,
and Mummu-Tiamat, she who bore them all,
their waters commingling as a single body.*

Babylonian creation myth, early 2nd
millennium B.C.

*In the beginning God created the heavens and the
earth. The earth was without form and void, and
darkness was upon the face of the deep; and the
Spirit of God was moving over the face of the waters.*

Genesis 1:1-2

3
Creation and Providence

Creation

That the OT pictures God as supreme over all the earth in no wise lessened the importance with which the Hebrews viewed the created order. In fact, it was because God made it and upheld it that the world could be important and substantial in its own right. Clearly, God is the absolute source of it all and the single will behind it. It exists for his purposes. In contrast to the accounts of beginnings in neighboring cultures (see the Egyptian and Babylonian myths above), the account of Genesis is simple and straightforward, displaying what someone has called "enlightened sobriety." In the OT there is no speculation on the origin of God as there is in so many Near Eastern myths. God is assumed at the start and in the end (Is. 41:4; see also Job 38:4).

Many scholars have taken the infrequent references to creation early in the history of Israel as evidence that the idea of God's creation of the world came rather late to their attention. These scholars argue that God's mighty work of redemption was the starting point for their reflection on creation. It is true that the early revelation of God to his people (as far as we can put together Israel's early history) does not contain extended reference to creation, and, similarly, that Moses and Joshua (in Deuteronomy and Joshua 24) do not mention God as creator where we might expect it. But before the conclusion is drawn that the experience of redemption preceded all thought of creation several things must be borne in mind.

First, very early portions of the Pentateuch (Ex. 15:16b and a later parallel in Deut. 32:6) speak of God's creation of Israel. It is true that the word for creation is not the same as that used in Genesis 1:1 and that the reference is to the creation of the nation of Israel by his mighty deliverance of them. Yet at the same time the idea is implicit that the exodus, which marks the creation of the nation Israel, is a creative act in which God again displays his creative power. Moreover, the language of Exodus 15 is similar to other references to God's original creation (Ps. 89).

Second, the commandment about the sabbath in Exodus 20:11 makes explicit reference to God's creation of all things before his own sabbath rest. Further, the commandment against making divine images certainly demands the background of the creation account to be properly understood (Ex. 20:4; Deut. 5:8-10; see Craigie, 153). Finally, the appearance of the creation account at the beginning of the Pentateuch indicates that all these materials (substantially dating, in my view, from Mosaic times) were traditionally understood in the light of the doctrine of creation.

It remains true, notwithstanding these considerations, that the full realization of God's creative power and greatness apparently came only later in Israel's history. It is not until the Psalms and the Prophets that God's power in creation is celebrated with any frequency. Israel perhaps first had to experience God's greatness in delivering them from bondage, preserving them and making them a great nation, to fully appreciate God's universal lordship. The step from seeing his greatness on their behalf to seeing his universal creative power was then a natural one. Perhaps we have here yet another example of God's revealing and impressing his truth on the people of Israel as they were able to receive it.

1. By Word and Work. Turning to the doctrine of creation itself, we note first that God created the world by his word and at the same time by his direct intervention. It is true that he spoke and the world was made (Ps. 33:6). But Genesis 1:2-3 also speaks of the Spirit hovering (like an eagle over her young), and Genesis 2:7-8 shows God making (in the sense of shaping) man and planting the garden. Creation by the word stresses God's transcendence—the primacy of his will and the ease of his work. The job of creating the world contained no struggle for God as it so often does in Near Eastern mythology. God's word was at the beginning, and continues to be, the basis of continuity between God and his work. At the same time, the image of the Spirit (or breath) of God in Genesis 1:2 suggests the intimacy of God's involvement in creation—his immanence. This serves as a suitable prelude for the personal relationship that God wishes to sustain with creation. It is wholly appropriate then that man and woman—the crown of creation—should be capable of address by this Creator-God as "thou." The word of the transcendent God comes to them in the form of a blessing and promise as near and intimate as their own breath (Deut. 30:14).

2. Ex Nihilo. By these Latin words Bible students have ordinarily expressed their belief that God used no previously existing material to create the world. There is strong support for such belief even if it is nowhere made explicit in the OT. First, in Genesis 1 the word for "create" *(bārā')* is used only of divine creation, and it never is used with the accusative of material. It is typical of God's creativity, then, that he brings into being that which previously had no existence. This was true of the nation of Israel; it was true of the original creation. What is at stake is the complete sovereignty of God over his creation. There is nothing that exists alongside of God with which he must struggle.

It is true, at the same time, that the Hebrew language, even as many languages today, was not equipped to speak in a technical way of nothingness. But even if the technical term *nothingness* is not explicit, the overwhelming strength of God conveys the same idea. What is to be stressed then is not the contrast of existence and nonexistence, but the revelation of an absolute power and the absence of such power. The prophets in a similar way employ such absolute contrasts to exhibit God's omnipotence (Is. 40:17 and Jer. 4:23-26). Here is creative power completely without analogy, power that is irresistible. As Karl Barth explains (speaking of Job 26:7): Creation *ex nihilo* "expresses the absolutely essential thing which is to be said of the creature of God as such, namely, that it derives from God and no other source, and that it exists through God and not otherwise. Hence it is not itself God, or an emanation of God" (*Church Dogmatics,* III/2, 155).

3. Note on the Two Accounts of Creation. The first two chapters of Genesis contain two complementary accounts of creation. The first (1:1—2:4a) is taken by critical scholars to belong to the late (Priestly or P) source, while the second (2: 4b-25) to the J (Jahwist) tradition. The view taken here is that the material all comes from the Mosaic period and reflects two perspectives on creation (perhaps coming from two older traditions) that complement each other. In the first account the approach is more systematic and the scope is cosmic. The emphasis is on the creative word as the means of creation, thus on God's transcendence over creation. It is progressive in nature leading up to the creation of man and woman as the climax. Though the intent is not scientific in the strict sense, the order of creation in general parallels the order that modern geology assigns for the relative age of the earth and its inhabitants. The broadest possible setting then is laid for all that follows. God is the Lord of all that is. In Calvin's words, everything that is, is a theater for his glory.

In the second account, as though with a zoom lens, we focus in on humanity in its unique environment. Here the work of God is seen on a more intimate scale and compared to the work of a potter at his wheel (the Hebrew word in 2:7

means "to shape" or "form" as a potter). God plants a garden for man, instructs him, makes a helpmate (meaning "one standing over against" to complement). History, properly speaking, begins here in chapter two—a history of relationship between God and humanity. With this beginning we already see the means that God will use to realize his glory, the communion he will establish with his people.

4. Summary: The Character of Creation. While the creation doctrine in the OT is not always made explicit, there are several points that run like threads through its pages. First, there is the assumption that creation is good. God was the first one to enjoy the beauty of creation as he pronounced it very good (Gen. 1:31). The idea is present in Ezekiel 28:11-15 as well, where the strength of the original perfection is implied. We will see that the Fall injured this perfection; but though the influence of sin is thorough, it is not complete. It does not alter the essential goodness of creation. Moreover, there is never any hint in the OT that creation is imperfect because it is material. Rather it is fashioned in such a way that it can become a vehicle of spiritual values, declaring the glory of God, reflecting his goodness in its own creaturely way. In its material character it has a life of its own, a beauty and goodness appropriate to it. Neither God nor humanity is ever frustrated by its material, earthly character.

Interestingly, it is the strength and steadfastness of creation that best reflected God for the Hebrew. Accordingly, the beauty of the flower, which in our more sentimental age reminds us of God, only spoke to the Hebrew of the transience of earthly glory (Job 14:2; Is. 28:1 and 40:7-8), though it did signal the arrival of spring (Song 2:12). More eloquent testimony of God's greatness is the rock (Ps. 62:2) and the storm, the wind and the mountain (Ps. 65:6-7 and Is. 55:12).

Not only is creation pictured as good in the OT, it is pictured as specifically ordered to work toward ends that God has planned for it. Though it has its own special character, God intends to work in it his purpose, that is, to exhibit his glory (Is. 6:3; Ps. 19). From the beginning (Gen. 1:26-30) creation ex-

hibits a symbiotic, cooperative interrelationship. Humankind and creation work together to accomplish the good purposes of God. We will see presently that the NT idea that all
things work together for good to those who love God (Rom.
8:28) is really based on the order that God made in creation,
which is so often celebrated in the OT (Is. 45:18-19).

Of course it does not always happen "naturally"; miracle
must intervene to restore the intended order. One could argue
that miracle in the Bible is simply God's effort to restore the
"natural" order of creation, though in the restoration he
makes a whole new order. Psalm 104 praises the course of
nature as an expression of God's faithfulness, concluding (v.
31): "May the glory of the LORD endure for ever, may the LORD
rejoice in his works." The arrangement of each part as well
as the whole is to display his glory, and if men and women
do not celebrate this, then the very stones will cry out. This
incidentally may help us understand some of the difficult
statements in the psalms. Psalm 104:35 says: "Let sinners be
consumed from the earth." That is, may the purposes of creation triumph in spite of evil people, may it be allowed to show
forth the eternal glory of God. This is no misanthrope who
cannot love his neighbor, but someone who has a glimpse of
God's great purpose and yearns for its triumph.

Finally, though the ultimate purpose of creation is the
glory of God, its immediate purpose is for men and women.
Why did God create? Edmond Jacob answers from the OT: "He
has created it [the world] for the covenant, that is to say because of his plan of love and salvation for man by means of
Israel" (Jacob, 137). Man and woman are the crown of creation and in them God's purposes are realized.

Myth and History in the OT

It is important to give attention to the question of myth and
history, not only because there are scattered references to
mythology in the OT, but more importantly because so many
people in Asia (and elsewhere in the Third World) understand
themselves in terms of myth. The elements properly con-

sidered mythological in the Bible have been the subject of great debate. Some feel that certainly the OT writers borrowed Babylonian and Canaanite mythical elements to use them in their picture of the world. Especially is this true, these scholars would say, in the case of the creation and flood stories. In Genesis 1:2 "the face of the deep" and "without form and void" are thought to be references to a chaos that existed before creation and with which God had to struggle to create. This same struggle is supposedly reflected in Psalm 104:7. In Psalm 74:13-14 God is pictured crushing the heads of Leviathan. This is believed to be the same as Lotan, the dragon of Canaanite mythology. Baal says, according to one myth, "I have slain the Crooked Serpent, the Foul-fanged with seven heads" (DOTT, 130). Likewise, in the account in Isaiah 51:9, God cuts Rahab and pierces the dragon. Job 7:12 may allude to Tiamat, who is kept in submission by Marduk. In the Babylonian account of creation these two "joined forces in battle. [Marduk] spread wide his net . . . and enveloped her. . . ." Then Marduk holds her at bay by an evil wind (DOTT, 9-10). Then, in a more fundamental way, other scholars take the whole paradise account, the flood, the sons of the gods (Gen. 6:2) and the prophets' vision of paradise and Fall (Is. 14:12-21) to be legends without any factual reference.

Before dealing directly with this problem it is well to clarify what is meant by *myth*. Certainly our modern idea of "something false" will not do. Better is the first definition of *Webster's New Collegiate Dictionary:* "a usually traditional story of ostensibly historical events that serves to unfold a part of the world view of a people" (1973). Myth then, in a broad sense, expresses a people's understanding of reality (Childs 1960, 17-21). This understanding is not simply of facts—though it usually includes these—but of the inner meaning of those facts. Myth expresses the force of communally experienced reality. In this sense then it is improper to imagine that only primitive people have such understandings. All people have their own particular myths that express the way they understand the world. In the West, for example, people im-

agine that history and nature are objective processes which
they can study and control. This is a part of their mythology
or world picture. To most people of Africa and Asia the world
is a living organism in which they are vitally involved. To
them it is the Western picture that is naive, imagining that
people are only spectators, viewing events externally. Who is
to say which view is more accurate?

In any event, the people of biblical times also experienced
the world in personal terms. The weather expressed the wrath
or pleasure of God, the heavens and the earth were all a part
of a grand drama which involved each person. In their practices of worship they celebrated their belief in the seriousness
of this drama, and in this they had much in common with
others of their day and of ours. But having admitted that this
view of the world is also found in the OT and that allusions to
pagan myths may be found in its pages, we must now look
more closely to see the absolutely unique way these elements
are used.

We have already seen that the consistent interpretation of
Genesis 1:1-2 is that God created out of nothing. Now nothingness as we also noted is an abstract concept for which Hebrew had no adequate terminology. The usual solution to the
problem of beginnings in Near Eastern mythology is to begin
with two forces struggling for supremacy, the creation result-
ing from their struggles. Sometimes the struggle is between
Tiamat and Marduk, sometimes between light and darkness.
While occasionally there are hints of such a struggle in the
Bible (Ps. 74:13-14), it is always clear that God is in no way
threatened by these other forces but triumphs over them by
his irresistible power. They are introduced not to suggest
competition but to illustrate the supremacy of Jahweh. There
is an interesting parallel phenomenon in the NT; in Colossians 1:16 many scholars see allusions to a gnostic view of the
spiritual levels of reality. As in the OT Paul does not mean to
specify that these levels actually exist, he is simply employ-
ing them in order to express Christ's absolute lordship.
Thrones, dominions, whatever exists is made by Christ and

for him. Similarly, all these OT allusions serve to remind Israel how much greater is their God than the gods of the heathen. In Babylonian mythology nothing is beyond the influence of Chaos; in Israel everything fled before God's mighty voice.

What about the paradise account? This motif—one paradise at the beginning of time and another at the end—has led some to see a mythological pattern of creation-fall-restoration which reflects a circular view of time. While it is true that some pattern is discernible and that time does focus on quality and significance rather than pure duration, it is not true that this reflects an unchanging cyclic view of time. In the first place, the end that the prophets envision is not simply a return to the beginning but is rather the emerging of a new reality determined by God. History and its events become by God's direction a real part of the goal that is in view. Meanwhile, the end that God brings about is a new creation (see Is. 48:6 and 65:17-19)—a new creation, and yet at the same time meaningfully and actually related to this world and its history. Now until the end, events of real significance *fill up* the time, which then becomes—so much more than a mere restoration—a *fulfilled* time (Childs 1960, 77-83).

In the OT places also take on special significance. Zion or Jerusalem is compared with Eden (Is. 11:6-9) and is pictured as the earth's center (Ps. 48:1-3; Zech. 14:10). Is this a mythology of place? Again we must remember that this is consistent with the personal view that the OT exhibits toward the world. The quality or significance, rather than the mere location, of the space mattered, and since the quality of Zion and Eden were similar they could be compared. But again there is an important difference in the Hebrew view. First Jerusalem had to *become* the symbol of the new Eden in the course of history. As Childs says: "The establishing of Zion is an historical, not a mythical event" (Childs 1960, 90). In the process of God's working in the events of history something new emerges, the fact and hope of Zion, which, while being like Eden, surpasses it in meaning.

It is clear then, on the one hand, that the Hebrews experienced the world in personal terms. Since they knew the Lord had revealed himself as the sovereign creator and sustainer of the world, they could not experience any part of it without seeing it in relation to him. Its terrible elements—earthquakes, clouds, lightning, darkness and thunder—were seen to accompany his appearances (Ps. 18:8-16; 68:7-9; Hab. 3:3-15). Its storms expressed his wrath (Ps. 29:3-9) and good weather his favor (Ps. 107:25-29). God is seen as a rider of the clouds (Ps. 68:4) and as Lord of the earthquake (Nahum 1:5). But in the deliverance of his people his wrath and his goodness are most clearly demonstrated (Ps. 77:16-20).

On the other hand, it is wrong to conclude from this that some of the events celebrated by Israel in their myths (creation, the flood) are only legend in the sense of not being factual. The OT focus on significance is meant to capitalize on these facts not to deny them. It may be the lived experience they wished to emphasize, but they certainly could not have felt the significance if they did not understand that God actually did create the world, deliver Noah, rescue the children of Israel and so forth. It is only in our modern world that we have allowed facts and meanings to be split apart; the OT understands them in their intimate interrelationship, both expressions of the faithfulness of God. The account of Israel's history, if it is to retain its full meaning, must be founded on actual events.

The world picture of the Hebrew is often described as quaint and unscientific: vaults, pillars, domes and fountains of the deep, and so forth. The observation is true in part, but its significance pales when we recognize that the Bible is written in the phenomenal language of everyday life. The fact that we speak this way ourselves (the four corners of the earth, the sun rising and setting) shows the danger of making ordinary speech the measure of scientific insight. It is certainly true that we know more of the vastness and complexity of the world than the Hebrews did. But this is sometimes suggested as a problem for the Hebrew view of God and the world, as though the dimensions of the biblical God were somehow limited by the inadequate descriptions of the physical world in the OT. I am sure this proposition would only puzzle a biblical writer. "For him the magnitude of the universe, had he known it, would have been even more ample evidence of the power and will of Jahweh to save" (McKenzie, 203).

There is one more distinction to be pointed out between Israel and her neighbors. For the Hebrew the unity and coherence of creation is the will of God. There is no concept of nature as a self-contained system in the OT. The will of God is both the limit and source for the created order. This suggests that for Israel reality cannot be understood in the same way as in Near Eastern mythology. As Edmond Jacob remarks, myth can never be a starting point for a movement in history (Jacob, 138). It is history, that is the order of events that God began and continues to direct, that gives meaning to the created order. There is natural process in creation—which we will consider below—but its purpose is seen most fully in the direction given to it by the free intervention of the Lord of creation. This direction is extended by the prophets to a new heaven and a new earth which will bring to a culmination both creation and history. There God will show himself completely sovereign.

In Mesopotamian mythology the struggle between the gods provided the greatest sense of insecurity to the world order. In Israel it was not God (or gods) but sin that threatened the created order. Because of this, God's judgment threatened (Zeph. 1:2; Amos 7:4; Jer. 4:23-26). But still he remained the ultimate source of security for his people and for the earth, for beyond this judgment there was a new heaven and earth, liberated from the forces of sin that now threatened (Zeph. 3:11-13). For God was ultimately the perfecter and not the enemy of the world.

Providence: God's Continuing Relationship to Creation
1. Completion of Creation. Here we are struck with the same tension of independence and dependence that we noted

earlier. On the one hand, Genesis 2:2-3 implies that in some sense God ended his work. But this does not mean that God turned away from creation (as deists believe), but rather that he turned toward it. God's relationship to creation is changed, but it is no less intimate. This new relationship is first of all a delight in creation—God pronounced it good—and then a rest (Ex. 20:11). Theologically this sabbath rest becomes an important symbol of salvation: rest from one's enemies, which Israel was one day to share. This rest God had to withhold because of Israel's sin (Ps. 95:11), but it will one day be enjoyed by all of God's people (Heb. 4:9-10).

2. Continuing Care. From creation on, God continues to care for his creation through processes he has established, which we call—somewhat inaccurately—natural laws. There are, in other words, built into creation the means of reproducing and generating life. These processes God uses to continue his care. But we misunderstand the OT teaching if we see these laws as operating independently of God and capable of temporary suspension if it suits his purposes. This somewhat mechanical conception is not even a proper picture according to modern science, and it is certainly not the biblical view of things. Bernard Ramm explains natural law this way: "In the process of time the Spirit working through-and-through Nature, *the command of God is fulfilled.* The laws of Nature, under the direction of the Holy Spirit, actualize over a period of time and through process, the plan of God" (*Christian View of Science and Scripture,* 1954, 116, emphasis his). This is a helpful way of stressing God's intimate presence and his use of these laws for his purposes.

The OT picture is of God working in and through the order of nature to realize his purposes. The image found there is a personal one. He sets bounds for the oceans (Job 38:10-11), decrees the weather (Job 28:26), creates the wind (Amos 4:13), directs the paths of the animals (Job 39:26) and gives them all their food and drink (Ps. 104:11, 21). We often dismiss this way of speaking as metaphoric. In a certain sense it is, because the OT sets itself against all forms of pantheism, which identifies God with his creation. But at the same time, God's use of secondary causes that we can understand in a scientific way (a reduced way of knowing after all) does not mean that God is any less intimately present in these processes, using them according to his plan. The most *natural* things we know in this world may be *supernatural* as well. It is difficult for us to see how there can be a real and regular process of nature in which God is also active. This may only reflect our inadequate view of God, and it may turn out in the end to poorly reflect the reality of nature as well.

3. Levels of God's Care. It may be helpful to think of God's activity in creation in terms of three levels. At the first level is the original creation which he made to exhibit his glory. It was made immediately, that is, out of no previously existing material. It perfectly reflected, in its creaturely way, its creator.

Growing out of this creation is a second level, which we ordinarily call providence. That is, God, having finished the original work of creation, continued to care for it in and through the life processes which he built into it. Though they operate on their own, they still depend on God's upholding care. At this level God allows the rain to fall on the just and the unjust. There is theological significance even in this regularity, for God is at work even there to bring people to repentance and to fellowship with himself. In Scripture there is a very important, though unobtrusive, theme: the order of nature on which man depends is a revelation of God's goodness, particularly his mercy and longsuffering. This is implicit in the OT in verses like Psalm 19:2-4: "their voice goes out through all the earth." But it is made explicit in the NT. In Romans 2:4 Paul asks: "Do you not know that God's kindness is meant to lead you to repentance?" To those who scoff at Christ's nonappearance, saying that nothing has changed since creation, Peter replies: "The Lord ... is forbearing toward you, not wishing that any should perish" (2 Pet. 3:9).

All this is made plain at the third level of God's care. As well as forming and preserving an environment suited to man,

God works directly to bring about salvation. At this level we refer to miracles, but we must not distinguish these too sharply from the other levels of God's operation. God does not contradict what he has already established. Rather, just as he reveals his goodness in the natural order, he freely intervenes to control events in special ways. In the Exodus celebration of God's deliverance from Egypt there is an echo of God's original creation, implying, as we noted above, that this act is another creative work. At the same time, floods, seas and winds, which we associate with the natural order, accomplish this miraculous saving work (Ex. 15:5, 8, 10). These special workings—the miracles of the prophets, Jonah, Samson, and the rest—all contribute to the deliverance and preservation of Israel as a special people.

All these are a part of the many and various ways that God spoke to his people (Heb. 1:1). In good and evil, blessing and punishment, God works freely (Lam. 3:37-39). But even— or we should say, especially—in these extraordinary events, it is the same faithfulness of God that is evident. Jeremiah, in fact, likens the covenant which has taken God's miraculous intervention to establish and maintain to the order of creation: "If I have not established my covenant with day and night and the ordinances of heaven and earth, then I will reject the descendants of Jacob and David my servant and will not choose one of his descendants to rule over the seed of Abraham" (Jer. 33:25-26). As Eichrodt points out, it is not the abnormal quality of the events that struck Israel but the "clear impression of God's care or retribution" within them (Eichrodt, II, 163).

We distinguish then three levels within God's care. But in a larger sense they are not distinct. They all reflect a single, purposeful will of a personal God. At all levels we are speaking about a single program for the world. In the vision of the prophets this program extends to embrace the whole world. All creation will again, and in a higher way, give voice to the great song of praise to God which is its highest privilege and final end (Is. 2:2-4).

Man, in contrast from all the rest of creation, has not merely been created by and through God, but in and for God. He is, what he is originally, by God and through God; he is also in and for God. Hence he can and should understand himself in God alone. Just as it is said of no other creatures, 'let us make', so also it is said of no other that it has been created 'after his likeness' or 'in his image'.

Emil Brunner, *Man in Revolt*

4
Man
and
Woman

The Creation of Man and Woman
1. A Special Relationship to Creation. Man and woman are the crown of creation; they are made to rule. Both in Genesis 1:26 and 2:7 the creation of man and woman follows a deliberate decision and definite act on the part of God. On the one hand, this means that man and woman are part of the created order. "Of the dust" implies that God took what was inanimate and lifeless to make the first man (see also Gen. 3:19). Note that God did not take an animal to form the man, but the dust. To take this for a metaphoric way of speaking of previously existing life, thus allowing for theistic evolution, would seem to stretch the text beyond reasonable limits. Humanity is thus separate from the animal world, yet part of the created order.

Man and woman's solidarity with the natural order, which they exhibit in their bodily existence, is an important emphasis of Scripture. Often God's covenant promises are given in the context of possession of the land. The worship of God by

his people must always be in an earthly context, even if that
will one day be a new earth. From Romans 8:19-22 we know
more of this interrelationship between the creature and its
final deliverance, but it is already present in the OT. When
the first man and woman sin a curse rests on the land (Gen.
3:17-18); sin defiles the land (Deut. 24:4). When the land becomes defiled it must eventually vomit its inhabitants (Lev.
18:25, 28). On the other hand, Jerusalem becomes a symbol of
the mountain of the Lord where all the nations will go up to
worship God (Is. 2:2-4). In that Day there will be peace in the
land; its integrity will be restored. Then the lion will lie down
with the lamb (Is. 11:6-9).

Yet despite their solidarity with the created order, human
beings transcend that order. Their fundamental relationship
lies with God, and in that relationship lies their fundamental independence of the creation. While they are made as a
part of nature, they are also made to rule over it. The first pre-
supposition of this is that for them creation is demytholo-
gized. That is, creation is not divine or endowed with divine
powers. Wherever human beings must live in fear of nature,
afraid to plant unless certain "gods" are appeased, afraid to
walk under a ladder or sleep on the thirteenth floor, there
they have not yet realized their essential lordship over creation. Man and woman are created to live and work freely in
the world. It can become an environment which can be molded
into symbols of their values; it was made to be their play-
ground, though sin has often made it seem their prison.

Adam, the first man, was told to name the animals (Gen. 2:
19-20). This was not merely to categorize all the animals, but
to discover their essential relationship to humanity and to
each other. None, however, was found as a fit helper for
Adam. To name was to give a place in the arrangement of
things (recall the importance of a name in the OT) and to show
Adam's own superiority in the created order. In naming,
Adam freed himself from the world and expressed his transcendence over it, thus reflecting in his creaturely way God's
transcendence. Even today naming is a basic component of

the descriptive method of science; in a sense it continues God's creative activity. Yet in discovering his role as ruler-worker, Adam felt at the same time the essential gulf that existed between himself and the rest of creation. "The gulf between man and nature was something inherent in the very deepest level of man's spiritual and personal being" (Eichrodt, II, 119).

2. The Special Relationship among Persons. Persons were made to love. Ultimately only another person will satisfy the deep needs of human nature. So God created persons male and female (Gen. 1:27). Karl Barth believes this statement is the definitive explanation of the image of God (*Church Dogmatics,* III/1, 195). Surely this duality is a vital part of their being: humans are made for relationship, to complement each other in love. From this verse it is clear that humanity is created as male and female such that each is incomplete without the other and both stand on an equal footing before God. Maleness and femaleness are basic to humanity, though clearly they belong to the created order rather than to God.

The bisexual nature of humankind suggests that love is the basic human relationship on the natural level. Interestingly, fertility is given in an additional blessing in verse 28; it is not necessarily implied in humanity's dual nature, and thus the fundamental relationship between the sexes is not necessarily sexual in the narrow sense. Already in Genesis 2:22-25, though, marriage is presented as the basic human institution. The ideal expressed is monogamous; the two become one flesh. It is true that in the course of the OT other arrangements are allowed, but these must be viewed as lesser goods which God allowed to care for problems which intervened because of sin: unmarried women, childless marriages and the threatening split of families and their resources. But as an image of God's love for his people, marriage is clearly monogamous to the core. It is spoken of as a covenant in Malachi 2:14 and Proverbs 2:17, and likened to God's relation to his people in the book of Hosea, especially. Genesis 1:28 expresses this as blessing and command: "Be fruitful and multiply." In this command "a tremendous motive power is implanted in human life, which inevitably drives it on to great goals" (Eichrodt, I, 110). Here as well the bodily nature of the person is created to express, not frustrate, man's love for woman and her love for him. This is clearly and beautifully expressed in the Song of Solomon and is implicit throughout Scripture.

But human relationship in the OT is broader than the marriage bond. Persons in fact are never considered separately but always as responsible members of a family or tribe. The individual is located as a member of a house, which belongs to a clan, united in a tribe, which all together finds its unity in the house of Israel (Josh. 7:16-18). This solidarity, which has been called corporate personality (H. W. Robinson 1946, 70), often causes references to shift between the individual and the group. See, for example, the shift from *I* to *we* in the ancient creed in Deuteronomy 26:5-10. Similarly, Jacob was the father of Israel, but later all Israel was referred to as Jacob (Mic. 1:5 et al.). To be alone, in fact, was to be afflicted (Ps. 25:15-16). In Psalm 102 a man dying and mocked by his enemies cries out "like a lonely bird on the housetop" (v. 7). Though even the lonely can find help in the Lord (Ps. 4:8).

There is an important exception to this group consciousness, and that is the call of God that comes to individuals for the sake of the group. Abraham is told to leave the comfort of his family and country in order to be the means of God's blessing to many (Gen. 12:1-3). Moses is called to come near to God for the sake of the people (Ex. 24:2). The high priest goes in alone to the holy place for the people (Lev. 16:17-19). Jeremiah must be alone for the sake of his message (Jer. 15:17). This individual calling serves as the backdrop for the calling of God that comes to Christ in the NT, who is sent from God to be a mediator of God's presence. Because of Christ the call of God now extends to all men (Acts 17:30-31; 1 Pet. 2:24-25). This calling is already anticipated in the OT, however, in the challenge of Joshua at Shechem: "Choose this day whom you will serve, ... but as for me and my house, we will serve the LORD" (Josh. 24:15; see Jer. 31:29-30). This personal and individual sense of responsibility before God—emphasized in the Reformation—lies behind the individual consciousness so evident in Western culture.

3. A Special Relationship to God. Ultimately their dominion over creation and their impulse to give themselves in love to one another speaks of man and woman's higher end: to love their creator. Persons are made ultimately to praise God and to find their highest end in that praise. This end is the supreme meaning of creation *in the image of God*. Human life in a unique sense is a divine gift, meant to reflect in some way the character of God himself. Precisely what this image consists of we are not told, except that it surely relates to dominion, for the reference to rulership immediately follows in parallel expression to creation in the image of God: "Let us make man in our image . . . and let them have dominion . . ." (Gen. 1:26). This connection is supported by Psalm 8 where human greatness is directly related to dominion over all the animals. It is not clear though whether the image consists in dominion itself, or whether dominion is that for which men and women are uniquely suited by virtue of this image.

Image and *likeness* are probably parallel terms meant to express a single idea. But the word for image implies more of a plastic, molded likeness, suggesting that the outward form of a person itself shares in the imaging of God. *Likeness* means rather a similarity than an actual copy, something resembling in ways not necessarily perceived by the senses. It has been suggested that the idea behind this is the custom of setting up a statue of the king as a testimony to the king's domination over that place (Dan. 3:1, 5). Human beings in this sense witness to God's own sovereignty over creation and stand in his stead as a "vicegerent" (Wolff, 160, and Eichrodt, II, 127). Human dominion thus reflects God's own lordship over creation. Certainly a further intention is to underline human creativity and responsibility with reference to creation. Human beings are not made for idleness but for purposeful work in which they are to take delight, just as God did in his own work. Though the Fall introduced the element of drudgery there is no endless work, for the sabbath gives people time to rest and enjoy the work of their hands.

In sum it can be said that the image of God implies the personal, responsible existence of men and women before God, suited to reflect their creator in their work, to know and love him in all that they do. Once again the body is not seen as a barrier to spiritual life, but rather the proper medium of it. Man and woman are known by God from their beginnings (Ps. 139:13-16), upheld by God in their lives (Job 10:12) and led toward their final end when they will look on God's face in the fullness of the life for which they are created (Ps. 16:11).

The Nature of Humankind

While there is obviously no systematic unity in the references, a careful study of the words and expressions used for the person can give us a portrait of concrete life. Wolff gives two helpful guides to the language the OT employs (Wolff, 7-9).

First, there is often the *stereometric* use of words, that is, the parallel and overlapping reference of words. Words close in meaning are used almost interchangeably to refer to the whole person from slightly different points of view thus giving a richer picture. For example, Psalm 84:2: "My heart and flesh sing for joy," or Proverbs 2:10: "For wisdom will come into your heart, and knowledge will be pleasant to your soul." Thus the way the words are used together throws light on a deeper content.

Second, there is the *synthetic* use of words, where one part of the body is made to stand for the whole. The part and its action are synthesized as in Isaiah 52:7: "How beautiful upon the mountains are the feet of him who brings good tidings." Thus "with a relatively small vocabulary, through which he names things and particularly the parts of the human body, the Hebrew can and must express a multiplicity of fine nuances by extracting from the context of the sentence the possibilities, activities, qualities or experiences of what is named" (Wolff, 8).

1. Soul (nepēš). The Hebrew word usually translated "soul" appears 755 times and actually means "soul" in only a few places. This word speaks primarily of the person as creature. In only 3 per cent of the appearances does it refer to God. In Genesis 2:7 God breathes into man and he becomes a living soul. That this is not unique to human beings is seen in the use of this term in the creation of animals in Genesis 1:20, 21 and 24 where it is usually translated "living creature." The meaning there is simply a living individual. Human beings live as souls; they do not "possess" souls.

The word is often used to express a person in need, usually in a purely physical sense. Sometimes it is used in the sense of a throat opened in greedy need (Ps. 143:6; "appetite" in Is. 5:14). It can be the organ that drinks (Prov. 25: 25) or that tastes (Prov. 16:24) or that craves (Jer. 2:24, Heb.; RSV, "heat"). Or it is simply the neck (Ps. 105:18 and Jer. 4:10, Heb.; RSV, "life"). In this sense the soul is the seat of the elemental needs of a person. By extension the word comes to mean "desire" in the sense of vital longing or striving, as in "our heart's desire" (Ps. 35:25; see also Mic. 7:1). This is perhaps the most common usage. Then its usage is enlarged to mean simply the soul in the sense of the center of spiritual experiences. "You know the heart [Heb., "soul"] of a stranger, for you were strangers in the land of Egypt" (Ex. 23:9; 2 Sam. 5:8; Job 30:25). It is used to mean simply "life" (Prov. 8:35; Ps. 30:3), or an "individual" or "person" (Prov. 3:22), or even a "corpse" (Num. 6:6).

Thus the soul is the living individual, not in the sense of an indestructible spiritual substance, rather in concrete, needy, physical life. It comes from God and is in constant need of refreshing; in itself it offers no protection against creaturely limitations. The OT believer cannot count on inherent immortality; this must come from God and be guaranteed by him (Ps. 16:10; 49:15). Humans are eager, thirsty for life and vitality, a life that cannot come from the creation alone. Human appetite for life suggests that deeper hunger for fellowship with God: "As a hart longs for flowing streams, so longs

my soul for thee, O God" (Ps. 42:1). Of course needy dependence can lead to desperation, but it ought to lead to dependence and praise.

2. Spirit (rûaḥ). This word, which appears 389 times, is more
often applied to God (136 times) than to persons or animals
(129 times). The basic meaning is physical "wind" or "breath."
It is wind that shakes the trees (Is. 7:2), or it is simply the
"cool" of the day (Gen. 3:8). It is the breath which the Lord
gives the people (Is. 42:5), or that can smell foul (Job 19:17,
literally, "my breath is strange to my wife"). By extension
the word comes to mean the vital powers—"strength"—when
referred to a person. The spirit can sustain a person in infir-
mity (Prov. 18:14), though it is those whose spirit is crushed
that the Lord promises to save (Ps. 34:18). For the spirit, while
it suggests strength, also points out limitation. It is God who
gives this spirit and when he takes it back the person returns
to the dust (Job. 34:14-15 and Ps. 104:29-30); in these verses,
in fact, the person's spirit and God's are all but inseparable.

Spirit is used of God to indicate his great power. It is by
his Spirit ("breath") that the earth is made (Ps. 33:6) or that
the waters of the Red Sea are piled up (Ex. 15:8). Accordingly,
when the Spirit of the Lord comes upon a person there is an
extraordinary endowment of power (Judg. 3:10 and 6:34) or
authorization (Is. 42:1). When his Spirit comes upon Ezekiel,
he is given the words to speak (Ezek. 11:5); in similar fashion
Bezalee is given artistic ability (Ex. 31:3). In most of these
cases spirit means the power that will supplement those
powers already present, making up what is lacking (Is. 11:2),
though not with elements that are strange or incompatible
with human nature. The gifts that God gives his people are
seldom supernatural in this sense. So when Pharaoh is looking for a man "in whom is the Spirit of God" (Gen. 41:38), he is
looking for a man who is wise and discreet, whose human
abilities are undiminished.

The word comes later to mean simply the organ of our
psychic life, what spirit ordinarily means today. It can
mean simply "mind" (Ezek. 11:5), "resolve" (Jer. 51:11) or

"will" (Is. 19:3). When the Queen of Sheba saw the glory of Solomon she was "breathless" ("there was no more spirit in her," 1 Kings 10:5). But the connotation remains that of "strength" or "vital powers" for which ultimately a person is dependent upon God and which cannot be claimed or held for oneself. H. W. Wolff summarizes: "That a man has spirit, is living, desires the good and acts as authorized being—none of this proceeds from man himself" (Wolff, 39).

It is evident already in the OT that only as persons know God and receive strength from him can they be fully human. David knew that a proper relationship with God would not be possible until God had put a "firm spirit" within him (Ps. 51: 10, Heb.). Although OT believers rejoiced fully in their God and enjoyed his gifts, they still looked forward to the day when God would pour out his Spirit without measure. The prophet Joel speaks of this day and connects it with the latter days (Joel 2: 28-29). Peter expressly connects the giving of the Spirit at Pentecost with this prophecy (Acts 2:16). This empowering gift of the last days now belongs to all believers; it is what Paul calls an earnest of our inheritance in heaven (2 Cor. 1:22). But all this is possible because we are somehow like God. Even this brief survey of "spirit" makes clear the marvelous affinity we have with God. The human spirit calls out for its divine complement; God for his part searches for worshipers who will worship him in spirit and in truth. This affinity is clear from the Christian's own experience, for God's Spirit bears witness with our spirits that we are the children of God (Rom. 8:16).

3. Flesh (bāśār). This word—usually translated "flesh"— appears 273 times, a third of them referring to animals and the rest to humans (it is never used of God). Thus at the outset *flesh* connotes what humans share with animals in contradistinction to God. The word can mean simply flesh in the sense of meat which people eat (Is. 22:13; Prov. 23:20), but more often it means flesh as characteristic of bodily existence (Job 10:11; Ps. 78:39). In an example of synthetic thinking, "great of flesh" becomes a strong image for lust (Ezek.

16:26), and when human flesh is particularly disgusting, it is likened to the flesh of animals (Ezek. 23:19-20).

As an expression of physical existence, flesh often stands for the human body as a whole. Though Hebrew has no term for body as such, this term served often in that sense. There is no soundness, says the psalmist, in his flesh (body) because of God's indignation (Ps. 38:3). The body (flesh) is to be completely shaved in the course of the Levite consecration (Num. 8:7). Even more generally flesh refers to bodily existence, or to the bodily mode of living. When the psalmist invites all flesh to bless God's name, he is inviting all people in their earthly physical life to seek the Lord (Ps. 145:21). A person of my flesh is physically related to me (Neh. 5:5; Gen. 29:14).

Significantly, there is no indication that the flesh as such is evil or even a source of evil. But a person as flesh is recognized as weak and lacking in strength. Especially is this true when flesh is compared with God. What flesh can stand before God and live (Deut. 5:26)? If I trust in God, what can flesh do to me (Ps. 56:4)? Cursed is the one who trusts in flesh instead of God (Jer. 17:5, 7). As with spirit, a person as flesh depends on the Lord for strength (Job 34:14-15). As Isaiah declares: "All flesh is grass. ... The grass withers ... but the word of our God will stand for ever" (Is. 40:6, 8). The flesh is the physical form of living, never opposed to the self, but rather the proper medium of spiritual and personal life. Though weak, it is not in itself evil or a source of frustration. For it is in this context that people can come to God and find strength and rest. To thee, the psalmist prays, shall all flesh come (Ps. 65:2). Along with my soul, my flesh longs for God (Ps. 63:1). The prophet Isaiah envisions all flesh coming to worship God (Is. 66:23), and Ezekiel predicts that God will take out of them a stony heart and give them a heart of flesh (Ezek. 11:19). Once again we are struck with the fact that God delivers from sin and brokenness, not from human characteristics. God's people are redeemed as men and women to stand before him as he intended at creation.

At the same time, as becomes clear in the NT, the weakness

of the flesh makes it an ideal target for temptation. While
the OT emphases are continued in the NT, flesh is seen there
as a special, but certainly not exclusive, seat of sin, so that
"fleshly" can become synonomous with "sinful" (1 Cor. 3:1).
Here lies the significance of Christ's coming in the likeness of
sinful flesh to condemn sin in the flesh (Rom. 8:3).

4. Heart (lēb). This, the most common of all terms in the OT
for a person and his life, appears some 850 times in all its
forms, almost always referring to humankind (only five times
to animals). If ever a word is misunderstood in its translation, it is "heart," which in our modern understanding carries
very little of the depth of meaning that it has in its biblical
context. In one sense it refers to the internal aspect of the soul.
But even this is limiting its scope; there is hardly a spiritual
process which is not brought into some connection with the
heart.

Following Wolff's method, we begin again with physical
ideas associated with the word and see how the meaning is
expanded from this basic framework. It is clear at once that
the OT has little interest in anatomy as such, for often "heart"
is used as an equivalent of "bowels," which were thought to be
the seat of deep emotions (Ps. 38:10; 26:2). In 1 Samuel 25:
37-38 Nabal's heart dies and he becomes as stone. But he
lives another ten days! Obviously it is his emotions and not
his physical heart that was affected. In Hosea 13:8, "to tear
out the heart" (Heb.; RSV, "tear open their breast") may have
a more literal meaning; in 2 Kings 9:24 the literal heart is
clearly intended.

More important to the Hebrews than the anatomical reference was the place of the heart in a person's being. It lay at
the deepest level of feelings and registered the most profound
responses to life. Jeremiah 4:19 describes the prophet's
anguish at the approaching war in such drastic terms that we
are tempted to think he has had a heart attack. When the
heart is faint ("overwhelmed" in many translations), a person
is at his lowest point (Ps. 61:2). Clearly this is the deepest
level of human need (Ps. 25:17). That this is true is evi-

dent from some of the metaphoric uses of the word where it implies the inaccessible or remote place ("heart of the sea," Prov. 30:19, Heb.; RSV, "high seas"). Thus it is the part of the person that only God can see. People can only look on the outward appearance (1 Sam. 16:7), but even in the heart we can keep no secrets from God (Prov. 24:12).

At this level of human nature then lies the area of wishes and—more importantly—the decisions of the will. Often we read of a person's heart's desire, that is, of his or her most deeply felt wish (Ps. 21:2). The imaginations of the sinful heart are evil continually (Gen. 6:5); the fool says in his heart there is no God (Ps. 14:1). When the heart is hardened, a person is obstinate and not open to counsel (Ex. 7:22; Josh. 11:20); but when the heart melts, the mind is changed (Josh. 14:8). Yet even though a person decides in his heart, it is God who directs (Prov. 16:9). Thus the firm decision is that which rests in God (Ps. 57:7; 108:1). This is the point of the human personality, then, at which surrender must be made to God. As Jeremiah explained, it is not our foreskin but our heart that must be circumcised (Jer. 4:4).

Lest we think this kind of decision is a pure act of the will, it must be pointed out that in the vast majority of the cases intellectual and rational functions are ascribed to the heart—what we would call functions of the mind. For all its importance as the center of personality (as we would put it today), there is no implication that humans are irrational creatures who operate on the basis of feelings and hunches. The highest gift that can be given a person is a heart (usually translated "mind") to understand. Moses lamented that the people had not grasped the significance of God's great deeds—they had not an understanding heart (Deut. 29:4). Solomon's great request is for an understanding heart (1 Kings 3:9, 12). "The mind [Heb., "heart"] of him who has understanding seeks knowledge" (Prov. 15:14). It is not surprising that the word appears almost 100 times in Proverbs alone, where wisdom is described as the living out of wholehearted trust in God (Prov. 3:5).

The modern distinction—so often discussed in connection with faith—between the heart and head certainly has no place in the biblical view. For as a man thinks in his heart, so is he (Prov. 23:7, though the Hebrew of this verse is obscure). It is the thoughts and determinations of their hearts that make people what they are. The biblical dichotomy that we are warned against is between outward profession and inward disposition—what we call hypocrisy. This is what Christ accused the Pharisees of: "This people honors me with their lips, but their heart is far from me" (Mt. 15:18; he was quoting Is. 29:13).

Finally, reference must be made to the heart of God. This is the standard of God's character against which people are judged. God seeks a faithful priest who will do what is in his heart (1 Sam. 2:35). A person after God's heart is one who does what God commands (1 Sam. 13:14). The heart is the place of God's planning and decision (Ps. 33:11; Hos. 11:8-9 may mean his decision is changed). When he wishes to stress that his presence will be in the temple (1 Kings 9:3), he promises his heart will be there. Ultimately it is upon the knowledge of God's heart that people must depend. For everyone's way seems right in his own eyes, but it is God that weighs the heart (Prov. 21:2).

The heart then is the focus of the personal life: the reasoning, responding, deciding self. Knowledge of the heart is by no means abstract or impersonal. It is expressed through personal participation and deliberate decision (Deut. 29:3-4). It is in such soil that the expressions of the book of James have their roots: faith without works is not real faith but merely profession. But to have genuine faith, to share the heart of God, involves a change so drastic that the prophets describe it as having a new heart, a fleshly one rather than a stony one (Ezek. 11:19). For this, he who is sent from the heart of God must first come.

5. Blood (dām). Appearing 360 times, the word *blood* refers to the physical life of man and animals, often meaning quite simply "the life of man" (Prov. 1:16, 18; Ps. 72:13-14). This word has no part to play in the emotional or intellectual life of man, though it is by no means unimportant in the OT scheme of things. When it is shed, it calls from the ground (Gen. 4:10) for revenge (Gen. 42:22). It is the blood that is to be saved from the passover lamb and sprinkled on the doorposts (Ex. 12). In Genesis 9:4-6 it seems to be synonymous with life and requires a reckoning when it is shed. This requirement is connected immediately with man's creation in the image of God (v. 6). So blood becomes a significant symbol of life and, by extension, the means of compensating for life (see Lev. 4, 16 and 17, which we will discuss in the chapter on worship). It is to be brought as a gift to the Lord. Proper contact with blood, then, brings one into immediate relationship with God who is the source of life. The meat can belong to man because it returns to the earth, but the blood, symbolizing life, belongs to God the giver of life (Lev. 17:6 and Deut. 12:15-16; compare Wolff, 61).

Certain crimes are crimes of bloodguilt (Lev. 20:9; Prov. 28:17) and must be atoned for by blood placed on the altar as an expiation (Lev. 4; 16:14). In this act the guilt can be transferred. Life, symbolized by blood, is a gift from God to be used in his service. All who misuse it must give account—not to human judges—but to God. This is the foundation for the high view of human life that has always been associated with the Judeo-Christian tradition. Life is not worshiped in itself—there is no fertility cult in the OT—but because it comes from God and belongs to him. Thus the treatment of life must be consistent with God's own standards of justice: "whoever sheds the blood of man, by man shall his blood be shed" (Gen. 9:6).

6. Members of the Body. Under this final heading we treat various references to the physical body and its functions. The physical form of the body in the OT is always seen as participating in the spiritual ends which human nature can realize. Bodily members are always media and expressions of personal values and never understood in their purely physical aspect. When God forgives, the bones that were broken rejoice (Ps. 51:8). The feet of the evangelist are beautiful (Is. 52:7).

Seeing and hearing, for example, can become expressions of the total human response to life and its demands. When these are threatened one's whole humanity is called into question (Ps. 38:13-14). Seeing and hearing what God has done is understanding and acting upon its significance (Deut. 29: 2-4). Hearing is often used as a synecdoche for taking heed and acting on what is heard. To hear, in this sense, is to obey: "Hear, O Israel: The LORD our God is one LORD" (Deut. 6:4). Isaiah notes that God has opened his ear in the sense that he was no longer rebellious (Is. 50:4-5). Similarly, in Psalm 40:6, the psalmist notes that God has literally, "dug" an ear for him, that is to say, God has given him a willing heart to do all that he has been told (v. 8). Of interest is the quotation of this verse in Hebrews 10:5, where the second part of the verse is changed to read: "a body hast thou prepared for me." This change— quite intentional—can easily be explained in terms of the synthetic use of language we discussed earlier. An open ear is a ready heart. Then taking a part (the heart) to stand for the whole (the body), we can just as easily say: a body thou hast prepared for me. This body, which Christ willingly laid down in obedience to the Father (a major theme of Hebrews), is a further and deeper elaboration of the meaning of the OT expression of God's desire for an open ear and a willing heart. This background also helps us to see the meaning of Christ's often repeated remark: he who has ears to hear, let him hear.

In the same way, seeing can be used for a believing understanding (Ex. 14:13-14). It is possible, of course, to have eyes and not see in this sense. For this insight comes only when God opens the eyes of his people (Is. 43:8-13). From the privilege of having seen the works of God, comes then the responsibility for speaking of his greatness (Ps. 97:4, 6). From this perspective one can better understand the rich biblical concept, developed in the NT, of the witness: one who has seen God's goodness and gives evidence of his gratitude in, and sometimes with, his life (1 Jn. 1:1-3). Surely the eye that

sees and the ear that hears in this sense are gifts from God
(Prov. 20:12).

Finally, the mouth and speaking indicate response to God's
initiatives. A confession in the OT is indicative of the giving of
the whole self to God (Ex. 19:7-9). What is in the heart comes
out of the mouth, whether it is cursing and bitterness (Ps. 10:
7) or blessings and praise (Ps. 109:30). The man and woman
of God meditate and repeat the law (Ps. 1:2), praise God continually (Ps. 71:24), put away evil from their mouth (Prov.
4:24), speak a word in season (Prov. 25:11) and are not hasty
in words (Prov. 29:20). Such proper use of the tongue is truly a
blessing from the Lord (Prov. 16:1). Rightly does James emphasize that the one who can control his tongue is able to control his whole body (Jas. 3:2).

Summary

This then is the human race: created in the weakness of flesh
from the dust, but with the capacity and appetite for God.
They are weak and needy, though need and physical limitation are never a hindrance to a walk with God. Rather these
strictures speak of dependence on the environment. In their
eating and drinking, men and women are reminded that all
they are, their life and their strength, comes from outside
themselves from the world and him who made it. So in the
partaking of the elements that satisfy their physical needs
they enact a parable of the source beyond themselves. It is in
this context that every creation of God is good if it is received
with thanksgiving (1 Tim. 4:4). It is this too which makes it
possible for the humblest nourishment—bread and wine—to
symbolize the communication of eternal life that comes
through faith in Jesus Christ, the bread of life.

Then, too, people do not experience their lives as individuals but as members of a community. They define themselves
by the traditions and values of the groups to which they belong. These relationships, especially marriage and family,
can also be bearers of a higher meaning when they are seen as
a type of the bond that ties us to God and of the love and faith-

fulness that ties him to us. The group can also express that special people of God that stands before him ("the congregation," Ex. 12:3 and elsewhere) and which comes to such sharp focus in the NT as the church, the body of Christ.

But though people live their lives in the body, they also transcend bodily existence. They remember the past and hope for the future; they love or despise what is around them and draw it all into their purposeful life. Thus all they are and possess become expressions and carriers of their values, of their emptiness or fullness. For the people of God use their feet to flee from evil, their mouths to speak of God's goodness, their hands to care for the needy, and with the objects of the created world they can shape and mold beautiful expressions of God's glory.

Men and women are always straining, reaching up, seeking in their bodily life to realize themselves in decision and action. In God they find the communion for which they are uniquely fitted. And though pride gives to this reaching-up quality the aspect of quest or flight, and though sin threatens life with death, they still can perceive that there is a divine environment where they will know rest and security. Only fools deny that God has anything to do with them.

At this point a few words are in order about human nature as a unity or a duality. In recent years it has become popular to stress man as a unity—body and soul together in their mutual interrelationship. We have seen some evidence to support this view. Spiritual states find expression in the body, and, on the other hand, individuals express themselves in and through their bodies. Their hearts express the unity of their thinking, willing and feeling. But, at the same time, important considerations weigh on the side of duality, that the individual is made of two parts, however interrelated they may be. For the body is clearly from the dust, and the life from God. God has put them together, and there is thus no place for the view that the body is the prison house of the soul. But at death the life of the soul leaves the body and goes to Sheol, where, bereft of the body, it must live a shadowy and diminished existence. The OT vitality of human life calls out for a further revelation of a bodily life that is a suitable vehicle for communion with God and praise of him. For this it needs the NT teaching of the resurrection of the body.

I taught my hand to observe the divine ordinances. . . .
Oh, that I only knew that these things are well pleasing to
god! What appears beautiful to man is abominable to
the god, and what is odious to man's heart is most pleasing
to the god. Who has learnt the will of the gods in heaven,
the gods' plan, full of wisdom, who can comprehend it?
When have stupid mortals ever understood the ways of the
gods?

Babylonia Wisdom

Transgression speaks to the wicked deep in his heart; there
is no fear of God before his eyes.

Psalm 36:1

5
Sin

The Origin of Sin: The Fall
1. The Boundary of Fellowship. A person's created nature represented no barrier to fellowship with God; it was not something—as in Greek philosophy—to be overcome. Thus when God finished his created work, he was able to say that it was very good (Gen. 1:31). But this did not mean, from a human point of view, that there were no limitations to life. Limitation was not incompatible with the created perfection of man and woman. They had to live out their lives in a body and to be dependent on the earth for their nourishment. Moreover, there was a limitation inherent in their relationship with God. They had to understand that he was their source and meaning and that they had to learn to live spiritually by his word. This is made explicit in Genesis 2:16-17.

God first of all instructs them that the goodness of the earth is made for their sustenance. God said: "You may freely eat of every tree of the garden" (v. 16). Here is sounded the note of affirmation that becomes an important theme of Scripture.

The created order is not to be spurned but enjoyed; it is God's gift. But, at the same time, there was one tree in the middle of the garden that was forbidden. This was the tree of the knowledge of good and evil. In Hebrew the "knowledge of good and evil" usually means simply moral knowledge; the point at which a child can discriminate between good and evil he becomes morally responsible (Is. 7:16). But we cannot immediately assume from this that the man and the woman were not morally responsible before the Fall, though some have described their innocence in this way. What perhaps threatened them was the experiential knowledge of good and evil (the word *knowledge* in Hebrew implies intimate knowledge). At any rate the question of obedience is raised, and the possibility of disobedience now exists.

It is fruitless for us to inquire as to the reason for this prohibition ("Who will say to him, 'What doest thou'?" Job 9:12). But at least we can say it made explicit for Adam and Eve the distinction that existed between creature and Creator, and the necessity that the relationship between them and God had always to be defined from God's side and not from theirs. Moreover, their life had to be lived in obedience. "Loving the LORD your God, obeying his voice, and cleaving to him . . . that means life to you . . ." (Deut. 30:20). The threat of death does not necessarily mean that they were created immortal. Perhaps their fellowship with God was sufficient to preserve them from the threat of death. Enoch and Elijah then might serve as examples of what God had in mind for all people. But we cannot be sure of this. Traditionally theologians have understood that the prohibition was a kind of probation. Gerhardus Vos calls the tree of knowledge "the god-appointed instrument to lead man through probation to that state of religious and moral maturity wherewith his highest blessedness is connected" (Vos, 31). It was, in other words, a test for the first couple, which, had they passed it, may have brought them to a higher state of moral responsibility. This may be so, though all this must lie in the area of speculation.

In any case this explicit limitation on Adam and Eve cannot

be construed as a restriction of their freedom. It is rather a definition of it. Man and woman will not find freedom outside of the order that is defined for them by God's word.

2. The Breaking of Fellowship. Sin enters by a free decision of Adam and Eve in Genesis 3. The first thing that comes to our attention is that the temptation to disobey God comes from outside them, but yet from within the created order. In this account, and we can assume up until the time of Moses, there is no indication whether it is Satan or merely a tool of Satan. We see it as merely one of God's creatures—a serpent. Only later (in the Wisdom of Solomon 2:23-24) is the temptation tied to Satan. But throughout the OT there is no speculation about the origin of this temptation (Is. 14:12-16 and Ps. 82:6-7 are the only passages that may hint of Satan's fall, but it is difficult to be dogmatic). It is only clear that evil comes not from God, but rather from an evil force within the created order. We know, however, especially from the NT, that Satan controls and directs these forces.

First there is a question, then a counterclaim (Gen.3:1, 4). That is, first the seed of doubt about God's goodness is planted, then an alternative claim is made. By Eve's answer (v. 3) it is already clear that she has reservations about God's instructions, for she adds the phrase "neither shall you touch it" to the command, thus compounding the prima facie improbability of God's word. "Your eyes will be opened" throws further light on the possible meaning of "knowledge of good and evil"; that is, life will be seen in terms that go beyond the limits that God has set for them. Here the root of all sin, self-seeking or hubris, appears. But note that it *follows* the doubting of God's word. Here is a deadly attack on the artlessness of obedience. Now Eve is placed in the position of an arbiter between the word of God and some yet unknown alternative possibility (von Rad, 1961, 85). Sometime after the serpent's words in verse 5 the actual acceptance of the alternative is made.

At this point sensuous charm exerts its power. God's word having become doubtful, a physical and sensuous charm of some imagined alternative could do its work. They ate and immediately (v. 7) their eyes were opened. Here the results of the Fall, that God later explained, were already being felt. The openness and naturalness of creation was destroyed. The first reaction (what Vos called "the reflex of the ethical"— Vos, 53) was shame. That is, they knew their guilt reached the most elementary of their relationships, and they tried pathetically to cover themselves.

Reading the account of the Fall with all of its dreadful implications, one does not feel any sense of inevitability in the event. It was the natural consequence of freedom that people could doubt and disobey God's word. "Man can pass from the condition of innocence into the state of free morality only by an act of self-determination" wrote G. Oehler (1880, 229). But it is a decision in which we are all implicated and which we repeat in our own turn.

3. The Protection of Fellowship. Here the great theme of God's redemptive judgment begins. Sin must be judged, but judgment is always mixed with mercy. The initial question implies God's forebearance: Where are you? Who told you you were naked? What is this you have done? God, of course, did not need the information, just as later he did not need to know about Abel when he inquired of Cain (Gen. 4:9-12). Rather, he seeks the repentance that will make restoration possible. But Adam responded by putting both the immediate (woman) and ultimate (serpent) causes outside of himself, just as Cain did. Already we see the *inclination* that sin has put within human behavior. Sin begets sinning as its natural consequence. When we understand the full implications of this interconnectedness of human acts (the acts of parents and children), we see how it is that original sin cannot remain an isolated phenomenon.

So God must judge the serpent, the man and the woman. First, in the case of the serpent, the enmity between it and the woman implies a corresponding reconciliation between God and her seed. Humanity and the forces of evil will never make a final peace. Man and woman will be continually exposed to attack. Nothing people do will be able to overcome this opposition; there will be no heroism. But there will be a fatal injury to the serpent which is only hinted at, though from the NT we know this to be a protevangelium or first glimmer of the gospel. It is Christ who will destroy the works of the devil (Mt. 1:23; Col. 2:15; 1 Tim. 2:15; Gal. 4:4).

For Eve God promises pains and particular hardship in pregnancy. That which is her joy and crown becomes at the same time her sorrow. Likewise, in her relationship with her husband there will be pain. Control has shifted from the loving and personal to the instinctive (Kidner 1967, 71). Though she will have this profound desire, and continue to seek fulfillment (Ruth 1:9), what she will find will all too often be humiliating domination. From this it is clear that domination and subjugation are not a part of that order, but are rather introduced at the Fall. The word *helper* (Gen. 2:18) means someone standing over against, that is, one who perfectly answers to man's need for fellowship. Though God certainly intended a certain "economic" (or "working") order, it was clearly within the context of full equality before God and mutual respect. The Fall has changed all that, and we still wrestle with its effects.

In the case of Adam the curse applies to his realm rather than to his person. In sorrow and sweat he will work. What a sad issue from the serpent's counterfeit promise that they would be as gods! The earth is to be cursed for the sake of, or on account of, Adam (Gen. 3:17). His fundamental relation to the earth, which existed from creation, now receives a new element—frustration and competition. His lordship over creation is challenged now at every turn. For his living he must work long and hard (strange—as someone has commented—that the curse itself should be so earnestly directed toward life!). To his work—which previously was perhaps only delight—is added the threat of frustration and failure. The negative character of the effects of sin can be seen in these curses. For to the order of creation nothing essential is added, rather a harmony is lost. The ecology of creation is upset. Now futility and hopelessness become a necessary part of the order of things (Eccles. 1:8). At every turn man must struggle for the order and beauty that belong to the birthright of creation. Now it all groans together, waiting for the deliverance to which Scripture time and time again looks forward (Is. 11: 1-9; Rom. 8:18-21).

A word may be in order about the historicity of the early chapters of Genesis, inasmuch as the question is of theological significance. Many modern scholars insist that this is not "ordinary history" but "primeval history," which is to say, it gives us the security of knowing we come from God when we feel threatened by the forces of chaos, but it does not tell us anything about what actually happened. Let it suffice to make these few comments. In the first place, it is hardly fair to say that this is not history as "we understand it"; after all, our understanding of history—in a scientific sense—is only some two hundred years old. That this history does not come to us in the form of scientific history is not to say that it does not give us information about what actually took place. Even if the form is stylized, there is nothing in the Genesis record itself to indicate that it does not purport to give us facts about our beginnings. Even if the account corresponds to myths of primitive people in certain particulars, this does not imply that it cannot have actually taken place as it is recorded. In fact, as Mircea Eliade explains, "a myth always narrates something as having *really happened,* as an event that took place in the plain sense of the term" (*Myths, Dreams and Mysteries,* 1968, 16). Furthermore, from the biblical perspective, the Genesis accounts derive their exemplary quality precisely from their actually having happened.

Furthermore, it is not put in a poetic form, nor is there anything in the rest of Scripture to lead us to think of it as a nice story that never actually happened as it is told. In fact Romans 5:12-21 puts the disobedience of Adam on exactly the same level as the obedience of Christ to describe our solidarity in sin and in righteousness. If we accept Paul's account, we cannot make one of the figures legendary and the other historical. The most important consideration remains that the events of these chapters—creation by God's word, the instruction and disobedience of Adam and Eve, and the curse and promise—are of inestimable significance for the whole development of God's redemptive work. It is of the essence of the biblical view of salvation that events in history are the stuff of revelation and the means to relationship with God. It seems gratuitous to assert this about Scripture as a whole while we deny it for the first chapters of Genesis (and, as many do, the account of events of the last times). Religious truth is not seen to rest on legend within Scripture. In short, there is no overwhelming barrier to taking these events as presenting a substantially historical account, and it would seem that no one would be inclined to deny this apart from certain philosophical presuppositions.

The Vocabulary and Definition of Sin

The OT has several word groups that it uses to indicate sin or transgression. They can be placed in roughly three major categories (see Grayston in Richardson, 227).

1. Deviation. The first category speaks of a *deviation* from the right way. The basic Hebrew word (*haṭṭā't* or *hēṭ'*) appears some 225 times as a verb. The theological orientation of the idea can be seen in the 25 times it appears specifically as "a sin against God" (the idea is present many other times by implication). Beginning with Joseph (Gen. 39:9) the idea reaches its highest point in David's confession: "Against thee, thee only, have I sinned" (Ps. 51:4). The basic idea of the word is to deviate from the correct way or to miss the mark (it is actually used of a sling missing the mark in Judg. 20:16). A similar idea is present in the word usually translated "iniquity" (*'āwōn*, Ex. 20:5 and elsewhere). The word group translated "perverse" or "perversity" (*'iqqēš*, Prov. 28:18 and elsewhere, especially in the wisdom literature) suggests a determined deviation from the norms of the community. A perverse man sows disharmony and strife in the community. He has deviated from the way of wisdom, which is the fear of the Lord.

Whether it is deviation from kindness or from a specific law, it is the Holy God who is concerned, and the end of such deviation is the dissolution of the soul.

2. Guilt. Secondly, there are words that refer to a state of being in sin: the *guilty* or the *ungodly*. One who is wicked (*rāšā'*) is guilty and thus deserving of punishment. This word is usually translated "ungodly." God "does not keep the wicked alive" (Job 36:6), their way shall perish (Ps. 1:6), they will not seek God (Ps. 10:4) but love violence (Ps. 11:5), and in the end they will be cut off (Ps. 37:28). Wickedness is the condition of one who cannot stand in God's presence and is liable to his wrath. Similarly, one who is guilty *('āšām)* has committed an offense and so is guilty before the law and in the sight of God. The word can mean "suffer punishment," "be condemned" (Ps. 34:21-22) or simply "be guilty" (Prov. 30:10). The meaning of the noun can be either "guilt" (Gen. 26:10) or "the offering that is brought to atone for guilt"—"the guilt offering" (Lev. 5:6). Even if one sins unwittingly, he still stands guilty and must bring a guilt offering (Lev. 4:1-3). Here the objective nature of sin comes to the fore. A man is responsible for all he does, and even a wrong committed unknowingly incurs guilt and must be compensated and atoned for. Guilt must be "borne" and so removed from the people. In this way God's holiness is reflected among his people.

3. Rebellion. Third is the idea of *rebellion* against a superior or unfaithfulness to an agreement. The word usually (but somewhat inadequately) translated "trespass" (*pesa'*) implies a personal act of rebellion (Job 34:37). In the secular sense it is used of rebellion against David's house (1 Kings 12:19). In Isaiah it is used of Israel rebelling against the God who raised them (Is. 1:2). The interconnection and solidarity in sin is emphasized in Isaiah 43:27: "Your first father sinned, and your mediators transgressed against me." The reference is probably to the sin of the patriarch (probably Jacob), rather than to Adam, though the latter may be included as well. Here the meaning of sin is enlarged to include willful turning against a superior or an agreement—unfaithfulness.

We are now in a position to suggest a definition of sin that includes these emphases. Sin is not misfortune or chance suffering, though these may result from sin and be included in its condition. Rather it is a personal and voluntary deviation from a norm, ultimately directed against God. Even when it is a matter of the transgression of the law, it is against God, for, as John Murray notes, the law is but a transcription of the perfection of God (NBD, 1189). Sin is also a state in which persons are guilty before God and liable to his punishment. In fact, there are indications in the OT that the state of guilt before God actually precedes and gives rise to the actual acts of transgression. David notes that he was brought forth in iniquity *(ʿāwōn)* and conceived in sin *(ḥaṭṭāʾt)* (Ps. 51:5). The extent of human inclination to sin was recognized early on: "Every imagination of the thoughts of his heart was only evil continually" (Gen. 6:5; see Jer. 17:9). Though the locus is in the heart, sin manifests itself in all that people do, they abound in transgressions (Prov. 29:22). Sin preys on that which is essential to being human and reflecting God's character. It leads to deterioration and ultimately to death (Prov. 11:19, and see Jas. 1:15).

The Character of Sin in the OT
1. Its Theological Character. Sin is first of all *theological;* that is, sin is always related to the holy purposes of God. In the OT there is the consistent feeling that what people are and do affect their standing before God; sin is always an obstacle to God's favor. How important this is can be seen by comparing the penitential psalms in the OT with similar prayers in other Near Eastern literature. Outside the OT there is merely the fear of the wrath of the gods because of the violations of certain laws, which needed to be absolved by prescribed ceremonies. The cult—as we will note further on—was religious rather than moral in character. That is, there was no awareness that the moral condition of the supplicant was in itself a barrier to the fellowship. They knew they were subject to the god's decrees, but they had no confidence these decrees

were just. Here is a portion of a Babylonian prayer:

> (Of) my Lord—may the anger of his heart to its place
>   return . . .
> What was forbidden by my god—unwittingly I have eaten;
> The transgression I have committed—I know not;
> The sin I have sinned—I know not;
> The Lord in the anger of his heart has looked at me;
> The god in the rage of his heart has turned on me;
> My transgressions forgive, and I will celebrate thy praises.
> May thy heart, like the heart of one's mother who bore—to
>   its place return;
> Of one's mother who bore and of one's father who begot to
>   its place return.
> (DOTT, 113-14)

Unwittingly he may have sinned, but he denies conscious guilt. How different the OT penitential psalms where the consciousness of failure relates immediately to God's righteous will (see Ps. 6, 15, 32, 51, 102)!

2. Its Objective Character. In the OT there is a consistent awareness of the *objective* nature of sin. Innocent guilt cannot be ignored (Deut. 21:1-9); it pollutes the land (Num. 35:33). Ransom must be made (1 Sam. 14:34-35). This objectivity reflects the standards of righteousness reflected in the created order as well as given in the revelation of God's law. There is a givenness to this order that cannot be circumvented or ignored. Proverbs 8 paints that striking portrait of wisdom who was with God before the earth was formed, and as he laid out its bounds was "before him always" (v. 30), so that it is certain that he who misses wisdom "injures himself" (v. 36).

3. Its Personal and Conscious Character. Sin in the OT is also *personal* and *conscious;* that is, though sin can be unwitting, it exists because the heart is in a state of rebellion against God. Every individual's "constitution is a permanent revolution" (Emil Brunner, *Man in Revolt,* 152). Sin at its heart is a voluntary act of rebellion against God and his word (Ps. 51:4). It is a forsaking of his lordship (Judg. 10:13). This personal quality becomes especially clear in the prophets, when the full richness of God's character is understood and the sense of individual responsibility before God is sharpened. Sin is a rejecting and then a forgetting (Hos. 4:6); it is a personal planning apart from God (Is. 30:1); and it is a conscious forming of idols who will stand in the place of God (Hos. 13:2). The unrighteous are in a hurry to sin (Is. 59:7).

4. Its Universal Character. Sin is *universal* in that it has invaded all of human nature and all men everywhere. It springs from a basic corruption of human nature that affects all that we do in one degree or another (see especially Gen. 6:5). Even our so-called goodness shares this perversion (Is. 64:6). This sin can of course manifest itself in various ways: Amos pictures ingratitude; Hosea, an inner hostility and aversion; Isaiah, a self-exaltation; and Jeremiah, a deep-seated falsity. There is no one who does not sin (1 Kings 8:46; Ps. 53:1). As Eichrodt notes, the fact that everyone is in sin simply underlines that everyone is indissolubly related to God and that this relationship cannot be done away with even by sin (Eichrodt, II, 408). Yet this does not lead to a morbid fatalism that believes one cannot do well and be accepted by God. As God explains to Cain: "If you do well, will you not be accepted?" (Gen. 4:7). One could be pleasing to God as Noah and Job were. One could say with assurance: "I have kept the ways of the LORD, and have not wickedly departed from my God" (Ps. 18:21). But this confidence did not belong to the natural order of things, but only to those who knew of God's mercy and had experienced his deliverance. For these things the individual could appeal to no inherent righteousness, but only to God's goodness (see Deut. 9:4-6).

5. Its Fixed Character. Finally, sin is pictured as so completely a part of the fallen order of creation that it is *fixed*. As a well keeps her water fresh so Jerusalem keeps her wickedness (Jer. 6:7). "Can the Ethiopian change his skin or the leopard his spots?" (Jer. 13:23). "Who can understand it?" (Jer. 17:9). So strong is this compulsion to sin that Jeremiah likens it to the drive of an animal in heat (2:24-25). It can only be said, as Israel often admitted, it is hopeless. On the level of human effort alone the OT (as the NT) presents no hope for righteousness. The only hope is to trust the promises of God and to look beyond the hopeless condition to God's provision of atonement.

The Results of Sin

1. Guilt. Guilt is the condition of liability to punishment at God's hands. This is not an automatic curselike retribution as in pagan religions, but the state of deserving God's wrath. It is an objective condition before it is a subjective awareness. As we have seen, this springs as much from the individual's nature as a sinner as from actual disobedience. If the holiness of God is kept in full view, it is not difficult to see how this condition can exist in a fully personal transaction with God. God must be consistent with his nature even as he calls men and women to himself. Guilt then is an objective condition, sometimes recognized and sometimes not. At times it is seen only in punishment (2 Sam. 21:1). In all events God does not forget (Josh. 22:22 and Hos. 13:12).

2. Punishment. The punishment of God finally follows as the certain response to sin. "Be sure your sin will find you out" (Num. 32:23). The basic element in punishment, even when it is also manifest in loneliness and suffering, is separation from God (Is. 59:2). Access is denied to God (1 Sam. 14:37-41). The final punishment is to be blotted out from the "book of the living" (Ps. 69:28); Sheol will be the home of the wicked (Ps. 49:14). We have noted before that God can use even evil designs for his glory, and we will see it again in our discussion of the cult. But it is worth noting here that God's purposes are advanced even in the case of the sinner (Gen. 45:8; Ps. 76:10), though it is safer to say that this is the result, rather than the purpose of sin.

You have seen what I did to the Egyptians,
and how I bore you on eagles' wings and brought you
to myself. Now therefore, if you will obey my
voice and keep my covenant, you shall be my own
possession among all peoples; for all the earth
is mine, and you shall be to me a kingdom of priests
and a holy nation.

Exodus 19:4-6

6
The
Covenant

Background of the Covenant Idea

A covenant is a solemn promise made binding by an oath which may be either a verbal formula or a symbolic action (Mendenhall 1962, 714). In the OT the covenant rests on God's promise and lies at the heart of the biblical notion of history. Though it is especially identified with the covenant made at Sinai, its full range extends from creation clear through to the prophets. It is the core of the Hebrew understanding of their relationship with God.

From the time of Julius Wellhausen—about one hundred years ago—it has been believed by all but a few scholars of the OT that the covenant idea came late into Israel's consciousness. The early relationship between God and his people was held to be a "natural" one. That is, God was considered as a tribal deity, almost as a symbol of the people. Basic to this line of thinking is the idea of development so dear to the nineteenth century. This early faith matured by the time of the classical prophets, who added the ethical element to religion, which then was understood in terms of a "covenant" between God and his people. This conception then was developed very late in Israel's history, though of course it was read back into the history that they subsequently wrote of their early life.

Beginning a generation ago the vast field of Oriental law and covenants was studied with a view to finding the context for the OT understanding of covenant. It was seen very early that the idea of covenant was an extremely important means of regulating behavior between peoples, especially in the area of international relations. Believing that they reflected a long and varied tradition of ancient law, G. E. Mendenhall studied Hittite suzerainty treaties from the late Bronze Age (1400-1200 B.C.) as a way of throwing light on the biblical idea of covenant (Mendenhall 1954). A suzerainty treaty was the formal basis of the empire. It spelled out the terms of relationship between the Hittite state and the vassals (lesser groups of peoples) which gave allegiance to the empire. The king would offer to protect a people in exchange for their support and tribute. This was the only choice for many peoples who were caught between larger powers, and it provided for them a means of security amid troubled times.

Mendenhall notes six elements that were nearly always found in the Hittite treaty texts (Mendenhall 1954, 58-60):

1. Preamble—"These are the words of the king of..."
2. Historical prologue—recorded the previous aid extended by the suzerain to his vassals and the debt which they owed him for this deliverance; past benefits called for future obedience.
3. Stipulations—spelled out the obligations of the vassal state, including the trust and tribute which was due.
4. Provision for temple deposit and periodic public readings—made certain that all the people were aware of their obligations.
5. Invocation of divine witnesses—those of both suzerain and vassals; even the mountains, winds and clouds were called to witness (compare Deut. 32:1 and Is. 1:2).
6. Blessings and curses—pronounced on those who obeyed

or neglected the treaty stipulations (compare Deut. 28). Now there is no single place in the OT where a precise parallel to this form is to be found, but OT scholars are generally agreed that this treaty form lies behind the OT understanding of the covenant. Similarities are immediately apparent in Exodus 20—23 and especially the book of Deuteronomy. Craigie, in fact, sees this structure as the basic organizing principle of the book of Deuteronomy. Aside from the fundamental difference that Israel bound herself, not to an earthly king, but to the Lord God, the form offers instructive parallels. The deliverance from Egypt established their relationship (Ex. 20:1-2), though later celebrations of their relationship expanded the context to the patriarchs (Josh. 24:2-13). In return they promised to obey the stipulations of the decalog (Ex. 19:8). The law was to be deposited in the ark which was sacred to the Lord (Ex. 25:16). The solemn renewal of the covenant, of which we have an example in Joshua 24 and which many scholars believe to have been an annual remembrance, fits as well. Even the tradition about the murmurings in the wilderness receives new meaning; the stipulations of the Hittite treaties specifically forbade murmurings against the suzerain! Like their secular equivalents, Israel was forbidden from entering into any agreement with neighboring nations (and, of course, from having anything to do with their gods). The promise of the king's protection was predicated on their exclusive obedience.

At the very least, scholars are now more open to the idea that the covenant concept goes back early into history; indeed, the covenant is now recognized as one way of accounting for the unity that this nomadic people was able to achieve so early (a "natural" relationship would not suffice). As Mendenhall concludes: "It can hardly be denied now that some kind of tradition of a covenant between a deity and the patriarchs was an important element in the pre-Mosaic heritage of ancient Israel" (Mendenhall 1962, 718).

Conservative scholar Meredith G. Kline (1963 and 1972) has drawn out the implications of this in terms of understanding the whole OT as a treaty document, and thus recognizing its inherent authority. The treaty, once validated, must not be tampered with or changed under pain of serious punishment. If the relationship was changed, the treaty was not altered; it was simply destroyed and a new one drawn up. Thus the covenant form was ready at hand for the Lord to use. The OT in its entirety, Kline believes, can be understood as a treaty document. "All inspired literature deriving from . . . cult and associated with that culture served the covenant and inevitably bore its stamp" (Kline 1972, 47). This then is the theme of the OT: God's relation to Israel based on the covenant.

Part of the accommodation of revelation, which we have seen before, is that God takes concepts that are current and uses them for his purposes. But the end result is that the idea is greatly expanded. So the covenant relationship, as it developed in history, became something that the original usage could not have comprehended. This is characteristic of God's redeeming action: God meets us where we are and takes us on from there. In the end, we will note, covenant comes to include the whole earth in its purview, and its validity is eternal. What human covenant could have been developed to express this breadth?

Development of the OT Covenant
1. The Covenant with Noah. The covenant idea is already implicit in the promise made to Adam and Eve in Genesis 3: 15, and it is reflected in God's merciful promise to Cain (Gen. 4:15) in marking him so that no one would slay him. But properly the covenant idea does not appear before God's promises to Noah. Notice that even before the flood God says to Noah: "I will establish my covenant with you . . ." (Gen. 6: 18). Then, as if to define the covenant, he tells him that he and his family are to come into the ark. Here the basis of the covenant as a solemn promise is apparent, for God takes the initiative to promise Noah and his family deliverance.

The covenant is then sealed (renewed?) after the flood (Gen. 9:1-17). Notice here the covenant is not merely a contract between two parties. God comes to Noah and his sons and announces that he will establish his covenant with them and with every living creature. The scope then of this promise is not limited to Noah and his seed, but is universal. (That all creation is included indicates how little God expected a conscious, favorable reply!) There are no conditions given, and the validity is to "all generations." As a sign of God's promise the rainbow becomes symbolic of the covenant between God and the earth (v. 13). It is very important to keep in mind the purpose of God's gracious activity, an intention present in the later covenant with Abraham: all the people of the earth are to be blessed. God narrows the line of his covenant people, not to exclude some, but that through those chosen all may come to know of his grace.

2. The Covenant with Abraham (Gen. 15 and 17). The basis of this covenant is present already in Genesis 12:1-3, where God calls Abram to leave his home and promises to make of him a great nation. In chapter 15, in response to Abram's question about his possessing the land (v. 8), God performs with Abram a solemn rite concluding in verse 18: "On that day the LORD made a covenant with Abram." Nothing could assure the certainty of this promise more than this solemn ceremony sealed by God's oath (see Jer. 34:18-22). First he promises to give the land (see also Gen. 17:8). (That this reference is to the Davidic empire is hinted at in 17:6, where God promises that "kings shall come forth from you.") Then God promises that Abram will become the father of a great nation, in fact, of "a multitude of nations" (17:4). Finally, God pledges to be God to them and to their descendants after them (17:7).

God's initiative is once again in the forefront. God is the suzerain (15:18; 17:7). The covenant is finally to be eternal (17:19) for all their descendants after them. Isaac is specifically included in this covenant (17:21), the first in the long line of descendants that will know God as their God and become his people. Ishmael is blessed but pointedly excluded from the covenant (17:20).

In this instance Abraham and his seed must "keep" the covenant (17:10-14). As a sign of this every male shall be circumcised (v. 10), and any that is not circumcised shall be cut off from his people. (M. G. Kline believes the cutting of circumcision to be symbolic of the curse pronounced on anyone who breaks the covenant—1968, 43.) Here is the first sign of reciprocity in the covenant. On the one hand, it is hard to conceive of circumcision as an obligation in the sense of a stipulation. Rather, it is a "sign" of the covenant "a guarantee through time of the validity of Jahweh's oath" (Mendenhall 1962, 718). As in the case of the rainbow, circumcision was to be an identifying marker of those who were later to share in God's promise. On the other hand, their grateful participation in the grace that God was extending was registered by their faithfulness in circumcising their children. It served as a type of the ordinances that were later to be signs of God's promises: baptism and the Lord's Supper. Circumcision was to be the symbol of the purification of all their lives—later explained in the elaboration of covenant law. All of this is an expression of God's desire for communion with his covenant people. And while the covenant was unconditional in the sense that God would never forget his promises and leave himself without a witness—that is, those who would respond in faith to these promises—the continuance of each individual in the blessings of these promises was contingent upon their response of faith. "Keeping is the condition of continuance in this grace and of its consummating fruition; it is the reciprocal response apart from which communion with God is impossible" (Murray, NBD, 265-66). Further on we shall see how both conditional and unconditional elements continue to characterize the covenant relationship.

3. The Mosaic Covenant. While this covenant tradition was to become the fundamental basis of the nation of Israel, the continuity with the earlier promises of God was obvious to all (see Ex. 3:15). The parallels with international treaty forms now become so striking that it is clear that Israel viewed this as the basis of her religious and social life. We saw earlier a fundamental variation from the secular form of treaty: God stood in the place of the king as their ruler, their suzerain (thus accounting for the ancient antipathy to kingship, Judg. 8:23). Unique also—and following directly from the first difference—is the placing of moral and spiritual values above political and economic considerations. The implications of this for Israel will be seen further along.

First, then, the people were sovereignly chosen in that they were delivered from the bondage of Egypt (Ex. 19:4). The motive for this is later expressed as God's love for them (Deut. 7:6-8). Yet as we noted, this choice was also an expression of his remembrance of his covenant with the fathers (Ex. 2:24). This continuity is particularly evident in the joyful recounting of God's protection in Psalm 105:8-15. The purpose of the exodus was redemptive, delivering the people from bondage and making it possible for them to worship God in purity and truth (which helps to explain the important but difficult statement in Ex. 3:12; see also Ex. 6:6-8 and 19:4-6). While the treaty parallel suggests a fundamental suzerain-vassal relationship between God and his people, it would be a mistake to limit our understanding of the covenant relation to this. The people are also adopted into a filial relationship with God (Ex. 4:22; Deut. 8:5). He was not only their suzerain; he was their Father.

In this covenant definite stipulations are present. Here keeping the covenant is enlarged to mean Israel's obedient response to God's initiative (Ex. 19:4-5; Deut. 26:16-19). We shall look more closely at these stipulations in the next chapter; they include both apodictic ("You shall not") and case law ("If . . . then you will"). As we will see, these stipulations are not to be viewed as one of the bases on which the covenant rests (the other being God's promise)—as though this were a bilateral treaty—but rather the condition of their continuing to enjoy the blessings the suzerain promised to them. But in this case, since the suzerain is God himself, the stipulations involve a life of obedience in which his holy character is to be reflected. This idea is summed up in Leviticus 19:2: "You shall be holy; for I the LORD your God am holy."

While the promise evident in the Abrahamic covenant is not missing, the emphasis here is on the stipulations which God imposes on his people. That is, the covenant is made and put in operation on the basis of God's (the suzerain's) decision. It is because of this prior fact—that they were God's people, his personal possession—that they are urged to reflect this reality by their obedient response. God's choice of them is fixed. Only their continuance in the blessings of that promise is a result of their obedience. This covenant challenge to Israel is a recurrent theme through the books of the Kings—sometimes called the Deuteronomic history. In these books their continued existence as a nation is made to rest on their faithfulness to their covenant obligations. For the northern kingdom the crucial event was the great sin of Jeroboam (1 Kings 13:33-34). Until the final catastrophe comes, the writer repeats the judgment against each king like a refrain: "He walked in the way of Jeroboam." When the blow falls and Assyria captures Israel, the reason is clear: "The people of Israel walked in all the sins which Jeroboam did; they did not depart from them, until the LORD removed Israel out of his sight" (2 Kings 17:22-23). The curses of the covenant are brought to pass because of Israel's sin. Her doom is sealed.

4. The Covenant with David. Running side by side with the threat to Israel in the Deuteronomic history is the promise to David. Here we are impressed again with God's pattern of taking up his promises and repeating them, each time in a larger and more comprehensive framework. God not only remembers his promises, but each time he speaks of them he throws in additional blessings for good measure. As Mendenhall puts it: "In David, the promise to the patriarchs is fulfilled, and renewed" (Mendenhall 1962, 718). The promise to David, spoken through the prophet Nathan, is found in 2 Samuel 7:12-17. The word *covenant* does not appear there, though the idea is present. In Psalm 89:3-4, 27-28, God's covenant with David is described in much the same terms as his covenant with Abraham. Again its immutable character based on God's initiative is evident—the promise element is to the fore (Ps. 89:3-4; 2 Sam. 7:13). Here, however, a new element is added: kingdom or empire. This includes both the "realm," the land that God promised to the fathers, and the notion of God's "ruling" over that realm. Thus God seems to say that he will take David's throne for himself and make it his own to ensure its permanence (2 Sam. 7:16).

The descendants of David are urged to keep his testimonies so that they will continue to sit on the throne (Ps. 132:12), but a novel element is added to the covenant promises: "When he [that is, your offspring] commits iniquity, I will chasten him with the rod of men, with the stripes of the sons of men" (2 Sam. 7:14; though there is a hint of this in Deut. 8:5). What kind of judgment could this be that would *ensure* the continuance of this throne?

Now, for a moment, we move ahead several centuries to the postexilic Chronicler, who again features the covenant of David. The theology of the books of the Chronicles is a part of the most interesting—and overlooked—sections of the OT. Written sometime around 400 B.C., the books are set in the midst of one of the great challenges to the people of Israel. The refugees have returned from exile and are faced with the immense task of rebuilding the nation. Where could they draw strength to live in such unsettled times? Would this remnant be able to find a source of strength in its own (southern) traditions? The answer given by the Chronicler is that the rebuilding must be a restoration. Only by recalling the covenant forms that David received from Moses and that were most perfectly realized in the temple worship could God be properly honored. They must remember, moreover, that God is their true king and that David's reign was a sign of this greater reign. Recalling Nathan's promise, the Chronicler reiterates God's intention for the Davidic line: "A son shall be born to you. . . . He shall be my son," God tells David, "and I will be his father, and I will establish his royal throne in Israel for ever" (1 Chron. 22:9-10).

This promise to David which features an eternal ruler is

picked up in Psalm 2:7: "You are my son, today I have begotten you." That this reference, which is so important to the NT interpretation of Christ (see Acts 13:33), has a messianic reference is clear from the following verse, where the son is promised the nations as his inheritance.

The idea that a child of God would be the mediator of an eternal covenant had earlier played a role in the servant songs of Isaiah. In Isaiah 42:1, 6, God chooses his servant ("my child" in the LXX) to bring justice to the nations. "I have given you as a covenant to the people," God says, "a light to the nations" (v. 6). Isaiah 55:3-4 refers to the everlasting covenant as God's "steadfast, sure love for David." Malachi calls this same figure "my messenger" (Mal. 3:1; "Who can endure the day of his coming?"). This rule will be a universal kingdom, involving all nations as God had promised Abraham (Is. 2:2-4), but bringing judgment (chastening) as well as blessing (Is. 2:9-12).

The prophet Jeremiah calls this kingdom a new covenant (Jer. 31:31-34). Writing in the midst of the destruction of all the outward symbols of God's covenant promises just before the exile, Jeremiah insists that God is not finished with his covenant people. One day God promises to make a new covenant, new in the sense that it will be unlike the former covenant which the fathers broke (v. 32). The Hebrew construction here implies that though the new covenant will succeed where the other did not, it will carry forward (as well as supersede) the reality of the Mosaic covenant.

What would be the nature of this covenant? First, it would be realized "after those days" (v. 33), that is, after another of God's redemptive acts described earlier in the chapter as a building and a gathering (see vv. 4, 10, 16). Second, it would involve placing the law in the heart, which is interpreted as knowing the Lord (v. 34). Israel's failure, Jeremiah knew, had been a lack of knowledge (see 4:22; 8:7 and 24:7). Now by inward revolution knowledge would be natural. Third, this new standing before the Lord would be for everyone ("from the least of them to the greatest," v. 34), not just for the prophets or priests. Finally, this new relationship would include the forgiveness of sins (v. 34). Sin, that is, would be dealt with in a final way and it would no longer be remembered. In the midst of personal and national tragedies Jeremiah lifted the hopes of the people and prophesied of a new and living way, the new covenant Christ would seal by his blood (see Lk. 22:20 and 1 Cor. 11:25).

Immediately after the exile Ezra and Nehemiah were faced on their return to Jerusalem with widespread syncretism and paganism. It was natural to focus on the covenant as God's reassuring promise and also to attempt to insure enforcement of the law by political means. If failure to keep the law had been the cause of their tragedies, they must ensure that the law be kept. (Mendenhall, however, believes this pattern of enforcement had already begun during Josiah's pre-exilic reform described in 2 Kings 23.) The people responded to Ezra and made an oath to walk in God's law: "Now therefore, our God, the great and mighty and terrible God, who keepest covenant and steadfast love, let not all the hardship seem little to thee that has come upon us. . . . Yet thou hast been just in all that has come upon us. . . . Because of all this we make a firm covenant and write it" (Neh. 9:32-33, 38). God was bound to his promise to Abraham as Israel was bound to keep the law given at Sinai. It was during this time that the Chronicler holds up before the people the hope to be found in the theocratic rule of David.

For the rabbis during the intertestamental period the covenant conception of the Chronicler was still central. They often spoke of God as king, who had solicited their worship by his saving acts. But the conditional element was also prominent. God's people had to accept God's kingship by obedience. In the covenant, God had provided for atonement by the keeping of the law which in turn established (or re-established) the covenant relationship (scholars often refer to this view as covenantal nomism). What Paul set out to correct was a misconception, not about the requirements of the covenant, but about the way that it is established. The new covenant is established, not by the keeping of the law, but through Christ's redeeming death and believers' faith response to him.

Before we discuss some theological principles that grow out of the covenant idea, two items call for comment. First, a question: was the covenant conditional or unconditional? From our brief survey we can see that it is oversimplifying to speak of either a conditional *or* an unconditional covenant. In a sense there are two sides to the OT covenant. One emphasizes the promissory, as in the promise to the patriarchs and to David; the other, stemming from Sinai and featured in the Deuteronomic school, gives more place for conditions or stipulations (though neither lacks promise or stipulations). But the two perspectives complement rather than contradict each other. The promise of salvation given to the patriarchs becomes the blessing of the Sinai covenant which Israel would enjoy through its continued faithfulness. Nathan voices again the promise of eternal blessing (2 Sam. 7), while Isaiah promises a faithful successor to David who will realize the covenant blessings for all his people. At this point the treaty form, while not excluded, is taken into a larger covenant ideal that will be brought about through the work of the Son of David, Jesus the Messiah.

The second item has to do with the nature of the covenant idea. In approaching the OT, systematic theologians have sometimes made the mistake of seeing covenant as a changeless idea. We have seen ample evidence that the reality of the covenant took a variety of forms in its historical development. The treaty form furnishes us with an important starting point and a background for our thinking. But we do well to allow for other patterns to help us as well. If we are to be biblical in our understanding of the covenant we must recognize its historical character and allow the biblical nuances to determine our theology.

Theological Implications of the Covenant
Lying behind the covenant is the sovereign will of the gra-

cious God: "I . . . will be your God, and you shall be my people" (Lev. 26:12). His will now directs a particular course of events. The importance of this can hardly be overestimated. Now the life of Israel (and thus of each person in Israel) has taken on a unique meaning; history itself receives direction and significance. This is because God has entered into history and tied himself to particular events, which he promises will have everlasting consequences. The end is only dimly envisioned, but this is because God sets the terms and fixes the goals.

This implies that for this people there is a new security to life. The covenant, as it is filled in by the law, helps man to know where he stands. He can count on things because a stable element has been added to his life and to history. Trust is possible; the paralyzing capriciousness of Near Eastern gods is totally excluded. At the same time, each man and woman, each family, is called on to surrender in obedience and love. Apart from such a response there is no bulwark of protection against this God. He has lovingly provided this means to communion, but, at the same time, he has excluded all other ways.

With such a foundation it now becomes possible to establish a well-defined moral and social order that will consistently reflect this foundation. This order, which comes to expression in the law and the cult, we shall examine next.

But the basic demand is to know the Lord, that is, to enjoy a living and personal relationship with this God. This is of more consequence than the sacrifices and offerings which are to *express* this relationship (Hos. 6:6). The spirituality of this bond, which is the goal of the covenant, has important implications. It embraces potentially all the people, from the least to the greatest, and makes possible a remarkable individual and group cohesion. Without diminishing individual responsibility, it makes real human solidarity possible. Moreover, all of life takes on the character of a response to God, a walking humbly in accordance with God's will (Mic. 6:8). From the start, then, there can be no split between the sacred and profane spheres of life; at least potentially every movement can be sacred unto the Lord. Finally, from its very beginning this association between God and his people hints of a universal application. It could not happen at once, but the covenant bond was not essentially exclusive. As Eichrodt puts it: "This association draws no clear line to exclude the stranger, but is continually absorbing outsiders into itself" (Eichrodt, I, 39).

Now it is possible to understand the biblical view of history. This relationship between God and his people arose in the course of actual events. It is not a bond inherent in nature, as with most primitive religions, but one that God has made in particular events. Events can now—when viewed in relation to this program—be decisive or *crucial* (in the original meaning of that word). There is a direction and a momentum to things that point us naturally to the crucial events of the life of Jesus of Nazareth.

Nothing is more natural than that the thing made should belong to its Maker and be subjected naturally to him. Nothing is more at variance with nature and first truth, than that a rational being adorned with the image of its Maker should not be the servant of God as his Maker, should be outside the law, should not be subject to him, should not obey him.

Cocceius, *De foed.*

7

The
Law

Background and Development of the Concept
The basic word for law, *tôrâh,* occurs some 220 times and comes from the word *yārâh* which means "to direct, teach or instruct in." Thus the basic meaning is "instruction." This kind of instruction is by no means limited to a legal setting; it is given by fathers (Prov. 3:1; 1:8), by wise men (Prov. 13:14), by prophets (Is. 1:10), but primarily by God with Moses as the usual mediator (2 Chron. 33:8).

As we have seen, the law is an expression of the covenant and always secondary to it. That is, the law is to express the character of life in the covenant. The giving of the law is a part of God's giving of himself to his people in the covenant and expresses the same loving purposes (see Ex. 19:5-6). The basis of the law in the covenant purposes of God is important for a correct understanding of law. In the structures maintaining any community there are ordinarily two elements: policy and procedures (Mendenhall 1954, 26-27). The policy, while more general, is the basis of the community. It is the legal understanding of how life is maintained. In the case of Israel, the policy of the community was its self-understanding as a covenant community. That is, its existence as a community rested on God's having chosen it and his promise to uphold it. The procedures then are the means by which the policy is put into effect. They simply express in concrete terms the reality that the community understands itself to be.

Accordingly, the law shows the people what conduct accords with its place as God's particular possession. The giving of the law initially with the covenant is a revelation before it is an instruction (Jacob, 272-73). Israel does not keep the law in order to become God's people, but because they already are. Both the relationship and the giving of the law which expresses that relationship are manifestations of God's grace. But, because God reveals himself as a redeeming, morally sensitive God, the proper response to his initiatives is faithful obedience. As we saw in our study of covenant, the promise of God is in one sense conditional, namely, the enjoyment of the blessings of the covenant are conditional upon the response of the people.

1. Development of the Law. In addition to the law given at Sinai, most probably the raw materials of what is now the OT law were single decisions taken in concrete dilemmas (NBD, 718-19). If Israel had a problem, they were to "ask the priests" (Hag. 2:11-13). The decision that the priest gave was called the *tôrâh* (Mal. 2:6-7). Then oral tradition brought these single decisions together into small lists of instructions which were collected and transmitted by the priests. This would lead to short statements of general instructions such as those found in Psalms 1:1-5 and 24:4-6. These lists no doubt contained some customs that were borrowed from local Canaanite laws (as in Ex. 22:2: "If a thief ... dies, there shall be no bloodguilt for him") as well as those laws that were given to Moses by revelation. These collections were put together and guarded by the priest at a sanctuary (Deut. 31:24-26). One such collection that may be very old—sometimes called the Book of the Covenant—is found in Exodus 21—23. We shall have something to say about this later. The final step in the formation of the books of the law was their collection and formation in the books of the Pentateuch. These five books later came to be called the Torah. There seems to be no substantial objection to seeing them taking shape under the formative influence of Moses (who is without exception recognized later as the mediator of the law) with certain materials added later.

2. Some Basic Legal Sections. It is not possible for us to review all the legal materials of the OT, but it is important to discuss briefly certain important sections. The first and most basic is the list of laws known as the Ten Commandments or the Ten Words (Ex. 20:1-17; Deut. 5:6-21). Following on the declaration of the covenant in Exodus 19, these instructions should be understood as the stipulations of the covenant relationship. Since God as their suzerain had delivered them from Egypt (20:2) and promised them his particular protection, he is in a position to ask them for this response. Note that nothing is promised for obedience (outside of long life for those who honor their parents); they are simply called to obedience without qualification (IDB, II, 81). It was understood that obedience was the way to life (Deut. 30:15-20), but this was simply because such a response is the substance of real life, not a mechanical means to that end.

All the commandments are to express in concrete terms the character of the relationship of God with his people. Notice that these laws deal with one's attitude both to God and to one's neighbor. No provision is made for the enforcement of these laws (some, such as the law about coveting, would be virtually impossible to enforce in any case). For it is of the nature of the relationship that it express the free, personal response of the person involved.

It is significant that with only two exceptions the laws are expressed in negative terms. "There is not commanded what establishes the relation to Yahweh, but prohibited what destroys it" (W. Gutbrod, TDNT, IV, 1037). This is consistent with the intent to preserve the spirituality of the relationship that is based on the free response of the individual. It is perhaps this character that has made it possible for these brief statements to have exercised their incalculable influence in the history of civilization. For the state learns from this that it can negatively protect the freedom to pursue human ends, but it cannot specify the nature of those goals positively. The attempt to do so is one definition of a totalitarian society.

The ancient code that follows the Ten Commandments is called by critical scholars the Book of the Covenant (Ex. 21— 23). This section contains both apodictic (Thou shall not . . .) and casuistic (If . . . then) laws. These both provide some of the procedure that is to implement the policy of Israel. Yet even here precise statements or regulations for use in law courts are lacking. Rather, they appear to be general statements and exemplary cases to serve as a guide for those charged with implementing them. There is nothing of the legalism that is to become so prominent later in Israel's history. Mention should be made as well of the so-called priestly code (Lev. 1— 7) which stipulated the procedure for offerings, and the *holiness code* (Lev. 17—26) which gave instruction for the maintenance of purity in the community life of Israel. Purity was to be reflected in the sacrifices (Lev. 17) and the family (Lev. 18), so that in their own human way they would reflect the character of the God who called them: "You shall be holy to me; for I the LORD am holy" (Lev. 20:26).

The collection of the laws contained in Deuteronomy 12— 26 reminds us of the continuing relevance of the law. This is perhaps the first example of the practice of reading and reaffirming the law at great tribal gatherings—this time just before Moses' death. Significant is the use of "this day" (Deut. 5:1-3; 26:16-19; 29:10-15). It was not enough that the law had been given and put into effect. Each generation had to reaffirm for itself its determination to obey the Lord. On the other hand, it was possible for each generation to stand in precisely the same relationship to God that the first generation did. So Moses made provision for a regular meeting at which Israel could register its response to God's gracious promise implied in the covenant law (Deut. 31:9-13, and see Josh. 8:30-35 and 24:1-33).

3. OT Law and the Law of Neighboring Peoples. The superficial resemblance of OT law to other law codes is undeniable, and it is instructive to ask what might be the relationship between them. We have already seen that in Israel it was God rather than the king who served as lawgiver. This put the idea of law in a unique perspective. In one sense all of OT law was religious. Israel had a keen sense of this difference: Moses asks, "What great nation is there, that has statutes and ordinances so righteous as all this law?" (Deut. 4:8). They knew that God "has not dealt thus with any other nation" (Ps. 147:20). But at the same time the similarities with neighboring law codes are also striking. These reflect not a wholesale borrowing, but "the influence of a single widespread customary law" (de Vaux, I, 146). Let us examine the relationship in more detail.

In the first place, because the law is to safeguard the covenant relationship, idolatry is severely condemned (Ex. 20:23; 22:20 et al.). Moreover, life is seen to belong to God (Gen. 9:5), so that when an ox kills a man, its flesh may not be eaten (Ex. 21:28, 32). As a result capital punishment is not nearly so common as it is in the case of the law code of Hammurabi (ca. 1800 B.C.). There a wife that does not guard her property is cast into the river (DOTT, 31); robbery is punishable by death (DOTT, 30) as is bearing false witness in a trial (DOTT, 29). Indeed, in general, the punishment stipulated in the OT shows a restraint of gross brutality.

The fact that all stood in the presence of God equally in the covenant relationship made it impossible for them to recognize a class distinction in their law. There is not one law for the free and another for slaves. Indeed, slaves come in for particular protection in the law against cruel and demanding masters (Ex. 21:2-6, 26, 27). By contrast, most of the Near Eastern law codes stipulate different punishments for a person dependent upon his station in life:

HC [Hammurabi Code] 203 If one of citizen status has struck

the cheek of his equal, he shall pay one mina of silver.
HC 205 If the serf of a citizen has struck the cheek of one of
citizen status, they shall cut off his ear. (DOTT, 34)

Because marriage is particularly important in God's sight
and instituted by him, any infraction against chastity is
severely punished. While promiscuity is punished in many
ancient law codes, outside the OT there are exceptions that
are authorized by the law. But in the OT if a slave is treated
improperly, she is to be treated just as if she were a wife (Ex.
21:7-11). If a man seduces a virgin, she shall become his wife
(Ex. 22:16). Otherwise, adultery and fornication are punishable by death (Deut. 22:22-24). The careful instructions in
Leviticus about proper relations between a man and a woman
are preceded by the warning that they are not to do as was
done in Egypt where they had been, nor as is done in Canaan
where they were going (Lev. 18:3-4). And the instructions
close with the plea not to defile themselves by these practices
for "I am the LORD your God" (Lev. 18:30). Ultimately, then,
even human relationships were to reflect God's character and
therefore were never to be understood only in terms of ex-
pediency. Unfaithfulness throughout the OT was such an
awful sin that God used it to illustrate the depths of Israel's
unfaithfulness with him (Hosea).

Specially unique in the OT law are the numerous provisions for the stranger or alien, and for those who are handi-
capped in one way or another. There were instructions for the
blind and deaf (Lev. 19:14), for widows and the fatherless (Ex.
22:21-22), and for the poor (Deut. 15:7-11). Strangers were
singled out for protection from oppression (Ex. 23:9), for, it is
explained, you should understand the heart of a stranger
since you were strangers in Egypt. God was especially concerned with the disadvantaged, of whom he says: "If . . . they
cry to me, I will surely hear their cry" (Ex. 22:23). One can
almost hear Christ's words: "Blessed are you poor, for yours
is the kingdom of God" (Lk. 6:20). Poverty is not considered
a virtue in the OT, but it is recognized there how unjust
the fallen order is, and those who are special victims of its

injustice provide God's people with a heaven-sent opportunity to express the mercy of God himself (see Kidner 1972, 26-27).

The Law in the Community
1. Priority of the Covenant. We have seen already that law as an expression of the covenant was the basis of the community life of Israel. As a reflection of the character of God it was to shape community life into a vehicle of God's presence in the world. This was an ideal from which Israel often fell away, but which consistently influenced the way the law was understood in the course of Israel's history. The responsibility of judging then took on a much broader meaning than it carries today. A judge, as de Vaux explains, "was more a defender of right than a punisher of crime. He was a just arbiter" (de Vaux, I, 157; see Job 9:33). Thus the place of law in the community was always on the side of the people as a whole, it was not to become a privileged possession of a certain class of people.

The priests were specially entrusted with the law. But the emphasis here was on teaching the law so that the people would understand what God required (Deut. 33:10). Then there were particular individuals who were charged with "judging," individuals like Moses (Ex. 18:16) and Joshua (Deut. 34:9) early in Israel's history. The so-called judges came later, of whom Samuel may be the best example (1 Sam. 7:15-17). Note it is said of him that he administered justice (v. 17). It is significant that when Israel had a king he was never considered a lawgiver. Nor was there a royal law. Indeed the king was under the law just as all his subjects (2 Sam. 11—12). Though he did function as a kind of supreme court in matters pertaining to the law (2 Sam. 15:2-6).

That the law functioned easily in the context of everyday life is seen best in the office of the village elders. They seem to have been entrusted with the responsibility of arbitrating disputes among the people (Deut. 21:19) and executing provisions of the law (Deut. 19:12; 25:7-10). Sometimes these were official appointees (2 Chron. 19:4-11), but ordinarily they were probably the older and more respected members of the community. They illustrate that the focus of the covenant was the home and marketplace; its provisions were to be realized in the family and among one's neighbors. Some scholars believe there grew in this connection a rural suspicion of the cities that furnished the soil that was to nourish the prophetic movement.

2. The Law in the Prophets. With the prophets a new level of understanding is reached of both the holiness of God and the meaning of the law. They have no sense, however, of being innovators but rather attack violations of the ancient covenant and its legal requirements. In our discussion of worship we shall ask if the prophets meant to do away with the ceremonial aspects of the law. Here it can at least be said that they had such a burning vision of God's holiness and its demands that by contrast the cult seemed of lesser importance. Indeed without the accompanying life of righteousness it could be denounced as an abomination (Is. 1 and Amos 5:21-24). If the law is properly understood as reflecting the inner commitment of the people to God, then the prophets were simply returning to the original intent of the covenant. At the same time, their vision of God and his demands is so sharp that the whole idea of the law begins to take on a new aspect. It seeks a more universal and internal frame of reference. All of this can be summed up in Micah's phrase "to do justice, and to love kindness" (Mic. 6:8). But for this there was needed a change so radical it reached to the heart. As Ezekiel put it, God's people needed a heart of flesh in place of their heart of stone (Ezek. 36:26-27). Jeremiah explains this as a new covenant in which the law will be written on our hearts (Jer. 31:31-34). Already then in the OT the impulse is present, not to do away with the law, but to establish it in a deeper way than Israel had found possible.

3. Postexilic Developments. If we ended our discussion of the law at this point, it would be difficult to understand some of the NT opposition to Jewish thinking about the law. Christ complained to the Pharisees: "You have a fine way of rejecting the commandment of God, in order to keep your tradition!" (Mk. 7:9). What were these traditions?

During the exile very important changes occurred in the life of Israel. All the institutions that supported the law were swept away—the king, the temple and regular priestly service. Because the written law was the major remaining tie with their past, they gave themselves fully to its study. During this period gatherings of people to study the law seem to have been common (Ezek. 33:30-33). It is here that the institution of the synagogue had its beginnings. Reading and study of the Torah took the place of temple sacrifices.

After the exile the law continued to have this primary position in the life of the community. We have already noted that the covenant that Israel affirmed before Ezra was "an oath to walk in God's law which was given by Moses the servant of God" (Neh. 10:29). Since they viewed their national disasters as God's judgment on them for their failure to keep the law, they determined that this would not happen again. They still understood the law in its relation to all of God's dealings with the fathers (Neh. 9) and as an expression of the covenant God had made with them, but their sense of obligation to the law and its requirements tended to outweigh all other religious concerns.

Moreover, as a result of their study and reflection an oral law arose that became equally authoritative with the written law. The reasons for this are not hard to find. On the one hand the central position of the law in postexilic Judaism made it all the more imperative to avoid breaches in the law. At the same time, the written law could not possibly cover all the circumstances that Persian and then Roman rule brought about. So there arose the tendency to interpret the law and adapt it to contemporary circumstances. While the attempt was always made to ground this tradition in Scripture (indeed Scripture itself foresaw the necessity of such adaptation—Deut. 17:8—26:19), its authority really came to rival that of Scripture itself.

Most important of all was the attitude toward this law. It

was regarded as the focal point of a person's life. Obedience to
the law was the means of securing merit before God. While
the danger of legalism was always present, we should remember that for many keeping the law was a delight; the faithful
found great joy in submitting to its demands. Moreover, obedience to the law had to be accompanied by a purity of intention (IDB, III, 94). This view which is called "nomism"—that
is, making the law the center and focus of one's life—is the
background against which Christ's criticisms of the Pharisees
and Paul's references to the law must be understood. Their
traditions were not so much wrong in themselves as indicative of a wrong perspective. When the law becomes the means
of maintaining the relationship with God, it is easily forgotten that the promise of God is the basis of our hope. In this
way the Pharisees tended to make "void the word of God"
through their traditions (Mk. 7:13).

The Character of the Law
1. Comprehensive Scope.
The law is comprehensive in its
scope. A proper understanding of the law leads one to see that
all of life lies under the controlling will of God, whether one is
getting up in the morning, sitting down to eat, walking along
the way or going to sleep. Whether one is concerned with life
in the state or in the cult, in business or in the home, nothing
lies outside the purview of the law. Since all of life lies open
before God, there is an inner unity between laws applying to
the state and those having to do with worship. Eichrodt explains that "there grew up an understanding of the total
ordering of the people's life as a revelation of the saving will of
God" (Eichrodt, I, 92).

Having said this, full weight must be given to the surprising lack of casuistry. That is to say, there is no attempt to
suggest laws for every conceivable occasion. Basic principles
are given and explained; application is left to what Eichrodt
calls a "healthy feeling for justice" (Eichrodt, I, 77). We saw
above how often a negative law is given in preference to a positive one. Thus the intent was to avoid errors so that there

would be freedom to pursue life in all its fullness. This is all summed up in the OT expression of the "way." Following the law was a way of going, a walking in the way of righteousness (Ps. 1). Its goal was simply the natural walk with God for which man was created (Is. 2:3).

2. Personal Appeal. While the law is comprehensive in scope, it is also personal in appeal. This means, in the first place, that it is propounded on the basis of what God had done for Israel. The terminology is not legal explication, but personal appeal. Often accompanying the laws is a clause which gives a justifying motive (Ex. 22:21; 20:5 and Deut. 22:24). Above all, they are to remember who it is that has called them, what great things he has done for them. They are to remember (an important word in the OT) and keep these words because "I am your God and you are my people" (see Deut. 10:16-22).

The deepest motive then for keeping the law must be a responsive heart, an inner and personal moral decision. "Choose this day," Joshua urged the people at Sechem (Josh. 24:15). External compulsion would never be enough, nor was this the design of God. As Christ explains in the NT, the whole law can be summed up in loving God (Deut. 6:5 and Mt. 22:37), and when it comes to expressing what is required of individuals in the community, all the law can be reduced to loving one's neighbor as oneself (Lev. 19:18). This kind of personal commitment to the Lord helps keep the law in its proper perspective. Reading the laws out of their context in the Pentateuch would never allow one to comprehend David's testimony that the words of the law are "more to be desired . . . than gold" and "sweeter also than honey and drippings of honeycomb" (Ps. 19:10).

3. Unconditional Force. The law is also unconditional in its force. Since it is based on the holiness of God, it demands perfection on the part of the people (Lev. 11:44). So everyone who does not continue in all the words of the law is cursed (Deut. 27:26). When Israel would turn against the law, it would inevitably bring on them the wrath and punishment of God

(Deut. 31:16). There was the realization that the law would not be kept perfectly. But as we will see in the following chapter this could not be simply overlooked. God's mercy does not consist in turning his back to sin. Rather there was a gracious provision for the ransom of the sinner, as we will see. Even in dealing with infractions of the law, the law itself must be left intact. So that the greatest lawgiver, Christ himself, could say that he had not come to destroy the law but to fulfill its demands (Mt. 5:17).

4. Universal Application. Finally, the law must be seen as universal in its application. Initially this meant that the law applied to all Israel without regard to social or political status. It is true that the law of Israel was unique among all the nations of the earth, but this was not because its relevance was limited to this people, but because no other people in fact knew of such a law.

From the beginning, the law moved toward transcending its national boundaries, as is clear in the case of Ruth. It was easily extended to apply to the visitor and the stranger. Even one's enemy was to have certain rights under the law: "If you meet your enemy's ox or his ass going astray, you shall bring it back to him. If you see the ass of one who hates you lying under its burden, you shall refrain from leaving him with it, you shall help him to lift it up" (Ex. 23:4-5 and see Prov. 25:21).

How much more universal is the application of such instruction than human ideas of law! Compare this with the words of Mao Tse-Tung, spokesman for those who claim to have the interests of all people at heart: "Today we cannot love the Fascists nor can we love our enemies. We cannot love all that is evil and ugly in the world. We must aim to eliminate them" (Speech in Yenan in 1942).

Israel was not always faithful to its role as a light and blessing to all nations. But their very existence and the covenant that lay beneath it spoke of a day when all, from the least to the greatest, would be able to know the Lord. In that Day all nations would go up to the mountain of the Lord to be taught of the ways of the Lord (Is. 2:2-4). It was as a vehicle of such a vision that Israel was a "covenant to the people, a light to the nations, to open the eyes that are blind, to bring out the prisoners from the dungeon" (Is. 42:6-7). To fulfill such a role there needed to be one greater than Moses, the Lord Jesus who in his first sermon quoted from Isaiah (61:1-2) and said that the giving of sight to the blind and release to the captive was fulfilled that day in their hearing (Lk. 4:18-21). He was to be the arbiter of the new covenant that Jeremiah foresaw in which the law would be written in people's hearts, and the tension between the external deed and the internal intent would be finally overcome (Jer. 31:31-34).

God did not command sacrifices in order to busy his worshippers with earthly exercises. Rather, he did so that he might lift their minds higher. This also can be clearly discerned from his own nature: for, as it is spiritual, only spiritual worship delights him.

Calvin, *Institutes*

8
Worship

The Need for Form
1. Form and Worship. Worship is the response of the believing heart to God. *Cult* is the term Bible students use for the formal and ritual aspects of the worship of the OT. Cult is simply the form of Israel's response to the revelation of God. The OT description of worship emphasizes that all Israel's life lay under the authority of God. They could not approach God any way they liked, though as we will see there was ample room for spontaneity. God must direct them even in this (see Ex. 20:24). Their relationship to God was made, reaffirmed and renewed in the cult.

The cult which God prescribed for Israel was to be the visible expression of their faith. Perhaps we should pause for a moment at this point, for evangelical Christians have trouble understanding the value of form in worship. Did not the Lord say that the true worshiper must worship in spirit and truth? Are not forms often identified with idolatry and meaningless ritual? All of this is true, and the truth was seen already in the OT. But any faith that is genuine wants to express itself outwardly. Belief strives for embodiment. Nor should we see external expression as merely a secondary matter. As Eichrodt reminds us: "For the men of the ancient world [and we might add for many people today] the outward form possessed a symbolic significance, totally different from the significance it has in the eyes of modern western man" (Eichrodt, I, 99). In this case we need to remember that God himself decreed that this people was to be characterized by a careful performance of certain duties (Deut. 30:16). And while the NT has made much of this form unnecessary, it does not do away with the need for structure in our worship.

Part of what it means to be human and created in the image of God relates to our ability to make concrete objects and actions symbolic of our values. This is true in at least two senses. One is that our behavior serves to confirm—and in confirming reminds us of—our faith and commitment. As Gustav Oehler put it, these outward signs become "instruments of tuition, or instruction, from the outer to the inner" (Oehler 1880, I, 264). On the other hand, these forms can also be the means by which the reality of God is brought home to us. The passover meal and ceremony made real to people of later generations the wonder of God's deliverance from Egypt; the sacrifices presented a picture of God's mercy. This did not mean there was any inherent value in these things, nor did this happen automatically, but they were potential vehicles of God's truth.

It is true that form limits our relationship with God. But this too can remind us of our creatureliness. Limiting is not suppression. The followers of God know that real freedom comes not when we do as we please, but when we walk in the paths that God has set for us. It was this that God wished his people to understand.

Of course it is foolish to ignore the danger that outward observance might replace inward reality. In fact the OT rarely pictures the balance between the outer and the inner properly kept. God, through Amos, told the people that he despised their feasts (Amos 5:21). But surely he meant that the forms counted for nothing when they no longer expressed a living faith. The danger of externalism always threatens worship, but that does not keep worship from always having some definite form.

One final word needs to be said about the basic character of the forms of worship. God had to instruct the people how to worship him not only because they did not know how, but because they were unfit to worship. They were sinners and so could not come into God's presence. The law provided for cleansing, for sacrifice—in a word, for redemption. That is, these instructions not only provided a way for Israel to express its faith, they also provided, from God's side, the way back to communion and fellowship once this had been broken. Atonement and redemption, as we shall see, are really the heart and core of OT worship.

2. The Place of the Cult in OT Religion. The formal aspects of worship were important then in embodying and expressing in outward form the realities of OT religion. They were the social and public expression of this religion, not something added to it and destined to fall away. This intimate relation between faith and response can be further explained by thinking of the cult as *symbolic* and *typical* (see Vos, 161-64).

The cult was symbolic in the sense that it represented in visible form the reality of spiritual communion with God. A symbol is an object or act that orients persons in their environment and by which they build their world. But the OT cultic acts had a deeper sacramental dimension that gave them their objective character. The temple, for example, reminded Israel of God's presence, but also—by virtue of God's promise and the sacrifices performed there—actually was a mediation of that presence. Inside the holy of holies the movement of the priest on the day of atonement was an expression of the real movement of the people toward God, which God in his mercy was allowing.

But the cult was at the same time typical. That is, it was

prospective, pointing in its very limitations to what would be real in the future. OT worship was heavy with its future. The temple made the Hebrew long for the day when at last God's dwelling place would be with men (Rev. 21:3). But the Christian, knowing of John's vision, cannot help but have a deeper appreciation for temple worship. He understands the joyful impulse: "I was glad when they said to me, 'Let us go to the house of the LORD!' " (Ps. 122:1). The reality of worship in the temple is not so much discarded as taken up into a higher order of things and thus seen in a new light. The law is fulfilled, consummated rather than destroyed. This is seen most clearly in the sacrifice of Christ, who takes up and completes the OT sacrificial system. If we do not appreciate the rich fullness of the prophetically typical—the shadow—we will not properly understand the antitype—the reality. So, for example, the cultic setting of the psalms is almost as important as the hymns themselves, for it is an example of the divinely ordered transaction that is enlarged on in Christ's sacrifice. As we saw in the introduction, this use of typology, so popular in the early church, has the virtue of giving full weight to the historical character of revelation. But, as Vos notes, something cannot be a type independently of its being in the first instance a symbol (Vos, 154). Holding these two aspects together—the present and future referents—makes it possible for us to avoid the temptation of seeing types where they do not exist.

Sacred Places

Although it was always clear that God dwelt in heaven (Gen. 11:5; Ex. 19:11 and 1 Kings 8:27), God did choose particular places where he would meet with his people. For the patriarch Jacob, Bethel—which means house of God—became a special place because God had met him there in a dream. Sinai became sacred in the traditions of Israel because God had appeared to Moses there. Numbers 14 tells of the glory of the Lord appearing to the people at Kadesh and warning them because of their murmurings against him. The tabernacle and the temple were honored because of their identification with God's presence. In the case of the temple God said: "My name shall be there" (1 Kings 8:29). This was another way of saying that he would be there, his name standing as a symbol of his presence. Yet these forms of his presence also express the fact that God is not limited to these places. In a sense, as Isaiah 6:3 says, the whole earth is full of God's glory. But there are times and places where, through mediating forms, this glory is especially evident to sinful men.

The danger was always present that Israel would believe that God was limited to these places. Jacob may have been thinking in these terms when he noted how awful Bethel was because God was there. Israel had constantly to be reminded that God chose to reveal himself in these places as an expression of his love and faithfulness to his promises. There was no necessary connection between God and the place. Nor could these places be used as talismans, as some people used the temple during the time of Jeremiah (Jer. 7:4). Here the faith of Israel is again set apart from that of her neighbors. Her God was never identified with the land or its natural processes. While God could appear in any place and nature was an expression of his goodness, he was Lord over all the earth.

Yet the unique way in which Israel remembered places where God's name was revealed was an expression of the concreteness and historical character of God's dealings with his people. God did not merely live in the heavens or rule over the earth in a general sense, but he showed his power and authority in the specific places where he appeared and intervened. Loyalty to a place then could be suited to express faith in the God who directed his people in history.

At the same time, the special places where God met his people spoke of meeting with God and standing in his presence as the highest objective of human life and the summit of happiness (see Ps. 15 and 24). The tabernacle, in fact, was called the "tent of meeting." But whenever a meeting with God took place the reaction was often one of fear. In the case of Isaiah the response was one of a deep sense of unworthiness

(Is. 6:5). All of this reminds us that real encounter with God must involve judgment before it offers joy. This is clear in the psalms mentioned above: "O LORD, . . . Who shall dwell on thy holy hill?" (Ps. 15:1). So the place that God provides for meeting must also be a place of cleansing and forgiveness.

In any event people could not meet God unless they made use of the places that God in his grace provided for meeting. This was because apart from God's condescension in coming there was no way for his people to know him. That is why the psalmist could write about his joy at the prospect of going to God's house (Ps. 122:1). It had to be that way until God's revelation of himself took another form and decreed by that form that places no longer had special significance. This revelation came with the One who said: "Destroy this temple [the place of meeting, though the text tells us he also means his body], and in three days I will raise it up [the resurrection]" (Jn. 2:19-21, and see 1:14 where the word *dwelt* means "tabernacled").

Sacred Times

Certain seasons of the year were designated by God as times of feasting and religious joy. All of Israel's neighbors also remembered the seasons with religious feasts, but their ceremonies were very different from those of Israel. In Mesopotamia and Ugarit the rites were to honor the gods so as to insure fertility of the land for another year. For the Hebrew, however, the seasons constituted a manifestation of God's goodness. The harvest reminded them that all good gifts came from God, and that was the reason the feasts were characterized by joy and celebration. In remembering they showed their obedience toward God and at the same time celebrated their God-given dominion over nature.

1. The Feast of Unleavened Bread. Three major feasts marked the Hebrew calendar. The first was the feast of unleavened bread, which was celebrated in the first month of the year and was early identified with the passover (Lev. 23:5; Ex. 23:14-15; Josh. 5:10-12; for the meaning of the passover, see Ex. 12:21-27). For seven days they were to eat unleavened bread, while on the first day no work was to be done and sacrifices were to be offered. During this feast they remembered the time when they were slaves and the Lord brought them out of Egypt. The celebration embodied a family service of memorial in which they re-enacted the passover ritual. To the question of the children: "What do you mean by this service?" the parents would answer: "It is the sacrifice of the LORD's passover, for he passed over the houses of the people of Israel in Egypt, when he slew the Egyptians but spared our houses" (Ex. 12:26-27). In this dramatic way they proclaimed the redeeming grace of God to one another and, for their part, reaffirmed their faith in him.

2. The Feast of Weeks. The feast of weeks, which was also called feast of harvest or day of the first fruits, was a feast where the first fruits of their crops were offered to the Lord (Ex. 23:16; Num. 28:26-31 and Deut. 16:9-12). This feast was also called Pentecost because it was celebrated fifty days after the beginning of the harvest. Later the date was calculated from the beginning of the Passover, and, by the time of Christ, some circles identified it with the giving of the law at Sinai and others with the renewal of the covenant. Interestingly, both of these find their fulfillment in the Pentecost of Acts 2. This too was a time of rejoicing in which freewill offerings from the harvest were offered to the Lord, as Deuteronomy 16:10 puts it, "as the LORD your God blesses you." Part of the instructions specified that they "rejoice before the LORD"— the family, the servants, and even the visitor who might be with them. Everyone was to rejoice together and remember not only that the Lord gave them a harvest, but that this provision was another expression of his loving care which included their deliverance from Egypt (Deut. 16:12). There was no sense that God could be laid hold of in the processes of nature or that he must be appeased by offerings. By contrast, as R. J. Thompson puts it, there was the joyful recognition that all belonged to God and the first fruits were offered thankfully in lieu of the whole (NBD, 1116). We will notice that this substitutionary character is important in all of Hebrew worship.

3. The Feast of Booths. The third great yearly feast was the feast of booths or feast of the ingathering. For seven days the people dwelt in booths made of tree branches (Lev. 23:39-43; Ex. 23:16 and Deut. 16:13). The first and the eighth day were days of rest. Again, a note of rejoicing was to characterize the celebrations for seven days. During this time they were to remember not only God's material provision, but his guidance and protection when they lived in booths after their departure from Egypt. Above all, this was to confirm to them that Jahweh was their God (Lev. 23:43).

4. The Day of Atonement. Then there were special days. The first, the day of atonement (Lev. 16), was to be a day of solemn rest, in which the Hebrews were to "mortify" themselves and atonement would be offered for the sins of all the people. This was a most important day of repentance and sacrifice. Now God had commanded that provision be made for daily and weekly sacrifices and offerings, but even these were not sufficient to cover sin. So on this day the high priest took the atoning blood into the holy of holies to make atonement for the priests and for all the people "because of all their sins" (Lev. 16:34). This was certainly a solemn reminder that all could not be joy in their relationship with God, for sin had to be dealt with. Significant on this day was the scapegoat, on whose head were put all the sins of the people before it was sent off into the wilderness. As it is explained: "The goat shall bear all their iniquities upon him to a solitary land" (Lev. 16:22). Again the substitutionary character of atonement is made graphically clear.

5. The Sabbath. Every seventh day the sabbath was to be observed (Deut. 5:12-15; Ex. 23:12). Though the accent was again on rest and refreshment (even for animals, servants and strangers), the primary purpose was to renew fellowship with God. As Eichrodt puts it: "No business, however pressing, should be allowed to keep men from regularly seeking his fellowship" (Eichrodt, I, 133). Again they are reminded that God brought them out of Egypt with a mighty hand,

and therefore they are to keep the sabbath (Deut. 5:15).

6. A Covenant Renewal Ceremony. Finally mention should be made of the supposition of some scholars (in different ways S. Mowinckel and H. J. Kraus) that there was a single major holiday not specified in Scripture that celebrated the national and religious experience of Israel. Some of the psalms seem to refer to such a celebration. Perhaps the early covenant renewal ceremonies (Deut. 27:11-26; Josh. 8:30-35) developed during the monarchy into a kind of New Year's celebration that served as a setting for some of the royal psalms (2, 18, 20 et al.). While these scholars may be too much influenced by the presence of such festivals among Israel's neighbors, the suggestion may account for certain expressions of worship (as, for example, Ps. 50) that do not fit easily into any other setting. In any case, this research has done much to deepen our understanding of the Psalms.

Special times, then, were reminders that all times were in God's hand and that he was working in time, in specific acts and in natural processes to show his goodness and deliver his people. Moreover, remembering the Lord was certainly no drudgery or meaningless ritual. It was a joyous expression of confidence that Israel's life had order and direction, that the Lord who delivered them in the past would surely continue to watch over them.

Sacred Actions

As a part of the response of worship God commanded that certain things be done by his people to act out their obedience and make their faith visible. Although the Mosaic period saw the greatest extent of ceremony, already the patriarchs were commanded to do certain things. First, as a sign of the covenant, every male was to be circumcised (Gen. 17:10). Note that this was something Abraham was required to do, but it was primarily to be a sign not of his faith, but of God's coming to be gracious to him, and also of the associated curse (Gen. 17:14). Only secondarily was it a sign of response and, eventually, a national sign of the Jewish people. Earlier God had made another request of Abraham (Gen. 15:8-11). When Abraham asked God how he was to know he would possess the land, God had him divide a heifer, a goat, a ram and a turtle-dove. The flaming torch that passed between these pieces (v. 17) was to be a sign that God would keep his promises. It was —like the fiery, cloudy pillar—a manifestation of his presence.

1. Purification Rites. Rites of purification were not unique to Israel and in fact we see them practiced before the explicit instructions were given during the time of Moses. Perhaps they were similar to those practiced by Israel's neighbors. As early as Genesis 35:2, we see Jacob telling his household to purify themselves and change their garments. But the context is especially important. They were going up to Bethel to make an altar to God. So there is the recognition, even if it is not clearly articulated, of the holiness of God and the necessity of preparing themselves to approach him. When Moses came down from the mountain (Ex. 19:14), he had all the people wash their garments and purify themselves so that they might be prepared to hear the voice of God. Then they took their stand at the foot of the mountain (v. 17). Again, this was an indication that if God would speak to them, they must prepare themselves, even though much specific legislation about purity had not yet been given. It is important to notice this, for awareness of God's holiness preceded the giving of the legislation and was not the result of it.

The primary purpose for the laws of purity was to set the people apart to the Lord. These laws were to be an outward expression of the fact that their God was holy and that they, therefore, were to be a holy (or separated) people. Secondarily, these laws set them apart from the peoples around them, especially from their animistic and demonic beliefs. It is for this reason that the pig may have been forbidden to Israel, for it was an ancient Canaanite sacrificial animal. Other unclean animals, mice, serpents and hares, were associated with pagan magical belief (Lev. 11 and Deut. 14:3-21; Eichrodt, I, 134). At the same time, these laws were to set them apart from

contamination that might issue from contact with a dead body
(Num. 19:11-13) or with leprosy (Lev. 13). But it must be remembered that hygenic considerations were not the primary
ones; other more contagious things, such as pestilence, did
not make one unclean. Primarily, for the Hebrew, "clean"
meant "qualified for approach to God" (Vos, 173). The basic
question in the faith of the OT was what effect a state had
on one's relation with God.

As with all the law the ceremonial instructions were to be
an additional lesson that only in following God's instructions
could one lead a joyful life that is pleasing to God. In the end,
however, it was seen to be inadequate to bring about the
purity of which it was the symbol. This cleansing was recognized very early to come from God alone. By the time of David
these rites were expressions of an inward purity that came by
the operation of God himself on the heart. "Purge me with
hyssop," David says (Ps. 51:7), when he really means, "put a
new and right spirit within me" (v. 10).

2. Sacrificial Worship. The meaning of OT sacrifice centers
around the Hebrew verb *kipper* usually translated "atone"
or "cover" (Lev. 1:4). The basic meaning could be "to cover"
(as in the Arabic cognate) or "to wipe away" (if from the Akka-
dian). Or the verb might indicate the process of ransoming
or atoning by payment of a sum or gift, reflecting the meaning
of the Hebrew noun *kōpēr* ("ransom price"). Given the full
biblical context (especially Lev. 17:11), this latter meaning
best expresses the Hebrew concept (R. J. Thompson, NDB,
1120). Leon Morris suggests that in the Bible the atonement
obtained is far greater in value than the ransom paid. "There
is always an element of grace in atonement" (Morris 1955,
162, 167). Notice further that both the subjective and objective aspects of sin are dealt with in the concept of atonement.
Basic to the sacrificial system are two elements. First, there
is a humiliation of the worshiper, symbolized by the laying
of his hands on the victim. Moreover, the worshiper makes
reparation to the offended party, usually God, so that the integrity of the personal relationship is maintained. Second,

there is a transfer from a state of defilement to a state of purity. Here the emphasis is on the objective wrong and the standards of God's justice on the one hand, and the process of becoming qualified for approach to him on the other. The first stresses what is brought near and offered to God, which can be symbolized by prayer. The second speaks of God's part in making man qualified to come to him, which can be thought of as the answer to prayer.

a. The burnt offering ('ōlâh). The different sacrifices and offerings can be divided into four kinds. First, there was the burnt offering (Lev. 1:4). This is perhaps the typical sacrifice of the OT, and we can use it to illustrate the elements present in most of the other sacrifices. Basic to it was its gift character; something was brought and offered to the Lord for and on behalf of the worshiper.

The worshiper began by choosing a particular animal from the flock, without spot or blemish, that is, free from anything that might detract from its value. This points out its character as a substitute—the purity of the victim stood in place of the impurity of the offerer (1 Pet. 1:19). Its purity also related to its gift character—only the best should be offered to the Lord. The animal then was brought to the tent (temple) where the worshiper laid his hands on (literally "leaned on") the victim. The significance of this must be related to the laying on of hands (Gen. 48:13-14; Lev. 24:14; Num. 8:10) which always signified a transfer from one person to another (Vos, 162). Thus the hands conveyed guilt to the victim which was otherwise innocent.

Next the offerer himself slew the animal "before the Lord." The victim suffered and died as a penalty for the sin which it now bore (Lev. 4:33; 17:11). The blood, then was collected and splashed against the altar, and parts or the whole of the animal were burned on the altar. The Hebrew word used for burning here does not mean destructive burning, but rather "refining," speaking of the life of the offerer given up in obedience as a sweet savor to God (which surely lies behind the reference to Christ's sacrifice in Ephesians 5:2). Finally, in some cases (as in the peace offering of Leviticus 7:11-18), a sacrificial meal followed in which either the priests alone or the priests and the worshiper together ate the meat. Meal fellowship everywhere in the Bible speaks of positive communion and blessedness. Thus the offering which is given to God is returned to the worshiper in symbol not only of ended hostilities but of the enjoyment of God's full favor. This fullness of fellowship is summed up in the OT idea of peace; that is, with the sacrifice peace is restored. This final step, meal fellowship, is God's gift-supper which is gathered up in the NT teaching on the Lord's Supper. Christ is our peace and we celebrate his offering around the Lord's table.

b. The meal or meat offering (minḥâh). The basic idea in the meal or meat offering was one of tribute or present made to obtain good will (Lev. 2). It had to be something valuable and something that the worshiper had worked for and prepared. It was a part of himself that was offered in symbol of the whole. The offering, when it was burned upon the altar, made a pleasing odor to the Lord. The sweet savor of the offering indicated its close connection with prayer, which was often spoken of in this way. Both this offering and prayer spoke of approaching God and surrendering oneself to his care. By the glad performance of these rites, the worshiper was reminded that God demands not only consent and confession but deeds as well. Even in the OT faith without external expression was dead.

c. The peace offering (zebaḥ *or* šᵉlāmîm). The peace offering (Lev. 7:11-18) was a sacrificial offering expressing thanksgiving to God or perhaps the payment of a vow. It too could be eaten in a special meal on the day of the offering.

d. The guilt or sin offering ('āšām *or* ḥattā't). Guilt or sin offerings (Lev. 4 and 7) became necessary when one became guilty of a ceremonial uncleanness. (Leviticus 4:2 specifies it was also for those who sinned unwittingly.) Sins against one's neighbor were more prominent in the *'āšām* and those against God in the *ḥattā't*. Here the element of expiation, or satisfaction of guilt, was prominent. This offering was for

everyone. Provision was made for the poor to bring things
that they could afford.

The Theology of the Cult

The sacrifices and offerings are all parables of the holiness
and justice of God. They express as well creation in God's
image and the ability to commune with God despite the Fall.
The sacrificial system was a part of God's means for creating a
people who would hear his voice and follow him.

We noted at the outset of this chapter that the forms were
to express an inner reality—repentance and faith. This inward character is reflected in the necessity that the forms be
accompanied by repentance and confession. At times confession is obviously the crucial element in the offering, as in
1 Samuel 7:5-11. This inner response is based in the first place
on the recognition that all that is belongs to the Lord. In
Genesis 22 Abraham does not question God's right to demand
the sacrifice of Isaac. If God actually had the authority that
Abraham believed he did, could he withhold his only son? Yet
when God saw Abraham's faith, he showed his lifegiving
character and provided a substitute to offer in place of Isaac.

The character of heartfelt response is evident also in the
scope left for offerings of thanksgiving. With the detailed
stipulations for offerings we sometimes lose sight of the fact
that OT worship allowed much spontaneity. Psalm 116:12
captures this spirit of response to God's goodness—"What
shall I render to the LORD?"—just as we might wonder about
a loved one—what can I give to show my love? The use of vows
in the OT may be mentioned in this connection. Though to
our modern ears vows sound crass and mechanical, to the
Hebrew they were the normal response to the Lord who owned
the heaven and the earth. A vow could be made to perform
(Gen. 28:20-22) or to abstain (Ps. 132:2-5) in return for God's
favor, or it could be simply an expression of zeal or gratitude
(Ps. 22:25). The vow was the sign that the integrity of the
individual's faith and response was somehow to be like that of
God, a kind of imitation which we will discuss in chapter ten.

The inward and personal character of worship, moreover, is seen in the fact that forgiveness could on occasions be obtained simply by calling on the Lord. Abraham interceded for Lot in Genesis 18; Moses, for the people in Exodus 32:30-34. The prophets as well often pleaded with God on behalf of the people. This suggests that God under certain conditions accepted other mediators in much the same way that he accepted the mediation of the high priest who entered the holy of holies once a year on behalf of the people.

All of this pointed toward the day when God's redemptive program would lead to a whole new inward disposition, which is expressed in the prophets as a new covenant or a new heart. But even before that, the Hebrew knew that the real form of worship was a matter of the heart. The one who says "I delight to do thy will" is surely moving toward fulfillment of all righteousness (see Ps. 40:8), and David when he says "purge me with hyssop" (Ps. 51:7) is referring not only to a ceremonial cleansing, but, as we noted, to an inward moral renewal.

How can we sum up the idea of sacrifice in the OT? The truth is no single picture comprehends the full meaning; rather a series of images together make up the idea of sacrifice. The central idea, as we have seen, is the process of ransoming or restoring to favor by means of suitable payment. This seems clear from Leviticus 1:4 as well as from Ezekiel 45 where a ransom sacrifice is the primary element in the ideal picture of worship. But in addition to this—if less prominent —is also the idea of propitiation. In the OT it is clear that the wrath of God—his consistent disposition against sin—must be expressed toward it. If people were to approach God, sin must be covered, but God's wrath must also be averted. If the people were found guilty of idolatry, they had to fear lest the anger of the Lord be kindled against them (Deut. 6:15). So for forgiveness to be complete, it had also to remove his wrath (Ps. 85:2-3 and Micah 7:18-20; see Morris 1955, 129-36). Further, OT sacrifices were substitutionary. We have commented already on this theme—the part for the whole, one for

the many. This idea runs through the instructions on sacrifice
and offerings. The most important image here is that of the
scapegoat, who bears all of the sins of the people out into the
wilderness. It is this element that best preserves the personal
element in religion. Blood in this case is not a magic element,
but is accepted by God as a substitute for the life of the worshiper. Finally, in all the instructions it is clear that God forgives for his name's sake. He cannot be bought off, even if in
his grace he takes the deed for the reality and forgives. But
it remains true that God is the one who will have mercy (Ex.
33:19). In Isaiah we read of the time when God will blot out
transgressions for his own sake, even when he is wearied by
the iniquities of the people (Is. 43:22-25).

In the end it must be seen that all the prescriptions of the
OT worship have a temporal character. They must be constantly repeated and so easily become formal duties. Then,
too, sins committed "with a high hand," that is, rebellion
against God, cannot be atoned for. Both human need and
God's character speak of a better way. Through all the regulations, the ordinances and statutes, there was really only one
hope: "O Israel, hope in the LORD! For with the LORD there is
steadfast love, and with him is plenteous redemption. And he
will redeem Israel from all his iniquities" (Ps. 130:7-8).

The hope for this plenteous and final redemption seems to
converge in the OT until it focuses on Isaiah 53. Here the
servant of the Lord becomes an object of hope even when his
appearance is unpromising. Here is the judicial element—"he
has borne our sicknesses and carried our pains" (v. 4, margin),
"the chastisement that made us whole" (v. 5). Here also is the
mediatorial—"wounded for our transgressions, . . . bruised
for our iniquities" (v. 5). Here too is the substitutionary—"the
LORD has laid on him the iniquity of us all" (v. 6). The context is clearly the expiation of sin by an offering—"he makes
himself an offering for sin" (v. 10). Finally, there is the impu-
tation, the transference of righteousness—my servant shall
"make many to be accounted righteous" (v. 11). Through it all
there is the hope of the final and eternal triumph of God—

"he shall prolong his days; the will of the LORD shall prosper in his hand" (v. 10). All of these are but glimpses, yet they speak of what is best in OT religion and presage something better. To fully understand their significance one must go beyond the OT to the One who came and took on himself the form of a servant and became obedient unto death (Mk. 10: 45 and Phil. 2:5-11).

Whom have I in heaven but thee?
    And there is nothing upon
earth that I desire besides thee.
My flesh and my heart may fail,
    but God is the strength of my
heart and my portion for ever.

Psalm 73:25-26

9
Piety

Theological Character of Piety

The piety of the OT is the response of the heart to God's self-revelation. When the eternal God shows himself as holy and loving, there must be response. The answer given, when it is genuine and heartfelt, takes into account, not only the gulf that exists between a holy God and the sinner, but also the joy of finding this God leaning down to love and care for his creature. The response of the OT believer is an active response that involves the whole of life. It is much more than mere assent or even confession. For Abraham it meant that he had to leave, to follow and, most importantly, to walk before God and be blameless. For Moses and Israel it was necessary to leave Egypt, to listen to God's voice and to dare to follow in the way he set. Let us consider some of the elements involved in the believer's walk with God in the OT.

1. The Fear of the Lord. The initial response to a revelation of power is fear. Rudolf Otto calls this sense of the numinous power of the holy the basic element in all religion

(The Idea of the Holy, 1923). But this initial terror is not what
the OT means by the "fear of the Lord." In fact, when Moses
tells the people what God had revealed to him, he explicitly
says "do not fear" (Ex. 20:20), and yet he goes on to say that
God came so that the "fear of him" may be before their eyes
(the root for *fear* is the same in both cases). Is this a contradiction? No, Moses wanted them to know that they need not
fear as if they faced something unknown or unpredictable
(the root cause of fear in pagan religions), but to live in the
sober awareness of who God is.

The Hebrew fear of the Lord was to be unique. In pagan
religions people live in constant fear of the spirits which they
must seek to appease. And so, as Gilbert Murray says of the
Greeks, "they are always afraid." Israel's fear of God was
rather an awesome realization that the holy God had turned
to them and had chosen them to be his people. Therefore they
were to walk in fear, but a fear that led to confidence and
trust, and not to paralyzing uncertainty. Wisdom, the art of
forming wise and successful plans, the psalmist said begins
with the fear of the Lord (Ps. 111:10). The parallel phrase
adds: "a good understanding have all those who practice it."
So fear was not primarily an emotion, but a way of life based
on a sober estimate of God's presence and care. Such an attitude includes emotion, but so far from being a disintegrative
force, this fear leads to life and satisfaction (Prov. 19:23).
Here too we should not expect that we will know the fear of
God perfectly now. For Jeremiah says that when the everlasting covenant has been made, the fear of God will be put in
their hearts, that they may not turn from the Lord (Jer.
32:40).

2. Faith in God. Genesis 15:6 says that Abraham believed
God who reckoned it to him for righteousness. Throughout the
OT only God is recognized as the proper object of trust: "he
who trusts in his own mind is a fool" (Prov. 28:26). In the OT
trust first implies a knowledge and understanding of God.
But this is more than a theoretical knowledge; it is always a
practical, experiential awareness. The psalmist asks man to

be still and know who God is, because, the verse before says, he makes wars to cease (Ps. 46:9-10).

An awareness of the reality of God leads, secondly, to a voluntary surrender to God for guidance. Like fear, faith is an all pervasive attitude that affects one's whole life. This is beautifully expressed in Psalm 37:3-5: "Trust in the LORD. . . . Take delight in the LORD. . . . Commit your way." Such a surrender leads finally to a trust in the promises of God, or perhaps we should say, an active obedience. Once God is known and commitment is made, life then becomes a matter of following. This is why the OT speaks so often of the "way of life." Psalm 26:1 says that the psalmist is not afraid to be judged by God, for he has walked in integrity. Then he adds simply: "I have trusted in the LORD without wavering." Notice he is not saying that he has confidence in his integrity, but that his integrity is offered as evidence of his trust in God.

Implicit in the idea of faith is repentance or, as it is simply expressed in the OT, turning. While the idea is not as fully developed as in the NT, it is present throughout the OT. Turning from one's own way and following the Lord and his statutes implies that the past way was wrong. Nor do we have a picture of a once-and-for-all turning to follow God. Rather, one confesses failure to God each time a sin is committed, that is, whenever a wrong turning has been discovered (Lev. 5:5; Deut. 30:2; Ezek. 18:30).

3. Love for God. The classic passage which describes the whole of human duty to God is Deuteronomy 6:5: "You shall love the LORD your God with all your heart, and with all your soul, and with all your might." We can recognize by now that this way of speaking in Hebrew means no less than a love arising from the whole person. Love is an inner cleaving that involves the whole self in all its activity. In a general sense love impels one to actions that satisfy awakened desires (Prov. 20:13). But, as we have noted, the basic thirst of the human heart is for God (Ps. 42:1). Love for God, then, is an inner force which attaches itself to God in a personal way and which naturally issues in a life of loyalty and commitment. Perhaps the highest picture of this relationship is found in the prophet Hosea, where this bond is likened to love between a husband and his wife. There the basic relationship is a manifestation of what Eichrodt calls a direct sense of mutual belonging; a man's or woman's love is always a response to God's loving initiative.

This loving response is the only proper correlative to God's faithfulness to man. As Deuteronomy 7:9 explains, God keeps his covenant with those who love him. Later Moses put loving God together with serving him and following in his ways (Deut. 11:13, 22). Notice again that love is not a feeling for God, though feelings will not be totally absent, but a strong inner commitment that is realized in outward obedience. In keeping his commandments one shows that he loves God (Deut. 13:34; see Jn. 14:15). Commandments become so important as vehicles of our love that the psalmist could celebrate his love for the law above gold (Ps. 119:127).

Hosea also emphasizes that love for God is a response to his prevenient love in choosing Israel. God says by the prophet: "I led them with cords of compassion, with the bands of love ... " (Hos. 11:4). The only reason given for God's choice of Israel is that he set his love on them, and that was certainly not in response to anything about which Israel could boast (Deut. 7:7-8). Jeremiah adds that it is God's everlasting love that is the basis for his faithfulness to them (Jer. 31:3). The preference for the term "know the LORD" in the prophets, specially in connection with the future kingdom, should be understood in the light of a loving response to God (Jer. 24:7; 31:34). Full knowing is the consummation of love ("to know" in the OT is often used to mean sexual intercourse).

Characteristic Expressions of Piety

1. Praise to God. The trust and confidence the Hebrew had in God led to a deep sense of joy that seems to pervade the references to worship in the OT. This joy led them naturally to outbursts of praise to God. The root idea of praise (Heb., *hillēl* or *yāḏâh)* is connected with making a noise or bodily gesture, or with playing and singing. From the accounts in the psalms it seems this aspect was rarely missing from worship. But in its usage praise came to be associated with the joyous recounting of God's gracious work as an expression of the gratitude of the worshiper. Early examples of this are Exodus 15, and Deuteronomy 26:5-9, where confession of faith and praise are offered together.

The awareness and remembrance of God's goodness gave to Hebrew worship its characteristic exuberance (see the psalms of praise, Ps. 92—100 and 103—118). For OT believers the reality of God was everywhere and immediately evident. They were confronted by it at every point in their lives. Deny God's existence and be a fool (Ps. 14:1)—so the OT describes the heart of the criminal. Yet God's presence was always personal. The psalms are filled with expressions such as: "come, let us praise our God," or, "I will sing of the mercies of the LORD," or "the LORD is my shepherd." As we will soon see, however, even the most personal feeling of thanks yearned for corporate expression.

Praise was often so exciting that worship could only be described as boisterous. There was dancing (Ps. 150:4), all kinds of instruments (Ps. 108:2), constant singing (Ps. 33:3) and even tumultuous shouting (Ps. 27:6). There was nothing dreary about OT worship! In fact one has the impression that in praising, men and women realize their highest end. Von Rad says insightfully: "Praising and not praising stand over against one another like life and death: praise becomes the most elementary token of being alive that exists" (von Rad I, 370). The "dead" worship of some contemporary churches strays far from God's desire.

2. Prayer. Growing out of the same intensely personal relationship between God and his people was the sense that appeal could be made to God. Though particular forms of prayer (such as the so-called sanctuary prayers in Psalm 24:7-10) developed later, the basic content of OT prayer was a spontaneous expression of trust called for by some personal experience. Abraham's servant (Gen. 24:42-44) knew that it was not necessary to pray only at sacred places but that

God could be confidently addressed whenever there is need.
There is considerable familiarity in OT prayer (Gen. 15:2-3;
24:12-14, 26). Very early, prayer was closely related to sacrifice, which was itself called "seeking the Lord." This connection
is important, for it suggests that one of the basic attitudes of
prayer is submission to the will of God, which, we have seen,
characterized the faithful keeping of sacrifices. The connection, however, is not a fixed one. Prayer as a natural expression of trust is appropriate at any time or place of life.

For the Hebrew there was no magic or any formula associated with the name of God. Exodus 20:7 forbids taking God's
name in vain, that is, thoughtlessly. This, along with the
spontaneous character of prayer, shows how far the Hebrews
were from the pagan notion of incantation. Eichrodt lists the
following elements common to pagan ideas of prayer which
were strange to the Hebrews: (1) in Israel there is no use of
God's name as a magic word; (2) there is no repetition of
phrases over and over; and (3) there is no whispering or mur-
muring in a prescribed way (Eichrodt, I, 174). Prayer in the
OT tends to spill over all fixed forms and mechanics. Just as
God's name is not kept secret but freely given to all, just so
God's people are free at any time to call upon the Lord.

Missing also is any mystical sense of losing oneself in God
and separating oneself from the world in praying. In fact, one
could say that prayer in the OT is not a means of retreat, but
a means to energetic cooperation with God in his work (see
Jacob, 176). This is all the more important when it is recalled
that the Hebrew saw the relation between God and the world
in the most intimate terms. God never called people out of
the world, but into it, for it was there that God was showing
himself Lord and Redeemer.

The full range of the religious life comes to expression in OT
prayer. It expressed the people's love and praise to God; it was
also a means of expressing love for their neighbors. One of the
main emphases was intercession. There are examples in
Moses (Ex. 32:32), Aaron (Num. 6:22-27), Samuel (1 Sam.
7:5-13), Solomon (1 Kings 8:22-53) and Hezekiah (2 Kings

19:14-19). That each of these was an important person suggests that such persons could serve as mediators between God
and man, and, while this does not preclude the use of prayer
by all people, it does illustrate a theme that becomes so crucial
in the ministry of Christ. A sinful people need someone who
will plead their case before God, though in the OT it was
recognized that sin required more than human intercession
(Ezek. 14:12-20). In a sense, all who trust God need one another
to intercede for them. For this reason the awareness of sin and
weakness was the constant context of prayer; expressions of
distress and confession often begin OT prayers.

Though prayer is the expression of the personal relationship between God and his people, we have already seen that
it finds full flowering in the communal worship of the temple.
The Songs of Ascents (Psalms 120—134) show the joy worshipers felt at the opportunity to go together to the house of
worship (Ps. 137:5-6). In the OT, private and communal prayer
are always complementary. As Eichrodt puts it: "There is no
need for a real and living piety to take refuge in private
prayer, but real adoration and lively religious feeling lend
force even to public worship" (Eichrodt, I, 175). That they
were used to joining together for collective prayer was certainly not regarded as a limitation by the Hebrews, though
they also knew that prayer was not to be offered only in the
temple.

3. Glorifying God. The biblical idea of glory, as we have
seen, is that of heaviness or worthiness. And glorifying God in
the biblical sense could be expressed simply as letting the
worthiness, the essence of God be manifest. The context of this
idea in the OT is the belief that the whole earth is an arena for
God's glory to show itself. Not only do the heavens declare the
glory of God (Ps. 19:1), but the whole earth is full of the glory
of the Lord (Is. 6:3). We have often seen how directly the Hebrew conceived the relation between God and the world. Theo.
Vriezen notes in this connection the parallel between the OT
view of the world and that of the Eastern Orthodox Church
which emphasizes the penetration of all things by the reality

of the Spirit of God (Vriezen, 282n). Yet the OT lacks the mystical reaction to the world common in Eastern Christianity. But there is in both the sense that God could manifest himself in the world, indeed that he could "see through" the world (Ps. 94:8-11). This relationship comes to clearest expression in the Incarnation.

However, because of sin people do not see God's glory in the world, and when God manifests himself it must be in judgment. Isaiah had to have his lips cleansed when he was shown the glory and splendor of God (Is. 6:6-7; compare Ex. 33:20). But beyond judgment (after sacrifice has properly been made) it is possible for the believer to behold the beauty of the Lord. Beauty for the Hebrew was primarily an experience of worship and was related always to the presence of God (Ps. 50:2). But this beauty was never something which was to be seen and enjoyed only. It was characteristic of God's manifestation of himself that when his glory was seen it was also communicated. Hebrew worshipers became like what they beheld. They were to reflect what they worshiped. Praise, as we have seen, was the means by which the believer remembered publicly what God had done. It reflected in this way the glory, the worthiness, of God. In expression, then, the worshiper spread the glory of God. As C. S. Lewis wrote about these things: "Praise not merely expresses but completes the enjoyment; it is appointed consummation. . . . Fully to enjoy is to glorify. In commanding us to glorify him, God is inviting us to enjoy him" *(Reflections on the Psalms,* 1958, 95, 97).

All of this has a future consummation. The prophets looked forward to the day when the glory of the Lord would cover the earth as the waters cover the sea (Is. 11:9). But in worship the believer anticipates that day, for there in the experience of worship the beauty and glory of God are manifest. Outside the temple there are those who do not see the glory of the Lord as they look at the heavens. So the prophets awaited a day when the glory of the Lord would be revealed in such a way that all flesh would see it together (Is. 40:4-5). Then all of the elements that are associated now with worship will be everywhere visible. That Day will be characterized by its beauty (Is. 33:17; Ps. 48:2), by its great joy (Is. 9:2-3) and its praise (Is. 12:1, 4). No one will have to lead in worship, urging us to know and praise the Lord, for we shall all know the Lord from the least to the greatest (Jer. 31:34).

This experience will be intensely personal without ceasing to be communal. Individual piety must be seen as the culmination, not the beginning of OT worship. We have often reversed this order in our modern individualistic understanding of religion. It is true that personal and individual communion with God was present from the beginning. Noah, Abraham and Moses spoke with God. But their experience was in some sense representative and mediatorial. They spoke for the group and God dealt with them for the sake of the group. It is important to remember that it is a people that God was calling to himself and that the individuals found their communion with God within the context of this people of God. In David we see the further stages of the development of personal religion (Ps. 51), but not until the prophets do we see its flowering. The experience of Jeremiah demonstrates the possibility of a personal relationship even as he looked forward to its universal extension (Jer. 31). Ezekiel too elaborated the idea of personal faith and responsibility to God (Ezek. 18). But let it be remembered that personal religion is the fulfillment and not the negation of social religion. In knowing God better we are free to love our neighbor more perfectly and share this knowledge together. To this concrete sharing of life we turn in the next chapter.

I am the LORD who practice steadfast love, justice, and righteousness in the earth; for in these things I delight.

Jeremiah 9:24

10
Ethics

The Basis of OT Ethics

When we divide material into chapters we always run the risk of implying a separation where there is none. In pausing to reflect on the various themes we have already considered, we need to remind ourselves of the underlying unity of OT theology. The covenant rests on the nature of God; the law expresses the covenant relationship; and the cult and piety grow together out of the covenant relationship defined in the law. But piety does not stand alone; it naturally expresses itself in the moral life of the community, what we will discuss here as ethics. Piety and ethics go together as faith and works do in the book of James. Nor is wisdom, discussed in the next chapter, unrelated to all of this. It is but the description of the concrete form of life in the covenant. This unified understanding is especially important in the OT where all of life relates to God and his purposes.

E. Jacob sums up the moral life of man in the OT in these words: "If the nature of man can be defined by the theme of the image of God, his function can be qualified as the imitation of God" (Jacob, 173). This theme of imitation, which continues in the NT, rests on important theological principles which we must now examine.

1. The Character of God. OT ethics are an expression of the character of God. This theological foundation, which we saw also in the case of law in general, is much more than a truism. First, it implies that religion and morality are related in the closest possible way. On the one hand, the OT knows nothing of morality apart from religion. That is, God is the source of the good, and if man is to do the good, it is because he knows God (Prov. 3:5-6). On the other hand, this knowledge of God must surely express itself in a moral life. Walking uprightly before the Lord is a common expression for moral living. So much is right living emphasized in the OT that during the intertestamental time Judaism took man's whole duty as keeping the law. Orthodoxy became only a matter of right practice *(orthopraxis)*. If a Jew obeyed the law, he was considered righteous whatever his beliefs happened to be. Thus there developed a wide variety of opinions about certain theological questions. It was the overemphasis on practice that the Lord spoke against when he debated with the Pharisees. Nevertheless, the importance of doing righteousness is constant throughout the OT, and Christ himself reaffirmed it in John 7:17: "If any man's will is to do his will, he shall know whether the teaching is from God" (see also Mt. 5:19). But practice ought always to be the expression of heartfelt confidence in God.

Since there is one personal will—expressed in the law—that is valid for all parts of the community at all times, there is a basis for a wholesome confidence in moral standards. There is only one yardstick for both the judge and the accused, and it will not shrink or expand at the whim of the powerful. By contrast, in primitive religions there are often hundreds of gods. Sacrifice must be made to appease as many as possible of these gods, and so one can never be sure that he has done enough. In Greek religion before the time of Christ, the gods were believed to be so concerned with their own struggles that their influence on human affairs was wholly unreliable. Polytheism sets many standards, monotheism sets one. This unity lies behind the centrality of the Ten Commandments in the law and Christ's summation of the law: love God and love your neighbor (Mt. 22:37-40).

This unity does not mean there are no experiential factors at work in the elaboration of the law. There are casuistic elements (If this happens, then . . .), and the wisdom movement represents a grand elaboration in terms of the life and times of the people. But these explanations were always to be understood in terms of the basic self-revelation of God: I am the Lord. This revelation too lies behind the categorical commands and gives them their central place in the OT reckoning (Ex. 20:1-2).

Since the law is ultimately one, the keeping of it is of a piece. The NT explains that if you are guilty of a part you are a lawbreaker (Jas. 2:10; James goes on to explain that this is because the same Lord gave all the law). But this was certainly no innovation. The OT as well understands the unity of God's demands. This is why Moses could tell Israel to "do all the words of this law. For it is no trifle for you, but it is your life" (Deut. 32:46-47).

2. Creation in the Image of God. OT ethics are based on mankind's creation in the image of God. The human orientation of the law is an expression of likeness to God. We have seen before that God is never frustrated by the created order, as though material objects were an obstacle to spiritual endeavor. Likewise, humanness is nowhere seen as a barrier to righteousness. True, in their fallen state, people have been estranged from goodness, but that is because of their sin, not their humanity. The laws of the OT are in sharp contrast to contemporary codes precisely at this point. The OT law is a law for people. In the Book of the Covenant (Ex. 21—23), human values are consistently championed over material ones.

People in the OT are linked to God because of his great mercy *(ḥeseḏ)*. They are marked out as those who are shown

God's mercy. At the same time they are linked to one another by this same mercy. As those who are the object of God's kindness, men and women are to show kindness in turn. What does God require? To do justice and love kindness (Mic. 6:8). People as image-bearers then are able by virtue of their creation to reflect God's character. This means that their relations with those around them can be more than merely fair or just, they can be creative and restorative, even as God's dealings are with us (see Job 29:12-14). What hinders is not humanness but sin.

In this context then we can understand God's command to be holy as he himself is holy (Lev. 11:44). This command is often shortened to "I am the LORD." This asserts not only God's right to command, but human ability to conform. This is why the law when properly understood is not an alien force standing over against people. The law expresses the real nature of human beings, and keeping it is not a mechanical exercise but a reflection of the I-thou relationship that they sustain with God. Of course men and women cannot be holy in the same way that God is holy, but they can be holy in their own human way.

Sin, however, has changed the human situation in a fundamental way. And so the instructions that God gives to people are not merely to keep them in line, but to restore them. The law is redemptive. Thus to follow the way of the Lord in the OT is to share materially in his redemptive program. This means not only that they will do righteousness, but that they may also suffer for righteousness sake. In Isaiah 53 the servant of the Lord will bear the sins of others and in this way heal them. This makes us think of Christ, of course, but also of the persecution that all those who desire to live godly lives will suffer (2 Tim. 3:12).

Obeying the law suggests a fellowship of wills. We willingly obey the law because it is an expression of God's good will. But already in the OT there is the recognition of the limitation inherent in obedience. The real goal of ethics is a movement beyond a fellowship of will to a fellowship of nature, that is to say, a restoration of the fellowship that existed between Adam and God. What begins with obedience cries out for something more: a new and obedient heart. By outward instruction God wishes to lead his people to the place where renewal and cleansing is possible. This process Paul records for us in Romans 7 and 8. The law brings us to the place where we can receive the renewal that is in Jesus Christ, who delivers us from this body of sin.

Development of the Principles of OT Ethics
1. Instructions and Ordinances Associated with Creation. In creation God gave principles that cover and regulate all of life. These principles become structures in which all of life will develop and which God's redemptive program will enrich and extend as well as restore. First, people are to exercise lordship in replenishing and controlling the earth (Gen. 1:28). The sabbath is to remind them of God's own creative work and his rest; therefore, it is blessed and hallowed (Gen. 2:3). Adam exercises his headship in creation through his work, tending and keeping the created order (Gen. 2:15). In his work he realizes his God-given potential. Then Adam and Eve are given to one another in a unique relationship that elsewhere reflects God's own relationship with his people. These are the basic structures in which man and woman are to live, and they are foundational for all that follows.

The Fall of course affects each of these areas. Weeds and briers challenge and frustrate human dominion and rest. Work becomes drudgery, something bringing sweat and tears. The relationship between man and woman becomes one of dominion and unbridled desire rather than mutuality and love. All of this makes ethics a problem and calls for instruction and guidance as well as deliverance. But this does not change the basic situation in which men and women function. It does not alter the basic relationship they bear to the earth, their work and their families.

Before we leave the discussion of the creation account we might look into the need for guidance. Did this need arise only after the Fall, or did it exist before as well? We know that God gave guidance before the Fall and even a prohibition (Gen. 2:16-17). As we commented earlier man and woman needed to know from the beginning that they could not live without God's word. Fellowship with God was basic to life. But these instructions were not meant to challenge man and woman or to give them anything like complete guidance; they did not need that. The relationship between God and the first couple was a completely natural one. They did instinctively what God required. These instructions were merely to confirm and elaborate the created structure in which they had to develop before God. It did add the possibility of disobedience, as some scholars hold, in the form of a probation. So in a sense it was a prototype of later ethical instruction.

2. Instructions and Institutions for God's Covenant People. The covenant, as we have seen, defined the life of Israel and expressed her relationship with God. All of the institutions of her life, furthermore, were elaborations of this covenantal relationship. As with the ordinances of creation, so with the institutions of Israel's life, morality was to be lived out and expressed through these forms. They impinged on the people at every turn and helped them to define themselves and served as the structure for moral decisions. John McKenzie goes so far as to say, "The individual man was moral only in society and through society. In a certain sense, he had no moral responsibility; moral responsibility fell upon the whole society which created the conditions in which the individual persons lived" (McKenzie, 239). This may be an overstatement, but it does point out the idea of corporate responsibility so important in the OT.

In the West modern man tends to disparage structure as a hindrance to the free pursuit of personal development. But it is obvious that individuals cannot live without certain structures. Some anthropologists, in fact, feel that the modern rejection of structures lies at the base of much anxiety and search for identity. The French Revolution shows how one modern movement seeking liberty and brotherhood at the expense of tradition contributed to the rise of totalitarian government. While individual development is surely the fruit of the personal liberation that Christianity made possible, it flowered most fully within the context of structures that protected and encouraged this development. The OT institutions provided such structure in the old dispensation; the church as the body of Christ provides it in the new. As we shall see, the OT is just as concerned (perhaps more so if McKenzie is correct) with the morality of the structures as it is with that of the individual within the structure. This must be constantly borne in mind when reflecting on OT ethics.

a. The Ten Commandments. We begin with the decalog which forms the core of biblical ethics. This law which was given at Sinai was not so much a new law as an authoritative formulation of already existing instruction (see Gen. 2:2-3 on the sabbath; 9:5 on murder; 26:9-10 on adultery). All of the relations between God and his people are covered. Note, however, that relations with neighbors are regulated after and in terms of the regulations having to do with attitudes toward God. God's people are to have no other gods before them nor to attempt to shape an image to represent God. The primary relationship of an individual is with God. When this is properly established it will become foundational for all other relationships. As Calvin puts it: "Surely the first foundation of righteousness is the worship of God. When this is overthrown, all the remaining parts of righteousness, like pieces of a shattered and fallen building, are mangled and scattered" (*Institutes*, II, viii, 11). The sabbath as well, though it is "for man," is an expression of God's rest from creation and becomes a small parable of salvation in which God's creative judgment (deliverance) issues in a rest of peace and fulfillment.

The command to honor parents deals with the whole area of human authority. Theologically, respect for parents rests on the prior fatherhood of God (Ex. 4:22). Our idea of parenthood begins here. Respect for authority then is to be continued and nurtured in the family. This is the place where one learns to

respect and obey regardless of personal merit. In this way, as
Derek Kidner points out, the family becomes a miniature of
the nation. If the one is sound, the other will be as well, and
the promise attached to the one may be extended to the other
(Kidner 1972, 12). The loyalty that is due to parents offers an
opportunity to learn loyalty. Brothers share troubles (Prov.
17:17). The family studies the law together (Deut. 6:6-9) so
that fathers and children learn mutual respect (Prov. 17:6).

The command not to kill, we have noted, rests explicitly on
creation in the image of God (Gen. 9:6). Christ pointed out the
relation of this command to the attitude of our heart (Mt.
5:21-22), but this inward perspective is not lacking in the OT
(Lev. 19:17-18). People's attitudes toward their neighbors
involve more than freedom from animosity; the fate of others
is never to be indifferent to us (Prov. 24:11-12). In our kindness to others we are able to reflect God's goodness to us.

Adultery is forbidden as a reflection of the dignity of persons, and ultimately out of respect for God. Faithfulness is the
basis of monogamy which is enjoined from the beginning
(Gen. 2:24). It is true that divorce is allowed because of human
weakness, but, as the newer translations bring out, Deuteronomy 24:1-5 is hypothetical. God is allowing this, not pre-
scribing it. Here is a case where the law allows for human
weakness in a way that keeps its evil effects in bounds (Kidner 1972, 17).

The command against stealing also goes back to the basic
structures of creation. When property is protected, the basic
responsibility for dominion is protected. There are many ways
that a person can be robbed as the OT well understood; oppression in the form of low wages is a kind of stealing (Lev.
19:13). The OT attitude toward material possessions is important here too. Ultimately all possessions reflect the fruitful-
ness of the earth and thus recall the goodness of the Creator
(see Deut. 11:10-12). Material possessions then are blessings,
reminding the people of God's care. Then too possessions are a
responsibility; special care, as we shall see, must be taken for
those who are unable to care for themselves. On the other

hand, all the things that God gives us are to be enjoyed to the full. The Hebrews were not ascetics. In fact Deuteronomy 14:22-26 commands the people to take the tithe they have saved and enjoy themselves with it ("spend the money for whatever you desire," v. 26). Here is a graphic example of the efflorescent character of God's instructions: what he asks of his people he gives back with interest. And what a fine picture of the joyous generosity that the OT asks us to show both to the Lord and to one another. Paul expresses this in urging the Christians to give *hilariously* (2 Cor. 9:7, which actually is referring to Deut. 15:10 and giving to the poor). We saw before how possessions could be symbols of response to God, elements of instruction, reminding the Hebrew at every turn of the source of life and its purpose. The OT understands well the prejudice of human imagination for that which is visible.

The command against bearing false witness has primary reference to the law court (Kidner 1972, 20) and seeks to prevent damage to an individual's reputation. The law provided strict penalties for what one "intended to do to his brother" by his lie (Deut. 19:19). Kidner discusses how the OT provides material for the much debated question whether it is ever permissible to lie. He suggests that when life is threatened there may be room for an evasive reply that is intended to deceive (Ex. 1:15-19 and 1 Sam. 16:2). Also when people so reject the truth that they become unworthy of it, God may deceive the insincere inquirer (Ezek. 14:7-11; Kidner 1972, 20-21). John Murray, on the other hand, believes that the presence of such situations does not mean God countenances lying. Rather, speaking of Jacob and Rebekah's deception, Murray says, "God fulfills his determinative purpose of Grace and promise notwithstanding the unworthy actions of those who are beneficiaries of that grace" (Murray 1957, 137). In this connection we need to remember that the OT idea of truth is faithfulness in relationship, supremely in the relationship of the covenant. It is because God is faithful to his Word and promises that these in turn can become our standards for truth. This faithfulness we in turn reflect when we in obedience speak truth with our neighbors (Eph. 4:25).

The final command against coveting is at once the most inclusive and the most difficult to enforce. But this is yet another example of how well the OT understands the motivational aspect of sin. Sin is a matter of the heart before it is a matter of behavior. Coveting was the basic sin of Adam, craving that which he did not have, desiring to "gain the world." Christ reiterated this instruction in Luke 12 when a man came to him complaining that his brother did not share his inheritance with him. "Beware of all covetousness," the Lord warned (v. 15), suggesting that here was a basic point at which a misunderstanding about the nature and meaning of life could take root. It is not insignificant that this is the last of the commandments, for it virtually calls out for its NT interpretation which Christ supplies: covet not these (earthly) things, "but seek first his [God's] kingdom and his righteousness, and all these things shall be yours as well" (Mt. 6:33; see also Lk. 12:31).

b. Problem areas. Slavery would seem to be in violation of many of the basic principles of OT ethics, and yet it is condoned, even specifically regulated. Why does God allow such a thing? The first thing to note is that slavery was as widespread as it was brutal in the ancient world. Slaves had no rights and were often treated as animals. But in the OT the situation is different. Basic rights are ensured the slaves under the law, even in rest and celebration. Thus slavery is allowed (as common as it was in the ancient world W. B. Greene wonders if a prohibition would have been possible at all—Kaiser 1972, 227), but it is carefully regulated and humanized. A Hebrew should serve no more than six years and go free with something in his pocket (Ex. 21:2 and Deut. 15:13). Masters were reminded that the slave was a person who was to be treated with dignity—the memory of their own slavery in Egypt was constantly before them (Deut. 15:15). A woman slave because of her special vulnerability was offered special protection (Deut. 21:10-14 and Ex. 21:9-11).

Thus there is a distinction between the institution of

slavery and the abuses to which it was subject. The latter were carefully regulated, but the former was not attacked. Kidner comments on the OT view: "By accepting the system, even while humanizing it, it allowed that society was not ready to do without it." God's way "was the long process of spiritual nurture, education and sharpening the conscience, rather than one of premature social engineering" (Kidner 1972, 33). Green adds—what has proved true in the church history—that the OT treats slavery in a way that "should both render it less oppressive and should foster a sentiment which would tend toward [its] abolition" (in Kaiser 1972, 227).

Israel's openness to outsiders is seen in her attitude toward *resident aliens*. These persons would always be at a disadvantage in Israel as the land was parceled out to the native population; visitors were excluded. Thus there is special provision for these persons. Though they were not allowed automatic release from debts in the jubilee year (Deut. 15:3, 12), in almost every other way they were to be treated as equals. They had equal protection under the law (Lev. 24:22). Their conditions were to be watched and they were to be paid promptly (Deut. 24:14-15). They could even have Hebrew slaves (Lev. 25:47). In short, all the good that would be due one's own people is due the stranger as well: "The stranger who sojourns with you shall be to you as the native among you, and you shall love him as yourself" (Lev. 19:34). The verse concludes: "I am the LORD your God." It is his character that is at stake, and his special interest in the disadvantaged is shown in this way (Deut. 10:17-19). Quite a contrast, this to the all too human tendency to welcome friends and ignore strangers! All this is clearer in the NT, but even in the OT loving care extends as far as one's enemies (Ex. 23:4-5 and Prov. 25:21).

Many people are troubled by the seeming endorsement of *morally repugnant behavior* in the OT. How can God require Abraham to kill his son? Israel to steal from Egypt during the exodus? Or Israel to totally destroy a people in war? How can Moses be authorized to say: "No Ammonite or Moabite shall enter the assembly of the LORD. . . . You shall not seek their peace or their prosperity all your days for ever" (Deut. 23:3, 6)? We see in retrospect that God's command to Abraham was a testing of his faith and a demonstration to him that everything belonged to God. God's ownership of all things may be shown during Israel's departure from Egypt as well. Israel was told to "ask" of the Egyptians with the intent of obtaining (Ex. 12:35-36). More than likely they asked for these things because of the anticipated needs for the celebration in the wilderness and for provision for their journey. At that point the Egyptians were perhaps more than willing to grant their request with no thought of return!

The question of the *war of extermination* is more serious. Part of the answer—who can say he understands completely? —must surely lie in the gross wickedness of the people of Canaan. This is implied in the phrase "devoted to the LORD for destruction" (Josh. 6:17). The destruction was no sadistic venting of frustration, but a policy that was demanded by the holiness of God. Exceptions were made for some of the defeated people who became slaves (Josh. 9:21). Finally after settling in Canaan there is never any sense that such vengeance was to continue. The destruction was limited, determined for the purpose of preserving God's holiness and protecting Israel as a nation. We have seen already that no animosity extended to strangers simply because they were foreigners, rather God's command was determined at that time as a demonstration of his power and his holy judgment. Indeed all this came about because the "LORD God of Israel fought for Israel" (Josh. 10:42).

The concept of a holy war should not be overlooked here either. It must be borne in mind that all of life was considered in relation to the Lord. There was no sacred and secular dichotomy as we understand it in modern times. Thus war was not simply a necessary evil, a means to a higher end, but could itself be sanctified. Probably one of the early sources of OT history was a book of the wars of the Lord (Num. 21:14; see NBD, 1315). The Lord was the captain of his people (2 Chron.

13:12) who fought for Israel. The presence of the ark was the primary symbol of God's assistance. Preparations for war were thus sanctified (Joel 3:9 and Jer. 6:4) and often battles were inaugurated by sacrifice or offering (Judg. 6:20). The battle cry of Israel, "For the LORD and for Gideon," could even have religious significance (Judg. 7:18, 20). Since Israel's enemies were God's enemies, the people were assured of success. The whole conduct of war became a symbol of God's righteous judgment, of Israel's faith and of the fearful end of those who withstand God. Deuteronomy 20 lays out the restrictions placed on Israel in the conduct of holy war—who was excluded from fighting, how surrender could be offered, and when cities should be plundered or destroyed. From such limitations—and from the NT—we know that the principle of extermination is in no way transferable to any and all wars but at that point in history it was God's means of instruction to his people.

Incidentally, it is worth noting that many tribal groups to this day conduct wars of revenge with religious sanction. Such "going on the warpath" is often preceded by elaborate ritual and accompanied with high standards of fair play as well as what we would call cruelty. (Interestingly, among the Crow Indians it is considered an act of exceptional bravery to touch an enemy while he is asleep, as David was able to do to Saul.) God could take such a custom that was (and is) so widely understood and place it in the higher service of his holiness. The holy war could then become a part of the redemptive process which, in the judgment on sin brought about by Christ's death, would eventually bring to an end all need for such revenge. This is the same goal that was seen already in the OT when the psalmist says of God: "He makes wars cease to the end of the earth" (Ps. 46:9).

This line of thinking may help with another problem, that raised by the *imprecatory psalms*. "Pour out thy anger on the nations that do not know thee," cries the psalmist (79:6). How could God allow such attitudes on the part of his people? Meredith Kline sees both these prayers and the wars in

Canaan as examples of what he calls "the ethics of intrusion." That is, in the covenant of redemption that God makes with his people there is an "intrusion" of God's righteous power and the reality of the consummation (or the end of history) into the affairs of Israel. At these points then we glimpse the perspective of God, who sees the end from the beginning and visits iniquity with his holy judgment. The psalmist then in these psalms sees this reality and expresses it under the inspiration of the Holy Spirit. OT ethics in general, however, are not ethics of "intrusion" but ethics of "delay," that is, of God's common grace. This delay expresses God's patience with sin and sinners and his desire that all should come to repentance. But even as we experience delay we are not to forget that God's judgment is really threatening (Kline 1972, 155-62; see 1 Pet. 3:8-10 where a similar idea is expressed). Thus the psalmist speaks from a unique perspective, but it is one that we are not privileged to share. But note, as W. B. Greene points out, the psalmist is not expressing a desire for personal vengeance, but "a longing for the vindication of the divine justice in the divine way. . . . [He] simply calls on God to do what he has said ought to be done" (in Kaiser 1972, 215). Delay expresses the mercy of the Lord everywhere in the Bible, and it is this longsuffering we are asked to reflect. Moreover, our perspective on these things is forever different since Jesus prayed on the cross, "Father, forgive them; for they know not what they do" (Lk. 23:34).

The Teaching of the Prophets
Israel was not always able to realize the high standard of ethics raised by the OT. Yet there is ample evidence of genuine moral behavior expressive of all the goodness God intends for his people. Abraham showed peacefulness and unselfishness. Joseph resisted a great temptation and forgave a great wrong. David refused to take revenge (1 Sam. 24:12) so that he could show the "kindness of God" to the household of Saul (2 Sam. 9:3). The continuing experience of Israel with God's self-revelation progressively sharpened her

sensitivity and her unique self-understanding. With the wisdom movement, which we shall look at in the next chapter, the laws were taken further into their everyday lives and deeper into their consciousness.

All of this reaches its climax in the teaching of the prophets. Here ethics become, as they are throughout the NT, a part of God's redemptive activity. This is true in the first place because moral norms now become inner attitudes and realities. We have often seen how this was the ideal from the first giving of the law, but the whole process of revelation in the OT is progressively to impress on Israel her heart relationship to God. In a way ethics takes a course from an external authority to an internal reality without leaving behind the importance of the act. The cult was to teach Israel about God's demands on the whole of life, though it could come to be a means of evading God's real authority. By the time of the prophets it was clear that God's primary demand was one of humility and self-restraint (Mic. 6:8), which would surely evidence itself in actual kindness (Jer. 22:16).

In the second place, there is a fresh awareness of what sin requires. When there is such wickedness among the people, there must be suffering, but not only the suffering of judgment. In Jeremiah and especially Hosea there is a revelation of the God who himself suffers because of sin. This becomes even clearer in the image of the servant of the Lord who, at the direct commission of God (Is. 53), suffers for and in the place of the people. The intent of such references is not perfectly clear (though most Jewish thinkers were sure this had nothing to do with the Messiah who would reign in triumph), but already there is the understanding, so vital in the history of redemption, that one can suffer for righteousness' sake. This is certainly one of the keys to understanding Jesus' own ministry and lies behind such statements as "For the Son of man also came not to be served but to serve, and to give his life as a ransom for many" (Mk. 10:45).

But here a new tension arose at the end of the OT. There was no doubt that righteousness was for all people and that it was to be realized with a new intensity—it was to cover the earth as the waters cover the sea (Is. 11:5, 9). But how was this to happen? In the tradition of the elders (seen already in Ezra), it is to be realized by the individual himself as he follows the law in his life. In their zeal for following the way of righteousness their traditions grew until by the time of Christ, as we have seen, they obscured the intention of the law entirely. On the other hand, there were those who believed the new order could only be established by God himself, who from outside this sinful history would intervene in the great Day of the Lord. This tradition, which goes under the name of Apocalyptic, can be seen for example in the apocryphal 1 Enoch. While its strong dualism and pessimism takes it beyond biblical teaching, it did serve to keep alive the hope that God would specially intervene and direct history, as in fact he did in the person and work of Christ.

All of this which the prophets perceived, however dimly, waited for reinterpretation as well as fulfillment. For the one it needed Matthew 5—7; for the other, the death and resurrection of Christ.

My son, keep sound wisdom
   and discretion;
let them not escape from
   your sight,
and they will be life for
   your soul
and adornment for your neck.
Then you will walk on your
   way securely
and your foot will not stumble.

Proverbs 3:21-23

Christ is the savior of all men, whether they
be intellectual or simple; those that are instructed and wise
can come here and be satisfied; those that are foolish
or sick or sinful can approach in order to be cured.

Origen, *Contra Celsius*

11
Wisdom

The Development of the Idea of Wisdom
1. The Wisdom Idea. The wisdom literature of the OT is a
literary type common to the Ancient Near East that included short sayings (Proverbs), longer reflections on life (Ecclesiastes) and dialogs which deal with the problems of life
(Job). The basic idea is reflected in the Hebrew word *ḥokmâh*
from a root meaning firm and well grounded. Related words
are usually translated as "understanding" (*bînâh*, Job 39:26)
and "insight" (*teḇûnâh*, Ps. 136:5). Basically wisdom is the intensely practical art of being skillful and successful in life. It
is knowledge in the service of life (Prov. 1:5). The seat of wisdom is the heart, which is the center of moral and intellectual
decision (1 Kings 3:9, 12 Heb.). If the cult is the form of worship in the temple or tabernacle, wisdom is the life of worship
extended to the home and marketplace. Wisdom is religion
outside of church.

Originally wisdom implied technical skill or expertise like
that of a seaman or craftsman, and it never lost this practical

connotation. Bezalel is endowed with wisdom (translated "ability") to devise artistic design (Ex. 31:3-4). Others are "skilled" in making idols (Jer. 10:9), or as metalworkers (1 Kings 7:14). A large measure of Solomon's wisdom was seen in building the temple (1 Kings 5:9-18).

This kind of practical wisdom was commonly collected in the ancient world in short sayings that expressed in a memorable way attitudes and observations toward life. We have some very old examples recorded in the OT:

Out of the wicked comes forth wickedness. (1 Sam. 24:13)

Let not him that girds on his armor boast himself as he that puts it off. (1 Kings 20:11)

During the monarchy there arose a class of wise persons that may have been connected with a school for officials in the court (2 Sam. 14:2). Perhaps they became counselors to the government officials. In any case, by the time of Jeremiah these wise people stood beside the prophets and the priests; these three were identified with counsel, the word and the law respectively (Jer. 18:18; see also Is. 29:14).

Recent research has made it clear that the Hebrew wisdom movement was part of a phenomenon common to the whole Ancient Near East. All over the world people gathered their collective wisdom in proverbs or riddles. As long ago as the third millennium B.C. this was already a distinct movement in the Near East. The Bible itself tells us about the wisdom of the Egyptians (Ex. 7:22 and 1 Kings 4:30), of Edom and Arabia (Jer. 49:7; Obad. 8), and of Babylon (Is. 47:10 and Dan. 1:4). That there is a relationship between the wisdom of these countries and that of the Bible became clear with the discovery of the "Teaching of Amenemope," which was published in 1923. At the very least this discovery demonstrated that the OT wisdom literature need not be as late as had been previously thought; the "teaching" almost surely dates from before 1000 B.C. Just what the relationship might be between this and Proverbs is not clear. Some feel both rest on a common source, while more recently it has been argued that the general similarities of wisdom forms of that period account for the parallels. In any case, the analogs with Proverbs 22:17—23:11 seem too close to be accidental:

Teaching:	Proverbs:
Give thine ears, hear what is said,	*Incline your ear, and hear the words of the wise,*
Give thy mind to interpret them.	*and apply your mind to my knowledge.*
DOTT, 176	22:17
Remove not the landmark at the boundaries of the arable land ...	*Do not remove an ancient landmark*
Nor throw down the boundaries of a widow.	*or enter the fields of the fatherless.*
DOTT, 179	23:10

But though the Egyptian work has also a religious orientation, the tone of Proverbs is different:

Give thine ears, hear what is said,	*Incline your ear ... for it will be pleasant if you keep them*
Thou wilt find it a success,	*within you, if all of them are*
Thou wilt find my words a treasury of life;	*ready on your lips. That your trust may be in the LORD, I*
Thy body will prosper upon earth.	*have made them known to you.*
DOTT, 176	22:17-19

The Queen of Sheba was only one of many visitors who came to savor the wisdom and splendor of the court of Israel. We know from Moses' experience in Egypt and Daniel's in Babylon that there was keen competition between each country's wise men. Surely the Lord's own people were not to be outdone and wished to show off the jewel of their faith in this setting. After all, it was he "who turns wise men back, and makes their knowledge foolish; who confirms the word of his servant" (Is. 44:25). As we have seen in the case of portions of Israel's law, Israel was not above borrowing from the glory of the nations to lay it under tribute and eventually to transform it altogether. For in the end it was all too obvious that by wisdom alone one could not know God, even if, knowing him, one had the key to wisdom and understanding.

2. On Learning to Be Wise. The curriculum of the school of wisdom was really all of life. Ordinarily it was the elder members of the community who had learned something from life and so could teach wisdom. They sat at the city gate (Prov. 1: 21) and gave their counsel. But if one were serious about learning wisdom, he went to walk with those who were wise (Prov. 13:20) or, later, even to live in their house (Ecclus. or Sirach 51:23). For learning wisdom was a personal discipleship. The key words in the learning process are all personal words: instruction, reproof, correction.

The goal was an intuitive insight into life, its dangers and joys. The process was typical for the Hebrew way of thinking. He did not begin with abstract principles but with the experience of foolish sons or loose women. He moves in the area of concrete life that everyone knows about and, with shrewd judgment, intuitively sees what is at issue. Thus wisdom becomes a means of revelation, not in the direct sense of the prophets who spoke the word of God, though indeed the prophets were often influenced by the wise men, but in inspired observation and deliberation.

After first coming by an indirect revelation through the events of life, wisdom may be transmitted by personal discipling. If foolishness is bound up in the heart of a child, he must be led away from it by one wiser than he. It takes first an insight into one's foolishness, then a "conversion," a "hatred of evil" as Proverbs 8:13 has it. After this the path of wisdom is one of devotion—"watching daily at my gates, waiting beside my doors" (Prov. 8:34). It demands careful perseverance and tending.

The wisdom literature never lost its fine balance between the practical and the general. True, Job and Ecclesiastes wrestle with larger philosophical questions, but they were equipped to tackle these bigger questions by the practical insights of the whole wisdom movement. Job deals with the ancient problem of the innocent sufferer. It faces squarely the reality of evil and human suffering but shows the futility of our calling God to account (Job 40:6-14). Not that there is no answer, but it would not be visible until Christ's suffering and final triumph. Meanwhile, the attitude of sufferers is more important than the answer to their questions. Job, then, prepares the way for the gospel on the one hand, and provides a corrective to human presumption and pride on the other.

Ecclesiastes also tackles the large question we have come to call the human predicament. Contrary to the common view, however, the preacher does not conclude that everything is hopeless. Rather he bases his thinking uncompromisingly on the Creator-God (12:1) and his ordered creation (7:13; 3:1-9). Thus one cannot predict his own future (7:14; 8:17) or control his own life (7:23-25). Vanity, then, is not characteristic of life in general so much as the attempt to treat the created world as an end in itself. Indeed one can redeem the time (11:1-6) and savor all life's joys (11:8-9) if he serves God while there is opportunity (12:1-4, see on this Kidner 1976). All of this, however, does not leave behind the practical wisdom of Proverbs so much as extend it. As we will soon see, wisdom is a seamless robe. It is one path from simple kindness to eternal life.

Theological Character of Wisdom
1. Wisdom Comes from God. Some scholars have been anxious to emphasize the purely secular character of wisdom which only later gained a place of religious importance. This view fits well with the older idea that Israel's religion evolved through various stages. Now it is certainly true that wisdom was sometimes used in a secular fashion—that is, without reference to God—especially during the time of Israel's unfaithfulness. It may also be true that a certain amount of Israel's wisdom was borrowed from the wisdom of her neighbors. But in Israel wisdom was understood in the closest relation to her faith in God and her covenant obligations. This is summed up in Proverbs 2:

My son, if you receive my words and treasure up my commandments with you, making your ear attentive to wisdom and inclining your heart to understanding; yes, if you cry out for insight and raise your voice for understanding, if you seek it like silver and search for it as for hidden treasures; then you will understand the fear of the LORD and find the knowledge of God. (Prov. 2:1-5)

In a word Israel believed wisdom belonged to God. "With God are wisdom and might," Job says (12:13). Isaiah pronounces woe on the Egyptians who trust in chariots but do not consult the Lord who is wise (Is. 31:1-2). All wisdom and power belong to God (Dan. 2:20-23). Since the world and all that is in it comes from his hand, it must all display this wisdom. "The LORD by wisdom founded the earth" (Prov. 3:19), and all the natural processes display his excellent wisdom (Is. 28:23-29; Ps. 104:24 and Job 28). Further, God's working in history displays his wisdom, his protection and judgment alike (Is. 31:2; Prov. 10:3). As H. W. Wolff comments: "That true knowledge of the world can be wisdom for man is founded objectively on the world as creation" (Wolff, 211). Indeed all that we know of as the "world" is in a way "a sustaining activity of Jahweh" (von Rad, I, 427).

For the Hebrew all that went on in the world had some direct relationship to God and his purposes (Ps. 145:10-12). Nothing was really left to chance, even the casting of a lot (Prov. 16:33). Since all earthly purpose was expressive of God's personal presence and interest in one's life ("The LORD ... watches all his paths" Prov. 5:21), there was ample motivation to see even in the ordinary events of life a reflection of a deeper significance. The surface features of life (the north wind, dripping water, a whip for a horse) could easily be likened to deeper realities (a backbiting tongue, a rod for fools) because they were two parts of the same truth. "Wisdom thus consisted in knowing that at the bottom of things an order is at work, silently and often in a scarcely noticeable way, making for a balance of events" (von Rad, I, 427).

2. Religion for the Common Man. There was wisdom in the whole of life, in the lofty and in the lowly. Wisdom had to do then with all people in whatever station they found themselves. Moreover, wisdom was nothing more than the real, solid, happy life that all people everywhere seek (which is the reason Israel was not ashamed to use the wisdom of other countries). It spoke to husbands and wives (Prov. 12:4), parents and children (4:1-9), masters and servants (29:19-21), rulers and subjects (28:15-16), rich and poor (19:4-7).

On the one hand, wisdom is plainly based on the natural gifts of men. It is common sense derived from common experience. That pride goes before a fall did not come from reflection on the nature of pride, but from the simple observation of proud people who stumbled. The difference between Greek thinking and Hebrew is clearest just at this point: the Greeks tended to begin with ideas, the Hebrews with experience. Their observation was obviously long and loving. The comments on ants, badgers, locusts and lizards (Prov. 30: 24-28) suggest a curiosity that is foundational for natural science and harks back to God's intention at creation.

On the other hand, if wisdom consists in generous portions of common sense, of both Israel and her neighbors, the key to it all is not to be found anywhere in the world. For the chief part of wisdom, Proverbs says simply, is the fear of the Lord (Prov. 1:7 and Job 28:28). You can watch and learn, but the light on the matter is from the Lord (Prov. 29:13). Close observation will lead you a long way, but the insight that will help you put it together must come from the Lord. The Lord gives wisdom (Prov. 2:6). But when you see the divine meaning of the whole, then all that you learn from experience becomes part of a grand path that leads to him. This may help us understand how the wisdom of neighboring nations can be included in the biblical record. To the Hebrews who knew the Lord and his wisdom, all that others had learned was like so much outside testimony to his greatness, and so could be taken and put into the context of special revelation.

3. The Two Paths: Wisdom and Folly. Wisdom then—or the lack of it—issues in a particular kind of life, a "way" (Heb., *derek*). But this is more than simply a "way of life," because it involves the total character of a person in all activities. Moreover, each act or word is seen as playing a part in shaping this way. Nothing is lost or forgotten. The full moral seriousness of life is drawn in large characters, from the rising up to the lying down. It is this sense of direction that distinguishes the Hebrew view of time from that of her neighbors. Life was a pilgrimage that led to a particular end. This character, which was unique to Israel, in the end transformed those insights that Israel took over from her neighbors.

First of all, there is the way of the *fool*. This way begins innocently enough with the person Proverbs calls the simple. Here is one who is easily led, gullible and often just plain silly. A fool will believe anything (14:15) and is basically irresponsible (1:32). Here Proverbs issues a warning rather than a condemnation. In similar fashion Jesus warns in a parable that a house that is swept clean will soon be infected with seven demons; so an empty mind is in danger of being led astray. The classical expression of the simple person is Proverbs 7 where he is met with falling into temptation. From Proverbs it is clear that life can be fun, even uproarious, but that is not the same thing as its being aimless.

The danger of the simple is that they are on the way to becoming fools. Basically fools are characterized by an aimlessness which has led to a snare, what Proverbs calls folly. To this they return "like a dog . . . to his vomit" (26:11). Since they are entangled in their folly (17:12), they cannot concentrate (17:24), and they will surely waste your time (14:7). In a word they have no moral sensitivity (14:9, which is best translated "every fool mocks at guilt," compare with NIV). Their basic problem is that they lack the beginning of wisdom: the fear of the Lord. A fool then is a practical atheist (Ps. 14:1). Von Rad characterizes foolishness as "a lack of order in a man's innermost being, a lack which defies all instruction" (von Rad 1972, 64).

The most striking aspect of Proverbs lies in its juxtaposing the most innocent matters with the most grave, as though it means to shock the reader into the realization that the slight offense sets one on a path that leads to death. "Bread eaten in secret is pleasant. But he does not know that the dead are there" (Prov. 9:17-18). Sheol is thirsty (30:16) and one had better stay well out of its reach. But the fool is so engrossed in his folly that he has no eyes to see where he is going. He does not choose a wicked life, he slides into it, a step at a time. For something as innocent as the lack of discipline he will die (5:23). While the abundance of laughter in Proverbs shows there is no reason to be overly serious, nor overbearing with those around, life still must be taken seriously. It is leading somewhere as surely as water drips down.

Second, there is the way of the *wise*. While the foolish resemble each other in their folly, the wise display a marvelous diversity; they are the friend, the good neighbor, the valuable wife or the thoughtful husband. They are whatever they are naturally and easily, for the way of the wise seems as light and easy as the fool's is rocky and hard. Their way is characterized by all the fullness of the OT view of life. Life is not its goal—as though it lay somewhere in the future—but its bone and marrow. The way of the wise "flourishes" (11:28); it sparkles with vitality, like an adornment for one's neck (3:22).

It should be clear by now that wisdom is a matter of character rather than intellect. It is the pattern of a life that is "tuned up" and harmonious. A person is considered to be wise only when the whole of life is shaped by the insights of wisdom. From one point of view the wise person is nothing extraordinary; he or she is simply someone you would like to live beside, or with, or meet on the street or the market. There is a caution and a reserve to the wise person (19:2; 13:11) which will lead to prudence (14:16). Then there is a restraint in speech (29:20; 17:27) which by itself produces pleasantness and health (16:24). How important words are in Proverbs! Finally, there is a control over life and its demands (Prov. 24:1-6) which we might call today "power." But what a subtle thing is the strength of one who "rules his spirit" (16:32). One thinks of Joseph in Egypt or Daniel in Babylon, not loud and noisy, but great just the same.

What is good for the farmer and tradesman is good for the

ruler. For wisdom is the foundation of both. Success is the common fruit on the tree of wisdom. If wisdom characterizes the practice of the ruler, his throne will be established forever (29:14, 16). This is because righteousness exalts a nation, not that exaltation is the reward held out by God, but that it flows from righteousness like water from a stream. This promise harks back to Nathan's promise to David in 2 Samuel 7. It reminds us too of the Messiah of whom Isaiah speaks, whose throne is established with justice forever (9:6-7).

We have noted that life is rather the companion than the goal of the wise, but their way just as surely leads them somewhere. The goal is also called life, a life that is defined also as fellowship with God, where wisdom will be perfectly at home (Prov. 8:35; see the excellent discussion in Kidner 1964, 31-56).

The Future of Wisdom

1. The Limitation of Wisdom. The problem with wisdom is that it soon reaches its limits. This is not a frustration, but a reminder of its partial character. Proverbs 25:2 hints at this when it says it is the glory of God to conceal things, but the book of Ecclesiastes speaks of it at length—all is vanity. Even wisdom, though it is better than folly, can in the end lead to vanity (Eccles. 2:12-19). No one part of God's creation, however good in itself, can supply the key to life (Eccles. 3:11). The truly wise understand this sort of limitation, and this recognition issues in humility (Prov. 18:12). They are not bothered by this weakness because their confidence is not in wisdom alone, but in the Lord who is the source of wisdom. "The name of the LORD is a strong tower; the righteous man runs into it and is safe" (18:10). The very evanescence of wisdom serves, then, to keep our mind on the fountain and not only on the water.

2. The Promise of Wisdom. While there is an inherent limitation because man is only man, there is promise also in the exercise of wisdom. This promise is seen most clearly in Proverbs 8, even if the exact reference lies in the future. Here wisdom is personified, probably as a poetic device (one should not read too much hypostasis into it). And yet the metaphor is a strong one that makes the call of wisdom even more urgent. Finally in verse 35 the chapter reaches its climax and identifies the quest with life itself and with favor from the Lord. Here for the first time we have what might be called a personal call to salvation, which, if it is not heeded, will lead to death (von Rad, I, 443). What is this wisdom—with God at creation, speaking truth and justice—which can offer so much? Here surely is an early expression of the important theme that comes to full expression in the life and ministry of Christ. He makes the call of God fully personal and promises to all who come to him rest and refreshment. And in Colossians 1:15-17, we see "that the personifying of wisdom, far from overshooting the literal truth, was a preparation for its full statement" (Kidner 1964, 79).

The man on and in whom the work of the Holy Spirit is done has to put himself seriously at God's disposal in his creatureliness. . . . There is no more intimate friend of sound human understanding than the Holy Spirit. There is no more basic normalizing of man than in the doing of his work.

Karl Barth, *Church Dogmatics*

12
The Spirit
of God

Vocabulary and Basic Meaning
It may seem strange to leave the treatment of the Spirit of
God until this point. But we have already seen that the spiritual conception of God did not come to full expression until
the NT. On the other hand, the operation of the Spirit has
been implicit in much that we have discussed already. And
it is on the operation, the work of the Spirit, that discussion
in this chapter will focus. The person of the Holy Spirit, while
implicit in OT developments, does not come into full view until he is introduced by Christ in John 14—16 and poured out
on his people in Acts 2.

The Hebrew word for spirit *(rûaḥ),* which appeared in our
earlier discussion of man, appears some 378 times in the OT
and ordinarily means "breath" or "wind" (the noun comes
from a verb that means to breathe out through the nose with
violence). Its basic connotation is power, often one that is destructive. The wind is often strong and violent; it is always
mysterious (Ex. 10:13 and Job 21:18). At the same time, it is

always under the control of God (Amos 4:13); as the psalmist says, it is one of God's servants (104:4). In its mystery and power, E. Jacob believes wind/spirit can virtually, if inadequately, express the totality of things divine (Jacob, 122). As breath, the word comes close to meaning life itself, or the life center (Ezek. 37:5-6, 8, 10).

Spirit when used of humans is a psychological expression meaning the dominant impulse or disposition of the person (Snaith, 143-53). The spirit in a person insures a particular type of action (as in Ex. 35:21). A spirit of jealousy or of bitterness dictates appropriate behavior (Num. 5:14, 30). The spirit in a person brings forth understanding (Job 32:8), and it is the spirit that is open to God's influence (Hag. 1:14). Snaith comments that an individual can control his soul *(nepēš)* but it is the spirit *(rûah)* that controls him, suggesting that it is here a person lies open to relationship with God.

When we consider spirit in relation to God, we see a special connection between God and spirit. The closest the OT comes to characterizing God as spirit is Isaiah 31:3: "The Egyptians are men, and not God; and their horses are flesh, and not spirit." But even here the contrast is rather between the strength of God and the weakness of men than between man and spirit. Strength lies in that which is spirit, and spirit, if it is not God himself, is uniquely under his control. He gives it and takes it away (Gen. 2:7 and Eccles. 12:7). In Ezekiel 37:6 the spirit or breath that God gives is almost equivalent to a life substance. In all events God must uphold a person's spirit, or it will fail (Job 10:12) and return to the earth from where it came (Ps. 146:4). In Ezekiel's vision (1:12-14) we have a significant glimpse of the role of spirit. Wherever the spirit goes, these winged creatures go. Here is clearly the directive empowering force that may be identified with the Spirit of God (Snaith, 152). In short, the Spirit of the Lord is the manifestation in human experience of the life-giving energy and creative power of God, played out against the background of overwhelming and controlling power. Spirit is at once somewhat alien to man, and yet something that he cannot live without. Inasmuch as all spirits are related to God (see Num. 16:22), Oehler comments that the Spirit of God becomes the "most powerful vehicle of the OT monotheistic contemplation of the world" (Oehler, 173n).

Theological Development

1. Early Period. In the earlier sections of the OT the Spirit of God is an intermittent power that comes upon a man and enables him to accomplish God's purposes. The earliest appearance is Genesis 1:2. Here the Spirit is hovering over the face of the waters as a mother hovers over her young. This same intimate relation of God to creation is further suggested in Genesis 2:7 where God breathes into man's nostrils the breath (spirit) of life. The spirit here becomes the perfect "symbol of the mysterious nearness and activity of the divine" (Eichrodt, II, 46). Man's continuing dependence upon God's presence is further elaborated in Genesis 6:3: "[God's] spirit shall not abide in man for ever." This limitation of the spirit's presence did not mean that man would die at once, but that he would experience a weakness that would limit his life span.

The relation of the Spirit of the Lord to human abilities was recognized early on. Pharaoh understood that only one endowed with the Spirit of God would exhibit wisdom as Joseph did (Gen. 41:38). Very interesting are the references to Bezalel, in Exodus 31:3 and 35:31, who is said to be filled with the Spirit of God to devise artistic designs for the tabernacle. The Spirit, then, works in man not only mighty deeds of deliverance, but along with these, aids in shaping lovely objects that will speak of God's own beauty and assist in worship.

In the person of Moses the operation of the Spirit comes into clearer focus. Numbers 11:17 and 25 indicate that there was a special measure of the Spirit given to Moses to enable him to accomplish God's purposes. Further, this measure could be shared with others who would participate in his leadership (v. 25). Thus Moses could be called a man of God (Deut. 33:1). Such usage of *the Spirit* suggests that it was thought of as an

almost physical substance that could be handed on (reminding one of *mana,* the personal-impersonal force in primitive
religions). In any case, it was uniquely controlled and given
by God for the accomplishment of his purposes.

A hint of the phenomenon of prophecy is given in the case of
Balaam (Num. 24:2-9). He goes out at the instruction of
Balak, the king of Moab, but instead of cursing Israel he
blesses her. When Balak complains, Balaam says: "What the
LORD speaks, that will I speak" (v. 13). One cannot transgress
the boundaries set by the Spirit.

2. Judges and the Monarchy. During the period of the
judges the coming of the spirit is still an extraordinary event
to empower a person to accomplish God's will. The judges are
introduced by the phrase: "the Spirit of the LORD came upon
him, and he judged" (Judg. 3:10; 6:34 et al.). Here the
leaders of God's people are empowered not only to judge as we
think of judgment, but to lead and deliver the people from oppression. The OT judge decides and delivers as a single activity. The redemptive character of God's enablement becomes
clear. In the case of Samson the Spirit is said to come upon him
mightily (Judg. 14:6 and 15:14).

Among the early prophets the experience is a similar one.
In 1 Samuel 10, Samuel tells Saul as he anoints him to be
prince over his people (v. 1) that "the spirit of the LORD will
come mightily upon you, and you shall prophesy with them
and be turned into another man" (v. 6). The promise is fulfilled in verse 10 when Saul begins to prophesy among the
prophets. When David is anointed, he too becomes the re-
cipient of the Spirit (2 Sam. 23:2).

1 Samuel 16:14-16 tells of the Spirit of the Lord departing
from Saul and the Lord sending an evil spirit upon him (see
1 Sam. 18:10). 1 Kings 22:21-23 goes so far as to say that God
can send a lying spirit with the purpose of deceiving. These
spirits clearly are sent by the Lord, though it is not clear
whether they are good spirits sent for an apparently evil
purpose or evil spirits. In either case they are under the hand
of God and do what he pleases. The same God who delivers the

humble also casts down the haughty (Ps. 18:27).

Interesting, too, is the account of Elijah and Elisha. When it comes time for Elijah to be taken up into heaven, Elisha asks him for a double portion of his spirit (2 Kings 2:9, 15). The spirit in question must surely be the Spirit of the Lord, but it is identified with the prophet and called "the spirit of Elijah" in verse 15. Again, the point where God's Spirit leaves off and man's begins is difficult to determine; man is utterly dependent upon God, and yet at the same time this dependence does not take away from his own individuality.

In the period of the monarchy the institutional aspects begin to predominate over the charismatic, and dependence upon the Spirit becomes less visible. Whether it is a cause or a result we do not know, but miraculous activity is noticeably reduced. Paradoxically, though, it is during this period that we glimpse one of the highest developments in personal dependence on the Spirit—the case of David in Psalm 51. A more permanent possession of the Spirit is implied in his plea to take not the Holy Spirit from him (v. 11). Surely in the light of later developments this is a valuable testimony of God's intention for personal faith. By the same token it is so unusual for its time that many scholars believe it is much later (see Vriezen, 217). But David must still be seen here in his representational role, after the manner of Abraham and Moses. Later testimony (for example, Joel 2:28-29) implies that this kind of personal experience with God was unusual and something that only a few enjoyed. We should be careful however about making generalizations. The Lord's encouragement to Elijah after his contest on Mt. Carmel—"I will leave seven thousand in Israel, all the knees that have not bowed to Baal" (1 Kings 19:18)—implies a personal knowledge that went well beyond Elijah's expectation.

3. The Prophetic Period. In any event it is not until the prophetic period that the work of the Holy Spirit becomes more personal, both in the experience of the prophets themselves and in their vision of the future. Strangely, as E. Jacob points out, the major prophets do not speak often of the Spirit in relation to their own ministry. In fact it is the false prophets that are connected with "the Spirit" (Jer. 5:13 and Hos. 9:7). Perhaps the false prophets were too free in claiming the Spirit, and the true prophets relied on the impact of their words (Jacob 1958, 125-26). It would seem that God's Spirit in the OT is related more to his saving power than to his revelation of himself. The teaching of the prophets about the Spirit supports this. They present his work more in an ethical context, more personal and intimate in his working, and at the same time potentially more universal in his influence.

a. Ethical import of the Spirit. In the prophets the Spirit continued to function as that which united man and God and enlisted human participation in God's redemptive activity. So it was that "God's transcendence became clearer without his immanence thereby being called into question" (Eichrodt, II, 53). This is true in at least two senses.

First, the Spirit progressively comes to be identified with God himself as an expression of his moral majesty, and is not merely seen as a force proceeding from him. As the Spirit comes to be more closely identified with God himself, he is seen more in an ethical context. One who makes a league not of my spirit is adding sin to sin, God says (Is. 30:1). There is a new vision of the holiness of God in the prophets and this vision is connected with the work of the Spirit (Is. 32:15). At the same time, Haggai 2:5 implies that this is not a completely new reality, but a new interpretation of the covenant God made with Israel when they came out of Egypt.

Second, the Spirit is seen more clearly as the power of God's moral excellence at work in the world (Is. 28:5-6). Above all, the Spirit is related to the vision of God's righteous people in the future. He is promised to the messianic king (Is. 11:2) and to the servant of the Lord (Is. 42:1 and 61:1). It is significant that the last reference became the text for Christ's first sermon in Nazareth (Lk. 4:18-21). Grieving God's holiness could be understood as grieving the Holy Spirit, which God had placed among his people (Is. 63:10-11). This is surely an anticipation of the work of the Holy Spirit in convicting of sin that is explained in John 16:8.

b. Personal presence of the Spirit. In the prophets the working of the Spirit becomes more than an intermittent and external influence. The idea emerges of the Spirit as an intimate presence working personally in the individual. The Spirit had worked previously in individuals, and often in an intimate way, but this was still the exceptional experience. Then the aspects of power and strength were to the fore, and the emphasis had been on external influence. Now the Spirit becomes the new foundation of personal life for the people of God. This experience is something real in the prophet's own life (especially in Jeremiah and Isaiah), and yet it is something still in the future in its broader fulfillment. As in the NT, there is with the prophets a present realization and a future hope, an "already" and a "not yet."

God promises one day to pour out his Spirit in a way that was never before known (Ezek. 39:29). There is in this vision an extravagance, a munificence that inevitably brings to mind the Lord's promise of springs of living water given to the woman at the well (Jn. 4:10, 14; and see Is. 44:3). This abundance has to do with extent first of all. It is to be for all people, not just a few (Joel 2:28-29). In Eichrodt's explanation the Spirit will be the "medium through which God's presence in the midst of his people becomes a reality and in which all the divine gifts and powers which work within the people are combined" (Eichrodt, II, 61).

The Spirit is not only for all people, but for the whole person. His work will be manifest in a complete transformation of the personality, what Eichrodt calls the central miracle of the new age. Jeremiah sees this as a new covenant written on the heart (Jer. 31:31-34), though he does not specifically associate this with the work of the Spirit. Jeremiah has no teaching about the Spirit of God, though the work the Spirit will accomplish is in full view. In Ezekiel, however, this same reality is the result of God's putting a new spirit within man (11:19), which is specifically identified with God's Spirit in

Ezekiel 36:26-27. As the psalmist expresses it: "let thy good spirit lead me on a level path!" (Ps. 143:10). From the very variety of expressions the prophets use—a new heart, a new spirit, a new covenant—it becomes clear how thorough and complete will be this transformation that God intends to work by his Spirit. Though the OT believer knew of the presence of the Lord, there was something more intimate and all-pervading to which they looked forward that is uniquely communicated by the Spirit of God. "Tremble . . . ," says Isaiah, "beat upon your breasts . . . until the Spirit is poured upon us from on high, and the wilderness becomes a fruitful field" (Is. 32:11-12, 15).

c. The universal work of the Spirit. This vision of the prophet, which is identified with the Day of the Lord, spills over the narrow banks of the nation of Israel and reaches out to the ends of the earth. And the unique instrument for accomplishing these universal purposes of God is the Spirit. He is the spirit of judgment and the spirit of burning that will cleanse the people of Jerusalem (Is. 4:4). All that God plans to do, the angel reminds Zechariah, will be accomplished "not by might, nor by power, but by my Spirit" (Zech. 4:6). He who understands the role of the Spirit in the divine economy will not despise the day of small things (v. 10).

Finally, as recorded in Nehemiah 9:20, 30, Ezra recognizes that God's instruction from the time of the wilderness through to the prophets was really an activity of the Spirit of God (so also Zech. 7:12). As the law was meant to give instruction for the whole of life and demonstrate God's sovereignty in everything, so here the domain of the Spirit is the whole of life. From here it is only a short step to the NT idea that to walk by the Spirit is to fulfill the law (Gal. 5:16-24). A short step, that is, for those who through faith in Christ are made to drink of this one life-giving Spirit. In Christ the gift of the latter days, the Holy Spirit, has already been poured out (see Acts 2:16-21).

It is the Spirit then that achieves the link between God and humankind. But however close to God human beings come, however deep the communion, there is never in the OT any idea of mystical identification, rather the reverse. The more intimate the relationship, the more natural persons become, the more they become "themselves." One could put it very well in the NT terms by saying the more persons lose themselves to God, the more they will discover who they are. As Martin Luther understood so well, it is only the person who walks by the Spirit that is free, free for a concrete life of obedience.

If we recognize the great and precious things which are given us . . . our hearts will be filled by the Holy Spirit with love which makes us free, joyful almighty workers and conquerors over all tribulations, servants of our neighbors and yet lords of all. *(The Freedom of a Christian)*

The prophet was an individual who said No to his society, condemning its habits and assumptions, its complacency, waywardness, and syncretism. He was often compelled to proclaim the very opposite of what his heart expected. His fundamental objective was to reconcile man and God. Why do the two need reconciliation? Perhaps it is due to man's false sense of sovereignty, to his abuse of freedom, to his aggressive, sprawling pride, resenting God's involvement in history.

Abraham J. Heschel, *The Prophets*

13
Prophecy

The Origin of OT Prophecy

The general phenomenon of prophecy is not unique to the OT. People possessed with a message they believe is from God and who mediate supernatural powers are familiar throughout the world, whether they be the sleeping preachers in Finland or the ecstatic prophets in ancient Greece. In the Bible too there is a historical tradition of prophetism that resembles parallel phenomena in neighboring countries—rural folk who often deviate from normal behavior in society and manifest ecstasy and clairvoyant gifts. But it is clear from the Bible that prophecy in Israel, however much it may resemble its neighbors at this or that point, is a fundamentally different phenomenon. Its controlling features are not these historical or personal factors, but theological factors that stem from Moses as the first and normative prophet. So in our discussion we will consider first those elements essential to the biblical idea of prophecy, and then discuss the historical development of the tradition of prophecy. Again we will find that God used a feature that was common to the Near Eastern world and filled it with a new content and used it to realize his redemptive purposes.

1. Moses as the First Prophet. With the office of the prophet the idea of a man or woman of God speaking the word of God comes to full expression. While it is true that Abraham is called a prophet (Gen. 20:7), the proper inauguration of the office comes with Moses. In his archetypical role as a prophet he bears careful study.

First of all, as recorded in Exodus 3, Moses receives a particular call from God. Whatever characteristics later become identified with prophecy, it is well to remember that the initiative in making a prophet lies with God. This call constitutes the basis of the OT prophetic office (see Young 1952, chapter two).

Moreover, the object of this personal call is to introduce Moses into the presence of God. Exodus 33:11 describes the unique relationship that Moses had with God: "Thus the LORD used to speak to Moses face to face, as a man speaks to his friend." It is only the one who has been introduced into the presence of God that is enabled to speak on God's behalf.

After standing before God Moses is to go and stand in the presence of his people. "The prophet stood before men, as a man who had been made to stand before God" (J. A. Motyer, NBD, 1037; see 1 Kings 17:1). Here the prophet is seen to function as a mediator. This role is well illustrated in Deuteronomy 5:24-28. Here the people say that they have heard God speak, but that Moses must tell them the meaning of it all. Eichrodt goes so far as to claim: "The prophet is the mediator through whom the divine life made its way into a world otherwise sealed against it" (I, 326).

Then, too, the prophet interprets events in which God is active. It is the prophet that makes possible the theological interpretation of history. Events that the prophet explains and looks forward to become vehicles of God's redemption *by their explanation.* To the event the prophet adds the word which is necessary to the full realization of God's purposes. All of this comes to classical expression in Deuteronomy 18: 9-22 to which we now turn.

The first point that emerges from this passage is the moral and ethical uniqueness of prophecy in Israel. Moses insists that Israel must not follow the practices of the nations they will drive out of the land. These have their own prophets—soothsayers, sorcerers, or charmers—to which they give heed (v. 14). Israel would be different, even if their prophets might bear a superficial resemblance to their pagan counterparts. These other prophets sometimes might tell the truth (1 Sam. 6:2-9), but that did not ensure that they speak from God.

The prophets that Israel will know will be unique. First, a prophet like Moses would be raised up by God (v. 15). Now this verse probably has a double reference. Its most immediate reference is to the office of the prophet in general, what E. J. Young calls the prophetic line (1952, 31; see vv. 20-22 which confirm this more general application). Again the normative elements that we noted earlier are present. God will put his words in their mouths (v. 18), and the people will give "heed" (from *šāma'*, meaning to hear with understanding with a view to obeying). Anyone that does not give heed to the words of the prophet will be held responsible by the Lord himself (v. 19).

The second reference to the prophet is eschatological, that is, it refers to the prophet that will arise in the last days. In the NT we learn that some people felt that this prophet would be the Messiah himself (Jn. 4:25 and 6:14). Others felt that he would be a great prophet not identical with the Messiah (Jn. 7:40-41). In either case many people wondered if Jesus was that prophet who was to come. From Jesus' own understanding of his ministry we know that he claimed as the Messiah to be that prophet who was to come (see especially Mt. 17:5). Thus Moses is speaking both of the prophetic line and of the Messiah who would come to fulfill all that God began by raising up the OT prophets. These all looked forward to the prophet to come and their work found its fulfillment in this one the NT presents as the Christ.

Finally, verse 22 makes clear the relationship between the prophetic word and the event. If the word does not come to pass, it is not from God. Here is the basis both of the forth-telling and the foretelling of God. The word that the prophet will speak from God will literally accomplish itself (Is. 55:11). The prophetic message does not simply refer to events, but becomes itself an element in the redemptive process. We will return to this point below.

2. The Prophetic Tradition. Now let us turn to the development of the tradition of prophecy in Israel. These characteristics of Moses were to become normative for all the prophets, but they were exercised against the background of a tradition that began in the wilderness and led straight through to the classical prophets.

The basic commitment of the prophetic tradition was to the covenant of Sinai, and its origins date back to this period in the wilderness. This covenant was apparently reaffirmed in periodic gatherings such as those recorded in Deuteronomy and in Joshua 24. Prominent in these events is the emphasis on "this day" and the need for recommitment on the part of the people to God's covenant promise. This kind of appeal was to become basic to the message of the major prophets. Scholars believe then that these traditions of renewal were preserved by a prophetic party associated with Gilgal and Bethel. These folk leaders were charismatic in nature and thus tended to be hostile to the idea of the monarchy (Judg. 8:23 and 1 Sam. 12:12). The northern kingdom may have been particularly fertile ground for this prophetic tradition (1 Kings 11:29-39 indicates that the prophets played an important role in the dividing of the kingdom). The north was more agricultural in character and this may have stimulated the spread of the Baal fertility cult. It was also more cosmopolitan in nature, so it was susceptible to influence from Phoenicia and Syria. All of this would have called forth a violent reaction on the part of those devoted to traditions of Israel's covenant faith. Such a tradition is perhaps best exemplified by the prophet Hosea who preached in the north around the middle of the eighth century B.C. (on the development of this tradition see Nicholson 1967, 58-76).

The early prophets were called *nebî'îm* (Heb. for prophets) or seers, or more generally men of God (after the very earliest period there seems to have been no distinction between the use of these terms). Sometimes they had gifts of clairvoyance, and occasionally they exhibited a group ecstasy (1 Sam. 10:5-6). But from the beginning their divine call was the key element. The phrase "the word of the LORD came to" is characteristic (2 Sam. 24:11; 1 Chron. 17:3; 1 Kings 12:22). They spoke on behalf of ancient traditions but conveyed "a distinctive expectation of salvation" (Eichrodt, I, 300). Form critical analyses of the message of the early and later prophets have shown the continuity of biblical prophecy. Throughout the OT the prophets' basic message remained the same: recalling Israel to her covenant faith.

These early prophets often went about in groups. They seemed also to have lived together as a band or school of prophets. Some of the early passages (1 Sam. 10:5-13; 2 Kings 2:5 and 4:38) sketch in for us the characteristics of these prophetic bands. First, the ecstasy was at times associated with music (1 Sam. 10:5), suggesting they performed a kind of sacred dance, "a form of expression through which God's power can be worshipped" (Eichrodt, I, 311). Then, as we have seen, they were proclaimers of the word of the Lord (1 Sam. 28:6; 2 Sam. 16:23 and 1 Kings 17:24). Finally, along with their message they were able to perform special miracles. This was especially true of Elijah and Elisha (1 Kings 17—21 and 2 Kings 2:9, 16). In these mighty works they gave a pledge of God's promises and at the same time became a type of the prophet who was to come (Mal. 4:5).

Many of the prophets exhibited behavior that we would today call deviant. They had unusual ways of dressing and eating (compare John the Baptist in the NT) and sometimes were made to perform unusual rituals (lying on their side, going naked and so forth). While this unusual behavior was not essential to their vocation of prophet, it is clear that God used even the eccentricities of the prophet to attract the attention of the people and communicate his message. Ecstasy, or the state of being beyond reason or self-control, was present sporadically in the whole history of the prophets, but this too was not a distinguishing mark of biblical prophecy. Nor were the prophets mystics in the usual sense of the word. A close study of prophecy has led some scholars to distinguish "absorption ecstasy" from a "concentration ecstasy," the latter being characteristic of the biblical prophets. Eissfeldt explains this as a "deep concentration of the soul on a single feeling or notion, [which] has the result of extinguishing normal consciousness and putting the outward senses out of function" (in Rowley, 137). But the consensus of scholarly opinion has discounted the role of ecstasy in prophecy. The prophets did not lose their identity while they received God's word. In fact, as Heschel points out, their individuality is accentuated: "In a sense prophecy consists of a revelation of God and a co-revelation of man" (Heschel, II, 146). Prophets were persons possessed by God's word, but they were not mystics losing consciousness in union with God. It is God's Spirit, and later his word, that enters the prophets to impel them to speak and act. They bear no resemblance to the delirious Greek prophets possessed by the gods.

3. **The Monarchy.** As we have noted, the true prophetic tradition was often critical of the monarchy, for during this time religion lost much of its vitality. Many prophets in fact became court functionaries, and the element of revolt dropped away. Along with the priests in the court, they stressed ritual rather than obedience, and served only to maintain the status quo (2 Chron. 20:14). As Eichrodt points out there is a basic and irradicable difference between those whose religious experience begins and ends with the cult, and those fired by an eschatological vision (Eichrodt, I, 497). The latter vision is at the heart of the OT religion and becomes a vital theme of the classical prophets. But during the monarchy religion was often limited to the cult. No one dared to suggest its application to all of life (Is. 28:7, 9 and Jer. 23:25-27). Rather than be-

ing someone dominated by God and obsessed by his word, the prophet became a religious technician. When this happened, the roles of both the prophet and priest were misplaced. Both were fundamental to OT faith. The prophet calls for obedience; the priest reminds the worshiper of the efficacy of the blood. As Motyer notes, "If we drive them asunder the former becomes a moralist and the latter a ritualist" (Motyer, NBD, 1044). This was the situation during the monarchy.

The Classical Prophets

1. Their Character. It is clear by now that the major prophets are not the originators they have sometimes been made to be. While the prophets after the eighth century B.C. were creative, they were at the same time heirs of an ancient tradition. As we saw in our study of Moses, the definitive experience of the prophets was their call to stand before God and to speak for him. Isaiah's dramatic call in Isaiah 6 is paralleled by that of Jeremiah (Jer. 1) and Ezekiel (Ezek. 1—2). Amos's case is particularly interesting (7:14-15) because he specifically dissociates himself from the prophets. This probably means he did not belong to the band of professional prophets that by this time was associated with the king. God, nevertheless, took him from his flocks and told him to go and speak to Israel. First of all, then, the prophets had a personal experience with God that gave them a fresh and living awareness of God's justice and mercy. This experience was to lead them to a head-on collision with the customs of their day. They did not intend to proclaim a new doctrine of God, or a new ethic, but a new sense of his majesty in the life of the people.

Though vision is common to these prophets, it is the word, both written and spoken, that is to be their primary instrument. The word of God which they introduced into their world radically changed things. Amaziah the court priest understood this very well, for he sent to Jereboam and complained of Amos: "The land is not able to bear all his words" (Amos 7: 10). This word of God Jeremiah calls the hammer which breaks the rock. God sends it forth and it will not return to him empty (Is. 55:11; 40:8 and see Jer. 23:29).

This message which the prophets bring seems to be directed against all of the institutions that Israel believed guaranteed their unique relationship with God, not only the monarchy, but the professional prophets and even the cult. The virile condemnation of the cult raises the particularly difficult question of the relationship of prophecy to the cult. Some scholars make prophecy a part of cultic worship itself. But although it is true that the prophet could at times be found at places of worship (even presiding, as Samuel at Ramah, 1 Sam. 9:12-14; 2 Chron. 20:14), they were essentially independent of it by virtue of their special call from God and thus free to criticize abuses that they saw. What, then, is the meaning of the strong denunciations of cultic worship that we find in the prophets (especially Is. 1:11-15 and Amos 5:21-25)? Were they out to destroy the cult and replace it with a more spiritual and personal religion? Here we must be careful not to read too much of the NT or our own religious biases into the OT. It seems safest to make the following comments.

What the prophets denounced was not the institutions—the temple, the law or the priesthood—but what the people had made of these things. The people had come to believe that these traditions assured them of God's favor, whatever their behavior might be. They imagined that God was bound to them and that these visible traditions were the guarantee of his favor. Thus they felt secure: "No evil will come upon us" (Jer. 5:12). In the awful words of Jeremiah both prophet and priest dealt falsely, "They have healed the wound of my people lightly, saying, 'Peace, peace,' when there is no peace" (6:14). The temple itself had become a kind of fetish (Jer. 7:4). Meanwhile, they continued their sinful ways; in Isaiah's words they were "laden with iniquity" (Is. 1:4).

In such a situation the prophets had to speak out. As J. A. Motyer explains, the prophets meant that "no religious activity avails in the context of a blatantly sinful life" (NBD, 1043). That Isaiah, for example, is not simply condemning the cult can be seen from Isaiah 1:16, where he actually uses an expression for ceremonial purification to symbolize their moral purification: "Wash yourselves; make yourselves clean." The prophet's intent was deeper than a critique of formal religion as such; it went right to the heart of the matter. Religion was to express a personal communion with God. It worked in the sphere of personal understanding, calling for personal decision and the surrender of the whole self. Most of all, it was to issue in a life of moral uprightness. "Take away from me the noise of your songs," says Amos, "But let justice roll down like waters, and righteousness like an ever-flowing stream" (Amos 5:23-24).

2. Their Message and Philosophy of History. The initial message of the prophets was to denounce the sin among the people. Their vision of a holy God had led them to grieve over the sins of the people (Is. 6:5). Having seen God they were unafraid to point to the king and say, "You are the man," as Nathan had done after David sinned with Bathsheba (2 Sam. 12:7). Much later Amos attacked social abuses in the north, while Hosea spoke against syncretism and apostasy. Then in the south Isaiah railed against external religion coupled with injustice (1:11-15), and Micah assailed false religion and inequity (Mic. 3:5-12).

But the sin of the nation was always viewed against the background of God's gracious acts of deliverance in the past. This mercy of God, expressed particularly in the covenant, Israel had spurned. They had broken God's covenant and thus earned his wrath. Amos reminds the people that God brought them out of Egypt, but they only responded by following the false prophets and telling the true prophets to be quiet (Amos 2:9-12). Their unfaithfulness had to be viewed in light of the fact that God had known only them of all the nations of the earth (Amos 3:1-2). In the moving imagery of Hosea God says: "When Israel was a child, I loved him, . . . I led them with cords of compassion" (Hos. 11:1, 4; see also Ezek. 16:1-14). In the case of Isaiah, the prophecy is influenced by the Davidic covenant, and he urges the people to trust God's promises "in quietness and in trust" (30:15). Thus they could expect discipline but not rejection (10:24-27). This hope focused on the figure of the Messiah (9:2-7; 11:1-9), which became the basis for normative messianic ideas in later Judaism.

At times there were important attempts to listen to what the prophets were saying and to mend their ways. Reforms took place under both Hezekiah (2 Kings 18:1-8) and Josiah (2 Kings 22—23). In the case of the former, the preaching of Micah (3:9-12) had found its mark (see Jer. 26:16-19). Though the reform was short-lived, the prodding of the prophets continued to bear its fruit. The people would not soon forget the conditional nature of God's promises. A little more than a half century later, Hilkiah the high priest came upon the book of the law while cleaning out the temple for Josiah (perhaps the cleaning itself was a result of a prophetic message). Zephaniah and the young Jeremiah were just at this time preaching repentance and promising the wrath of God if the people did not repent. By far the most extensive reform of Judah's history followed, and the law of God was again placed in a prominent position. But we know from Jeremiah that even this reform left something to be desired (Jer. 6:16-21 and 5:20-23). While officially standards were high, underneath the sins continued. The people seemed content to pursue their sins "like a horse plunging headlong into battle" (Jer. 8:6). Religion all too easily led to security rather than repentance.

The fortunes of Judah went from bad to worse. In 609 B.C. Josiah died in battle and Judah's precious independence was lost. In 597 many of her leading citizens were carried away into exile. Then in 587 the death blow struck and Jerusalem was destroyed. What had become of God's covenant promises in the light of such disaster? Was this a contradiction of God's promises? Here, at this most serious challenge to Judah's existence, the prophets spoke God's word. Disaster was no denial of God's goodness, but rather an expression of his righteous judgment. Any nation which had fallen into such evil ways called upon itself God's wrath. The fierce anger of the Lord could not be turned back from them (Jer. 4:8; see also

Ezek. 8—11 and Hab.). Here the important theme of God's retribution comes to the fore. As Isaiah had put it earlier: "They shall eat the fruit of their deeds" (Is. 3:10). In Habakkuk's words: "He whose soul is not upright in him shall fail" (Hab. 2:4). That is, the wicked carry within them the seeds of their own destruction.

God's judgment then is a righteous one. But more than that, it is redemptive. As Isaiah had put it, God's hand is turned against his people to refine them (1:25). Even in wrath, God remembers mercy (Hab. 3:2). This restorative character of judgment is explained by B. D. Napier: "The act of judging is one in which wrong is righted whether by punishment of the aggressor or by restitution to the victim or by both" (IDB, III, 913).

This leads to the final element of the prophets' message: God's promises are never to be given up. In the midst of severe judgment, when hope seems to be gone, one can still trust in God's word. Jeremiah can buy property in his native land. Ezekiel can calculate the dimensions of the future temple. Even when "there be no herd in the stalls," says Habakkuk, "yet I will rejoice in the LORD" (Hab. 3:17-18). Here the personal character of prophetic faith shines through. In spite of their awesome portrayal of wars and disaster as the rod of God's anger, there is a definite preference for personal analogies in the prophets. There is the husband-wife relationship in Hosea; father-son in Isaiah 1:2; owner-vineyard in Isaiah 5:7; shepherd-flock in Ezekiel 34:6; potter-clay in Jeremiah 18. Judgment then is never to be considered a blind fate. It is always the expression of a real person in the context of a personal relationship. Because of this there is always hope in God. He will not be angry for ever (Jer. 3:12), for how can he give up his people whom he loves (Hos. 11:8)? Thus the message of the prophets leads surely to a living hope for the future: "For a brief moment I forsook you, but with great compassion I will gather you" (Is. 54:7).

God's promises are secure, but they also extend beyond the borders of Israel. We have commented before on the tendency of God's mercy to work through Israel to her neighbors (even sometimes to her enemies). The story of Ruth underlines this earlier in the OT, and later the prophet Jonah furnishes a classic example. Here is a man of God who flees from God's call (Jon. 1:1-3) before he finally consents to prophesy to the pagan city Ninevah (3:3—one thinks of Peter's scruples in Acts 10:14-15). The people of Ninevah repent, and much to Jonah's chagrin God spares the city. Here the great pity of God (4:11) is in full view and his desire that all should come to repentance is clear. In some way yet unclear, the prophets knew that all nations must one day glorify God (Is. 2:2-3).

Before we turn to this vision of the future in the next chapter, two things call for comment: the prophets' philosophy of history and then the question of foretelling versus forthtelling. First, do the prophets present a philosophy of history? The fundamental conflict in the prophets is a moral battle between God and the forces of evil, but the arena in which this struggle is carried on is human history. It is here that God intervenes to show his mercy in delivering Israel from Egypt, and it is the same history that sees Israel and Judah sent away into exile. As H. W. Robinson points out, "History itself creates the values by which it is to be judged, by which it judges itself" (Robinson 1946, 133). The moral struggle between evil and righteousness is not carried on with a sort of cosmic inevitability (as in the Hindu doctrine of karma), but the course of peoples and nations lies under the control of a sovereign and loving God. Beyond this the events of history were moving toward—one could say were calling for—a final decision in which all of creation would be involved and which would be eternally decisive.

"Thus every element acquires its own eternal importance, and at every moment human conduct is subjected to the binding obligation of decision" (Eichrodt, I, 383). Time and moral decisions are taken with absolute seriousness. One is called to decide for God and hear his voice at every point in time. Nevertheless, the determining factor, as far as the prophets are concerned, is not man's decision alone, but God's redemptive intervention. "Behold, I am laying in Zion for a foundation a stone ..." (Is. 28:16), which will reveal God's purposes for the whole earth (Is. 14:26). At this denouement, history as we know it will be broken off, and a new age will be established by God. It is this final settlement between God and man that we will examine in the next chapter.

Finally, we turn to the question of foretelling versus forthtelling. Was the primary ministry of the prophets to speak about the future or to address their own contemporaries with the word of God? There has been much emphasis recently on the latter element, and it is a wholesome corrective to remember, after all, that the prophets did have their own contemporaries in mind when they spoke. They were not speaking for later generations. At the same time, when one reads the prophets again, one is impressed with how much of their message does have to do with the future. It is important, however, to understand carefully the theological significance of these predictions.

In the first place, one must bear in mind that the prophets, in speaking God's word, spoke an effective word; that is, what they said accomplished—as well as spoke about—God's purposes. In a very real sense, therefore, the prophets were themselves a part of God's sovereign and redemptive working. This is seen most clearly in their symbolic acts—Jeremiah's buying land, Hosea's marriage, and so forth—which actually present the truth of their message. As H. W. Robinson explains: "[Symbolic acts] serve to initiate the divine activity amid human affairs by performing in miniature that which Jahweh is performing on a larger scale, from the first utterance of his judgment to the final overthrow of the city" (Robinson 1946, 185).

Then, too, one must remember that though the prophets' primary address was to their own day, as we have said, that day was never seen in isolation from the past and the future. Rather, it was itself a working out of God's promises in the past, and it found its meaning in terms of what was yet to come. Thus if the people were to exercise a proper moral responsibility in the present, they had to have an understanding of the future (see Is. 30:15-18). As people of the Lord of history, who is just in all his ways, they had to see their present in the light of his future.

Finally, the close personal relationship between the Lord and the prophets made it very reasonable that these collaborators would learn something of God's program for the future. Amos goes so far as to say that God does nothing without revealing it to the prophets (Amos 3:2). After all, it is God who reveals secrets and gives wisdom (Dan. 2:21-22). Why would he not tell his servants the prophets something of his wise plan? To the content of this revelation we turn next.

*It appears that all that is ever spoken of in the Scripture
as an ultimate end of God's works is included in that one
phrase,* the glory of God. *In the creatures' knowing,
esteeming, loving, rejoicing in and praising God, the glory
of God is both exhibited and acknowledged; his fullness
is received and returned. Here is both the* emanation *and*
remanation. *The refulgence shines upon and into the creature,
and is reflected back to the luminary. The beams of glory
come from God, and are something of God and are refunded
back again to their original. So that the whole is of God,
and in God, and to God, and God is the beginning, middle
and end in this affair.*

Jonathan Edwards, *Dissertation Concerning the End
for which God Created the World*

14

The Hope
of Israel

The Vision of the Kingdom

One does not have to look to the prophets to find the shape of Israel's vision of the final kingdom. From the very beginning of their experience with God they had learned to trust him to bring them to the land promised to Abraham (Gen. 12:1-3). Thus for Israel hope always had a very concrete, visible aspect: God would one day give them the Promised Land. But the means that God would use to lead his people to this place of rest sometimes were seen to involve destruction and judgment, sometimes construction and growth. Let us examine these two streams of thought that during the time of the prophets broke their narrow banks and flowed together to form the single vision of the universal kingdom of salvation.

First, there was the irruptive, warlike stream that identified hope with God's intervention. Early on, Israel understood that God must fight for them and triumph over their enemies. Already in Genesis 3:15 there is reference to a struggle and a

victory. Then in the Song of Moses (Ex. 15) Israel celebrated
God's strength and intervention on their behalf in bringing
them out of Egypt:

Thy right hand, O LORD, shatters the enemy. . . .
Thou didst stretch out thy right hand,
    the earth swallowed them.
Thou hast led in thy steadfast love the people whom
    thou hast redeemed,
        thou hast guided them by thy strength to thy holy abode.
(Ex. 15:6, 12-13)

From this source developed the idea that God was a mighty
warrior who would fight for his people, a line of thinking
seen clearly in the book of Judges (see especially the Song of
Deborah in Judg. 5).

The prophets often emphasized the cataclysmic nature of
God's intervention when they spoke of the Day of the Lord
(for example, see Amos 5). Here the emphasis is on the kingdom of God as a new creation springing directly from God's
creative act. As Isaiah 43:19 puts it: "Behold, I am doing a new
thing; now it springs forth, do you not perceive it?"

But even in this promise of Isaiah the second stream of
thinking is present as well. That is, the future that God brings
about will also be a perfection, a springing forth of what already exists. This line of thought implied that the kingdom
might come about by peaceful means, that it was already
present in the covenant that God made with his people and in
the covenantal institutions. One day these forms would grow
to perfectly reflect God's ideal. We see this already in the
blessing of Jacob in Genesis 49:9-10. He says of Judah: "The
scepter shall not depart from Judah, nor the ruler's staff from
between his feet, until he comes to whom it belongs" (v. 10).
The monarchy itself came to rest on such hopes, as is evident
in Nathan's repetition of this promise to David in 2 Samuel
7. From such soil sprang messianic expectations. Here then
was the hope that already within the institutions of Israel and
Judah—in the monarchy and the priesthood—were the seeds
that would one day flower in the divine kingdom.

It is worth noting that both versions of expectation continued right up to the time of Christ. On the one hand, the loss of the prophetic voice after the exile led to the expectation, called by the name *apocalyptic,* that God would intervene mightily and destroy this evil order, while he brought salvation for those afflicted. This point of view is especially evident in the apocryphal books of 1 Enoch (which is quoted in Jude 14) and 2 Esdras and is certainly influential in Paul's eschatology. On the other hand, there were those who felt that by strict observance of the law they would prepare the way for the Messiah and the introduction of his kingdom. This point of view was represented by the people of Qumran and to some extent by the Pharisees of the NT times.

There were elements of truth in both perspectives, but, strangely enough, the classical prophets attacked both forms of hope. This was because both had become a way for Israel and Judah to feel safe even when they were being disobedient to God. No matter what they did they could trust that God would intervene for them. After all did they not have the temple, the law and the king whom God had put on the throne? The prophets had to tell them that their hopes had become false hopes.

As for the Day of the Lord, Amos warned it would be a day of judgment and not of peace, of darkness and not of light (Amos 5:20; see also Is. 7:17). They had said, the Day is coming and God will save us. Ezekiel responds: "Behold, the day! Behold, it comes! Your doom has come, injustice has blossomed, pride has budded" (Ezek. 7:10).

At the same time, the prophets insisted that they could not trust in their institutions to save them. Looking too much to these visible expressions of God's goodness, the people came to think they could bring about the kingdom by their own strength. These things—the temple, the law, the monarchy—were means to the end of fellowship with God, but when they were seen as ends in themselves they were misunderstood. They had become mere fetishes that the people clung to superstitiously. Jeremiah warned: "Do not trust in these deceptive words: 'This is the temple of the LORD, the temple of the LORD, the temple of the LORD' " (Jer. 7:4). A new understanding of God's future was needed. This is what God gave through the prophets.

1. The Prophetic Picture of God's Kingdom.

a. Based absolutely on God's decision. The first character-istic of the prophetic picture of the future is that it will come about because God wills it. Thus one must look to him alone for a proper understanding of the future. This is to say, on the one hand, that the kingdom will come about for the sake of God. God says through Ezekiel: "It is not for your sake, O house of Israel, that I am about to act, but for the sake of my holy name, which you have profaned among the nations." (Ezek. 36:22). Thus the kingdom is to vindicate, to express and to demonstrate—as the next verse says—the holiness of God. God's people had forgotten the majesty of God who would not share his glory with another (Is. 48:11). On the other hand, the kingdom will come about by God's strength alone. His word will not return to him empty. It is a word which accom-plishes what he purposes (Is. 55:11). For the mouth of the Lord has spoken it (Mic. 4:4).

This does not mean that God's promises have nothing to do with human decision or with this world. In this connection it is important to remember Jonah. For when the people re-pented, God did not bring the judgment that he promised. As the Lord says by Jeremiah after warning against the misuse of the temple: "If you truly amend your ways and your doings . . . then I will let you dwell in this place" (Jer. 7:5, 7). Here too the sovereignty of God has to do with the place that God is preparing for his people.

b. A new creation. What God intends for his people is a *new creation*. Here each word is significant. The kingdom had to be something *new* because the point had been reached wherein the old order could not simply survive. Things had reached such a state that there had to be destruction. "Eschatological hope of salvation does nothing to limit the seriousness of the judgment; on the contrary it is what gives it its full seriousness" (Eichrodt, I, 379n2). Here those looking for God's intervention were correct. There can be no future hope without a break with the past. There can be no salvation without miracle.

But it will be a new *creation*. Because God is creator his judgment is also creative; it vindicates his righteousness and makes possible a new order. (This is very beautifully described in the Magnificat of Mary in Luke 1:46-55.) Moreover, this was a new creation in the sense that the kingdom was to be realized in a visible and a concrete way. It is important that we understand this earthly character of God's promises if we are to fully appreciate the new order that Christ came to establish. Nothing is spiritualized: "For eye to eye they see the return of the LORD to Zion" (Is. 52:8). It is true that many images are employed to picture this new order. It is called the mountain of the Lord (Is. 2:2-4 and Mic. 4:1-3), Zion (Is. 51: 11), and Mount Zion (Obad. 17). In all events what is clear is the earthly and bodily content of the prophetic hope. What is in view is not an unmaking but a remaking of the earth. The creation will answer God's creative word with grain, wine and oil (Hos. 2:21-22). God's people will be planted on their land and never plucked up (Amos 9:14-15). This imagery reaches its glorious climax in Isaiah 9 and 11. Martin Buber puts this quality of the OT hope in these words:

> So it is not only with his thought and his feelings, but with the sole of his foot and the tip of his finger as well, that he may receive the sign-language of the reality taking place. The redemption must take place in the whole corporeal life. God the creator wills to consummate nothing less than the whole of his creation.

(The Writings of Martin Buber, 1956, 265)

c. *A mediator.* In the prophetic picture of the future God is seen to make use of a mediator through which and in which the reality of the new order will be realized. Again several images are used. There is in the first instance the *remnant.* Beginning early in the OT there is the idea of a righteous remnant for whose sake God will withhold his judgment.

Noah and his family were preserved by God in the flood. Abraham's pleading on behalf of his nephew Lot—"Suppose there are fifty righteous . . . suppose ten are found there"—leads to the saving of Lot and his family (Gen. 18:22-33). Elijah had been comforted with the assurance that there were still seven thousand who had not bowed the knee to Baal (1 Kings 19:18). But it had become all too easy to identify with this righteous remnant. And so God found it necessary to tell the people that they could not be assured of their survival. In Amos the remnant itself became a sign of the destruction that God would bring about. Those dwelling in luxury in Samaria would be "rescued, with the corner of a couch and part of a bed" (Amos 3:12; see also 5:3). In fact not one would escape (9:1). Here again the creative act of God is necessary to preserve, or better, to re-create, the remnant that would survive. In Zephaniah God pleads for those who are humble to seek righteousness and "perhaps you may be hidden on the day of the wrath of the LORD" (2:3). Zephaniah goes on to declare: "For I will leave in the midst of you a people humble and lowly. They shall seek refuge in the name of the LORD. . . . For they shall pasture and lie down, and none shall make them afraid" (Zeph. 3:12-13). It is God who will preserve this remnant, he will carry and save them (Is. 46:3-4).

Then there is the mediation provided by the *servant of the Lord*. This servant is pictured in the so-called servant songs (Is. 42:1-4; 49:1-6; 50:4-9; 52:13—53:12). Here the prophet looks forward to the coming of one who would embody perfectly the ideal of God's people. This title was also used of some of God's servants from Israel's history—Moses, David, Job—but in Isaiah 41:8 it is explicitly used of Israel as a nation. All of these designations are taken up in the servant songs, which, in G. A. Smith's words, seem to progress in their descriptions from a personification to a person. Jewish interpreters were not agreed as to whether the servant was a historical figure, the prophet himself or the nation as a whole. In any case there was the perception that some figure(s) would be able to bring about the righteousness that Israel longed for, to bring them near to God. Clearly, as C. R. North points out, the picture that results embodies "exactly those qualities which accorded with messiahship as Jesus understood it" (IDB, IV, 293).

Finally, there is the figure of the *Messiah* who takes a central place in later Jewish expectations. While the word *messiah* (which means "anointed one") is found only in Daniel 9:25 and 26, the idea of a special anointed representative of God was an important theme in the OT. It is implicit in the idea that it was God who chose and would preserve Israel's king: "Great triumphs he gives to his king, and shows steadfast love to his anointed, to David, and his descendants for ever" (2 Sam. 22:51). In a different context the idea is seen in God's choice of Cyrus to accomplish his redemptive purposes (he is called God's anointed in Is. 45:1). Then, too, the idea of the Messiah was naturally related to significant figures in Israel's history whom God used to accomplish his purposes. The messianic future gathers up several OT themes. It recalls the perfection of the garden of Eden and Adam's perfect fellowship with God (Amos 9:13 and Ps. 72: 16); it speaks of a deliverance like that of Moses from Egypt (Hos. 2:14-23); and it proclaims a better kingship than that of David. In fact the imagery of the shoot from the stump of Jesse (Is. 11:1, 10), that is, the remnant of the house of David, is the most familiar image of the Messiah. The Messiah is a son of David (Ps. 2:7), seated at the Lord's right hand (Ps. 110:1) and is himself divine (Ps. 45:6). God's delivering purposes designated by a unique birth are set forth in an intriguing prophecy: "Therefore the Lord himself will give you a sign. Behold, a young woman shall conceive and bear a son, and shall call his name Immanu-el" (Is. 7:14). In its immediate context this verse speaks of God's purpose to destroy Israel by a force from the north, but at the same time the prophet "holds up before the troubled gaze of the doomed community the hope of Immanuel's distant but certain birth" (J. A. Motyer, NBD, 815). God himself will be with Israel to deliver her; no alien purpose will triumph.

There is a larger sense in which the hope identified with
the Messiah is the fulfillment of the original endowment
given to man by virtue of his creation in the image of God
(Gen. 1:26), and that is further elaborated in Psalm 8. Mention should also be made of the son of man (Dan. 7), who
received universal dominion, a dominion that his people will
share. Here the pattern recurs that is familiar in OT references to Messiah. He is human and yet possesses divine qualities; he will accomplish universal rule in spite of opposition.
In short, he possesses all the characteristics of the Messiah
Jesus of Nazareth.

d. *The goal of God's redemptive work.* Now we are in a position to glimpse the final goal of God's redemptive working.
By his action, through the mediation of his servant, God will
realize the salvation of his covenant people. His people will
dwell securely in the land God will give them and exhibit the
righteousness of their Lord. All of this is summed up in the
oft-repeated phrase: "I will be their God, and they shall be my
people." Jeremiah explains this to mean everyone will know
the Lord from the least to the greatest (Jer. 31:31-34). Hosea
speaks of God's people being married to the Lord, betrothed
in righteousness (Hos. 2:19). This involves a change so radical
that it can only be described as a resurrection of dry bones
(Ezek. 37:4-10), the giving of a new heart (Ezek. 36:26), which
is explained as the placing of God's own spirit within them.

On God's side, his sovereignty will be absolutely established. He will be king over all the earth. The Lord alone will
be exalted in that Day (Is. 2:11). In that Day the Lord will be
one and his name will be one (Zech. 14:5-9). God will personally reign on the earth (Is. 11:9).

Here is a grand vision of God's future victory, his vindication and his reign. The images are so manifold and lively that
they defy systematization; they break out of all the narrow
categories in which they are placed. All was not clear; but
what was clear was exciting indeed. In the midst of the destruction and misery that lay around them there was hope in
the air. Jeremiah could write in the midst of his lament over

a destroyed Jerusalem: "But this I call to mind, and therefore I have hope: The steadfast love of the LORD never ceases, his mercies never come to an end; they are new every morning; great is thy faithfulness" (Lam. 3:21-23).

Such faith, unfortunately, was not destined to survive. As we have noticed before, very shortly such hope was domesticated. The voice of prophecy was no longer heard in the land. Eichrodt observes:

> *Thus at the close of its career the form of the OT hope cries out for a critique and a reconstruction* which will be able to reach out and grasp the unchanging truth hidden under its bewildering diversity, and set this in the very center where it can dominate all else, while at the same time unifying its struggling contradictions, its resting in a timeless present and its tense waiting for a consummation at the end of history. Both these needs are fully met in the NT confession of Jesus as the Messiah. (Eichrodt, I, 490, emphasis his)

2. The Idea of Judgment. Central to the vision of God's future intervention on behalf of his people is the idea of judgment. We have seen already that the OT word "to judge" (*šāpaṭ*) has a much wider usage than merely "passing judgment." To fully appreciate the scope of OT judgment we should think of the totality of God's government in which he executes judgment, rather than of moral decision alone. The core idea is related to "retribution" and "vindication" that we discussed in the wisdom literature. God's judgment is a making right in such a way that the aggressor is punished and the victim is compensated. Judgment, then, is a part of God's redeeming activity. It is God's activity of restoring the fallen created order by punishment on the one hand, and deliverance on the other.

In the first place, judgment is the prerogative of God alone by virtue of his character. In one sense all God's activities pertain to his judgment because they all express his righteous government. Since judgment is God's (Deut. 1:17), those who wait for his judgment are blessed (Is. 30:18). All his judgments are true and righteous (Ps. 19:9). His right to rule, therefore, grows out of his character as judge. As Leon Morris points out, it is easier to see how *rule* arises from *judge* than the reverse (Morris 1960, 10-11).

Judgment, in the second place, is a dynamic work of God involving discrimination and action together. In human judgment, passing judgment and executing judgment are separate functions; the one must consider the evidence and make a decision, while the other enforces the will of the judge. Since God's wisdom and power are perfect, he neither has to weigh the evidence nor struggle with means to execute his judgments. God knows our hearts immediately and works righteousness without delay. He delivers the weak and fatherless (Deut. 10:18 and Ps. 82:3-4), and he punishes the wicked (Ezek. 7:3 and 25:11). Since individuals in the covenant are to reflect God's character, this quality of action is uniquely appropriate to Israel's covenant relationship (see Zech. 8:16 and Mic. 6:8). From the human point of view, then, the "doing of justice," which characterizes God's judgments, becomes essentially a religious obligation. To know God is to do justice.

All of this, however, speaks of the final settlement. All too often in Israel's experience the wicked prospered and the judges could be bought off. But there was a day coming when both God and his people would be vindicated. The majority of the uses of the word "to judge" in the OT are in the future, uncompleted tense. God is the one who will come to judge. The Day of the Lord, or the final judgment, for which Israel waited was above all a decisive judging. A deep disharmony pervaded the created order that caused the OT believer to cry out to God (Ps. 88). The hills and the mountains, the beasts of the fields, men in their sin—all called out for deliverance:

Say among the nations, "The LORD reigns!
Yea, the world is established, it shall never be moved;
He will judge the peoples with equity...."
Then shall all the trees of the wood sing for joy
before the LORD, for he comes,
for he comes to judge the earth.

He will judge the world with righteousness,
and the peoples with his truth. (Ps. 96:10, 12-13)
The mystery that surrounded judgment in the OT, which
comes out so clearly in Amos, was how such a bright reality
could come about through the purifying fire of God's judgment. How could darkness bring light? For this to be clear we
have need of the great NT change of tense, in which the
coming judge has come and executed judgment. In God's judgment on his Son, humanity—indeed the whole created order
—finds deliverance (Jn. 12:31-32).

Death and the Afterlife
Our comments on the prophetic hope have demonstrated that
OT hope was a collective hope. The same is true when we turn
our attention to the view of the afterlife: immortality is first
of the group and then of the individual. It is only as a person
finds himself in the people of God that he or she can be assured
of eternal life.

1. Death and Sheol. All the peoples of the world understand
that death is a natural end to life on earth. As the Gilgamesh
Epic puts it:
When the gods created man
They passed out death to him.
Life they kept in their hands.
In the OT, however, death is related to sin and thus reflects
something unnatural about the world as it stands, something
over which God alone can triumph.

From one point of view, the Hebrews too understood how
natural it was to die. Bodies made like ours must one day die
"as a shock of grain comes up to the threshing floor in its
season" (Job 5:26). At times death is spoken of as simply the
end (2 Sam. 14:14). Death is like water spilt on the ground; it
cannot be gathered again. We must return to the ground, for
we were taken out of it (Gen. 3:19). Here the Hebrews shared
a large body of ideas about death that were common in the
Semitic world. By simple observation one sees that death can
be either the absence of vigor (sometimes simply the absence

of breath— Ps. 104:29), or the reduction of physical vitality
that makes us think of sleep. "Lighten my eyes," the psalmist
prays, "lest I sleep the sleep of death" (Ps. 13:3). In spite of its
naturalness, death is a dark shadowy thing that people shun
(Ps. 55:4). The melancholy vanity of Ecclesiastes lies in the
fact that all human activities end in the grave; only the living
have hope (Eccles. 9:4). Nowhere in the OT is death simply
the door to paradise (Jacob, 299). Its character as enemy
is everywhere evident.

Death was both a symbol of the destruction sin brought into
the world and a part of the destruction itself. In this sense
death was not a normal part of the world, but something alien
to God's good purposes. In fact in Genesis 2:17 man is promised that in the day that he eats of the fruit he will surely die,
and Genesis 6:3 confirms that man's unrighteousness is related to his end. Just before their entrance into Canaan,
Moses urged the people to choose life or death, by deciding to
obey the commandments of the Lord, or by turning to serve
other gods (Deut. 30:15-19). The OT does not as a rule make a
distinction between physical death and spiritual death; man
as a whole is subject to death. But underneath the physical
aspect there is the deeper reality of spiritual death—a con-
firmation of the separation from God and from the joy of his
presence that was begun in the choices of life. So Moses could
say: "I call heaven and earth to witness against you this day,
that I have set before you life and death, blessing and curse;
therefore choose life, that you and your descendants may live"
(Deut. 30:19). While this refers to earthly life, it clearly has
implications beyond that.

The Hebrews knew they had such a choice to make because
they understood that life and death were under God's control.
While man could choose life, it was God who must give it. God
is the one who kills and who makes alive (Deut. 32:39). It is
he who brings down to Sheol and raises up (1 Sam. 2:6). But
there is nothing in the OT conception that leads to fatalism. It
is God who decides, but man must also choose. Moreover, the
God who decides is a personal God responsive to the prayers

of those who call on him. As he says through the prophet Ezekiel: "For I have no pleasure in the death of any one, says the Lord GOD; so turn, and live" (18:32).

The place of the dead in the OT, Sheol, was often pictured in visible terms as a shadowy, nondynamic existence. Here as well the Hebrews shared many ideas with their Near Eastern neighbors. Sheol is not identified with any location, but is rather thought of as a kind of existence, which, in the case of the Hebrews, is basically opposed to God. Sheol is the place of bare survival. One is sleeping with his fathers (Gen. 37:35 and 1 Kings 2:10). It is a place where praise is impossible (Is. 38:18 and Ps. 6:5). It is beyond the reach of earth and its institutions, but it is not beyond the reach of God (Ps. 139: 7-12; Amos 9:2). While it is a place of hopelessness from a human point of view, God can ransom from the power of Sheol the one who trusts in him (Ps. 49:15).

But what is the meaning of the hope that God would not allow his people to go down into the pit? There is no conviction that though the body dies, the soul may survive. E. Jacob goes so far as to say "no Biblical text authorizes the statement that the 'soul' is separated from the body at the moment of death" (IDB, I, 803). No, as Eichrodt notes, the Israelite hope was too full-bodied for any kind of fulfillment in the realm of the spirit alone. It wanted nothing less than the renewal of bodily and earthly life as they knew it (Eichrodt, I, 491).

2. The Resurrection of the Body and the Hope of Eternal Life. Ideas of eternal life in the OT have been difficult to assess. Traditionally scholars have believed that while the Hebrews had some vague sense of immortality, they had no clear idea of resurrection. Recently Mitchell Dahood has made use of Ugaritic parallels in his study of the Psalms to show a much more confident expectation of resurrection and immortality. In Psalm 16:10-11 he believes an Enoch or Elijah-like assumption is in view (see also Ps. 73:24 and 49:16), and he translates Psalm 17:15b "at the resurrection" (RSV, "When I awake"), which he takes to be "the plain sense ... when one compares it with the eschatological passages

Isa xxvi 19 ... and Dan xii 2" (Dahood, I, 99; see also pp. xxxvi, 91 and E. B. Smick in Payne 1970, 104-10). This clearly leads in a fresh direction that promises a deeper understanding of the OT material. It is certainly characteristic of OT faith that its delight in God and in his provision is so robust that it simply will not hear of any temporal limitation. Communion with God is so real that it transcends earthly experience. Primarily we see this in three separate themes that gather strength through the pages of the OT and lead, almost inevitably, to the NT doctrine of the resurrection. Though for that to be clear, we need the concrete example of our precursor in death and resurrection, the Lord Jesus.

a. Theological foundation. While the theological foundation for eternal life could profitably be developed at length, it is enough to point out that the OT view of God itself decreed the survival of those who trusted in him. This belief was rooted in the conviction that God is the unique source of life: he gives it and he takes it away (Gen. 2:7 and Ps. 36:9). Life belongs to God essentially, and it springs from him. "With thee is the fountain of life," says the psalmist (36:9). So when one encounters God and begins to share his life, one acquires an indestructible element. This is pictured in many ways in Psalms and Proverbs. God is a strong tower in which the righteous are safe (Prov. 18:10); he is a rock that protects and cannot be moved (Ps. 62, note in v. 2 that *rock* and *salvation* are placed in parallel construction); and he is a fortress (Ps. 46:1, 4). So while there is never any illusion about human weakness and proneness to death, there is the firm confidence that God will protect all those who trust in him. "My flesh and my heart may fail, but God is the strength of my heart and my portion for ever" (Ps. 73:26). Notice—*for ever*. That is, his strength is such that its protection knows no limit. It simply must be that the one who fears God will not see Sheol (Ps. 16:10-11). Nowhere is this more beautifully presented than in the simple words of Psalm 23: "The LORD is my shepherd." Though I will go through valleys reminiscent of death, the psalmist confesses, I have experienced the overwhelming provision of God to such an extent—my table is lavishly spread, my cup is spilling over—that I believe goodness and mercy will pursue me, I cannot escape them (Dahood, I, 148-49). The simple corollary is that I will surely dwell in God's presence forever (see a NT parallel in Jn. 14:1-3).

b. Ethical foundation. The source of the ethical foundation for eternal life is the OT idea of retribution that we have discussed earlier, especially evident in the wisdom literature. There is a certain kind of fruit that follows from a life of righteousness or of evil. The fool walks on a way that leads to death, the righteous on one that leads to life (Prov. 11:30). God's judgment which is always righteous will surely bring about a righteous end. He will requite the righteous and punish the wicked. The fact that life is called the fruit of a righteous life indicates how deeply ingrained is the idea of justice. It was something like a law of nature. This comes to expression in the NT in Paul's words: "Whatever a man sows, that he will also reap" (Gal. 6:7). Thus God could be counted on to vindicate the righteous with life. Truth must stand because of the order of things. It is the sense of retribution that lies behind Job's plea, so prophetic in its character. "Oh that my words were written!" he cries, "For I know that my Redeemer lives, and at last he will stand upon the earth" (Job 19:23, 25). The word *redeemer* here could also be translated "vindicator." For Job knew that even after his flesh was destroyed (v. 26), God's vindication would preserve him. It is as though, by the Spirit's inspiration, he is reaching beyond what he knew to a truth that his experience with God made necessary, the truth that God's protection of his flesh after death would be a vindication of God's own righteous order. Here the faith of the OT reaches to the very threshold of God's further revelation in Christ.

c. Historical/eschatological foundation. We have emphasized earlier in our study the "this-worldly" quality of Israel's faith. They did not have to speculate as to how God treated his people; they had ample occasion to witness it with their own eyes. They had seen that God had taken Abraham and brought his seed into the Promised Land. They had seen God deliver them from oppression: "You have seen what I did to the Egyptians, and how I bore you on eagles' wings and brought you to myself" (Ex. 19:4).

All of this gave them confidence that God would yet deliver them in the future. The experience they had of God's concrete care and provision led them naturally to believe that God would preserve them. God's word through the prophets confirmed this faith and assured them, despite any evidence to the contrary, that God would bring about a final and definitive victory for his people. Moreover, they had before them the examples of Enoch and Elijah, men who had walked with God and enjoyed his special protection. All of this led the Hebrews, when they came to reflect on the future, to believe that God's final victory would certainly include within it the final victory over death. They had no clear idea of how God would do this, but *that* he would do it they had no doubt. The final settlement, Isaiah notes, will include the swallowing up of death (Is. 25:8). Associated with the coming of Michael and the time of troubles, Daniel tells us, "Many of those who sleep in the dust of the earth shall awake" (Dan. 12:2).

There is no question of denying the reality or the terror of death; it is rather a matter of getting things in perspective. When one fully understands the character of God, when one sees the way the moral order of the world operates, when one has seen God deliver his people, then death after all is seen to be the small and weak thing which it is in the eyes of God. When the victory finally comes, there is no question but that death itself will fall. Here too, though, the OT seems to stand on tiptoes; it reaches for a complement and embodiment of all that it knows with the highest certainty to be true. That embodiment is the new creation that Christ came to reveal. The truth they only knew in part, Christ has come to make even clearer to us: that by his death and resurrection we may be his people, and he our God, forever.

Basic Bibliography for OT Theology

Documentation in the text which lists an author without a title refers to a work listed here. The system used is explained in the introduction (p. 21).

Albright, W. F.
1957   *From Stone Age to Christianity*. New York: Doubleday.

Baker, D. L.
1977   *Two Testaments: One Bible*. Downers Grove, Ill.: InterVarsity Press.

Barr, James
1961   *The Semantics of Biblical Language*. Oxford: Oxford Univ. Press.

Bright, John
1960   *A History of Israel*. Rev. ed., 1972 Philadelphia: Westminster.

Brown, Colin, ed.
1976   *History, Criticism and Faith*. Downers Grove, Ill.: InterVarsity Press.

Bush, F. W.
1976   " 'I Am Who I Am': Moses and the Name of God." *Theology News and Notes* (Fuller Seminary). December 1976, 10-14.

Childs, Brevard S.
1960   *Myth and Reality in the Old Testament*. London: SCM.
1974   *Exodus*. Philadelphia: Westminster.

Craigie, P. C.
1976   *The Book of Deuteronomy*. Grand Rapids: Eerdmans.

Dahood, Mitchell
1966, 68, 70   *Psalms I, II, III*. The Anchor Bible. Garden City, N.Y.: Doubleday.

Davidson, A. B.
1904   *The Theology of the Old Testament*. Edinburgh: T. & T. Clark.

Eichrodt, Walter
 1961, 67   *Theology of the Old Testament.* 2 vols. Phila-
                         delphia: Westminster.

Ellison, H. L.
 1967   *The Message of the Old Testament.* Exeter: Pat-
                         ernoster.

Hasel, Gerhard F.
 1975   *Old Testament Theology: Basic Issues in the Cur-
                         rent Debate.* 2nd ed. Grand Rapids: Eerdmans.

Harris, R. Laird
 1971   *God's Eternal Creation: A Study of Old Testa-
                         ment Culture.* Chicago: Moody.

Harrison, R. K.
 1969   *Introduction to the Old Testament.* Grand Rap-
                         ids: Eerdmans.

Heschel, Abraham J.
 1962   *The Prophets.* 2 vols. New York: Harper and
                         Row.

Jacob, Edmond
 1958   *Theology of the Old Testament.* New York:
                         Harper and Row.

Kaiser, Walter C.
 1972   *Classical Evangelical Essays in Old Testament
                         Interpretation.* Grand Rapids: Baker.
 1978   *Toward an Old Testament Theology.* Grand Rap-
                         ids: Zondervan.

Keel, Othmar
 1978   *The Symbolism of the Biblical World: Ancient
                         Near Eastern Iconography and the Book of
                         Psalms.* New York: Seabury.

Kidner Derek
 1964   *The Proverbs.* London: Tyndale.
 1967   *Genesis.* London: Tyndale.
 1972   *Hard Sayings: The Challenge of Old Testament
                         Morals.* London: Inter-Varsity.
 1976   *A Time to Mourn, and a Time to Dance.* Down-
                         ers Grove, Ill.: InterVarsity.

Kitchen, K. A.
1966   *Ancient Orient and Old Testament.* London·
                        Tyndale.

Kline, Meredith G.
1963   *The Treaty of the Great King.* Grand Rapids:
                        Eerdmans.
1968   *By Oath Consigned.* Grand Rapids: Eerdmans.
1972   *The Structure of Biblical Authority.* Grand Rap-
                        ids: Eerdmans.

Koehler, Ludwig
1957   *Old Testament Theology.* London: Lutterworth.

Kraus, Hans Joachim
1966   *Worship in Israel; A Cultic History of the Old
                        Testament.* Richmond: John Knox.

Lindblom, Johannes
1972   *Prophecy in Ancient Israel.* Philadelphia: For-
                        tress.

McCarthy, D. J.
1972   *Old Testament Covenant: A Survey of Current
                        Opinions.* Richmond: John Knox.

McKenzie, John L.
1976   *A Theology of the Old Testament.* New York:
                        Doubleday.

Mendenhall, George E.
1954   "Ancient Oriental and Biblical Law." *Biblical
                        Archaeologist* 17, No. 2, 26-46.
                        "Covenant Forms in Israelite Tradition." *Bibli-
                        cal Archaeologist* 17, No. 3, 50-76.
1962   "Covenant." IDB, I, 714-23.

Morris, Leon
1955   *Apostolic Preaching of the Cross.* Grand Rapids:
                        Eerdmans.
1960   *The Biblical Doctrine of Judgment.* Grand Rap-
                        ids: Eerdmans.

Mowinckel, Sigmund
1962   *The Psalms in Israel's Worship.* Nashville:
                        Abingdon.

Murray, John
    1957   *Principles of Conduct*. Grand Rapids: Eerdmans.

Nicholson, E. W.
    1967   *Deuteronomy and Tradition*. Philadelphia: Fortress.

Oehler, Gustav F.
    1880 (1875)   *Theology of the Old Testament*. 2 vols. Edinburgh: T. & T. Clark.

Pannenberg, W., ed.
    1968   *Revelation as History*. New York: Macmillan.

Payne, J. Barton
    1962   *The Theology of the Older Testament*. Grand Rapids: Zondervan.

Payne, J. Barton, ed.
    1970   *New Perspectives on the Old Testament*. Waco, Tex.: Word.

Pedersen, J.
    1926   *Israel: Its Life and Culture*. 4 vols. Oxford: Oxford Univ. Press.

Pritchard, J. B., ed.
    1955   *Ancient Near Eastern Texts* (ANET). Princeton: Princeton Univ. Press.

Rad, Gerhard von
    1961   *Genesis: A Commentary*. Philadelphia: Westminster.
    1962   *Old Testament Theology*. 2 vols. New York: Harper and Row.
    1972   *Wisdom in Israel*. Nashville: Abingdon.

Richardson, Alan, ed.
    1950   *Theological Wordbook of the Bible*. New York: Macmillan.

Ringgren, Helmer
    1966   *Israelite Religion*. Philadelphia: Fortress.

Robinson, H. Wheeler
    1913   *The Religious Ideas of the Old Testament*. London: Duckworth.

1946   *Inspiration and Revelation in the Old Testament.* Oxford: Oxford Univ. Press.

Rowley, H. H., ed.
1951   *The Old Testament and Modern Study.* Oxford: Oxford Univ. Press.

Ruler, A. A. van
1971   *The Christian Church and the Old Testament.* Grand Rapids: Eerdmans.

Snaith, N. H.
1964   *The Distinctive Ideas of the Old Testament.* New York: Schocken.

Spriggs, D. G.
1974   *Two Old Testament Theologies: A Comparative Evaluation of the Contributions of Eichrodt and Von Rad.* London: SCM.

Thomas, D. Winton, ed.
1958   *Documents from Old Testament Times* (DOTT). New York: Harper and Row.

Vaux, Roland de
1965   *Ancient Israel.* 2 vols. New York: McGraw Hill.

Vos, Gerhardus
1948   *Biblical Theology: Old and New Testaments.* Grand Rapids: Eerdmans.

Vriezen, Theo. C.
1970   *An Outline of Old Testament Theology.* 2nd ed. Newton, Mass.: Charles T. Branford.

Westermann, Claus, ed.
1963   *Essays on Old Testament Hermeneutics.* Atlanta: John Knox.

Wolff, H. W.
1974   *Anthropology of the Old Testament.* Philadelphia: Fortress.

Wood, Leon
1970   *A Survey of Israel's History.* Grand Rapids: Zondervan.

Wright, G. E.
    1950   *The Old Testament against Its Environment.*
                             London: SCM.
    1952   *The God Who Acts.* London: SCM.

Young, Edward J.
    1952   *My Servants the Prophets.* Grand Rapids: Eerd-
                             mans.
    1959   *The Study of Old Testament Theology Today.*
                             New York: Revell.

Youngblood, Ronald
    1971   *The Heart of the Old Testament.* Grand Rapids:
                             Baker.

Zimmerli, Walther
    1978   *Old Testament Theology in Outline.* Atlanta:
                             John Knox.

Scripture Index

(Only those passages actually discussed or those crucial to the discussion are listed. Page numbers following book names indicate discussion of the book as a whole.)

Old Testament

Genesis
1:1 *64-65*
1:2-3 *65, 203*
1:26-30 *67-68, 79, 81, 83, 175, 234*
1:31 *67, 99*
2:2-3 *51, 74, 175*
2:7-8 *65, 79, 202, 240*
2:15 *175*
2:16-17 *99-101, 176, 238*
2:19-20 *80*
2:22-25 *81*
3:1-7 *101-2*
3:8-9 *26*
3:14-19 *102-3*
3:15 *58, 116, 227-28*
3:17-18 *80*
3:19 *237*
4:6, 9-10 *27*
4:15 *116*
6:3 *203, 238*
6:5 *107, 109*
6:18 *116*
9:4-6 *92, 116, 177*
9:13 *117*
12:1-3 *27, 82, 227*
15 *27-28, 117-18*
15:6 *162*
15:8-11, 17 *152*
17 *27-28, 117-18*
17:10-14 *118, 151-52*
18:14 *50*
18:22-23 *232*
20:7 *212*
22 *156*
24:42-44 *165*
26:9-10 *177*
28:13 *28-29*
28:17 *50*
35:2 *152*
49:9-10 *228*

Exodus
3 *30-31, 212*
3:5 *52*
3:15 *118*
4:22 *177*
6:1-2 *32-33*
6:3 *46*
12:21-27 *144*
12:35-36 *182*
15 *64*
15:2, 6 *50, 228*
15:11 *53*
15:16b *64*
15:18 *47*
19:3-6 *33-34, 119, 129, 242*
19:8 *115*
19:17 *152*
20—23 *115-16*
20:1-17 *131-32*
20:1-2 *33-34, 173*
20:7 *45, 166, 177*
20:8-11 *64, 177*
20:12 *177-78*
20:13-15 *178-79*
20:16 *179*
20:17 *180*
20:20-21 *162*
20:24 *144*
21—23 *130, 132*
21:2 *180*
22:31 *52*
23:12 *150*
23:14-15 *148*
23:16 *149-50*
31:3 *203*
33:18-23 *34*
34:5-10 *35*
35:31 *203*

Leviticus
1:4 *153-54*
2 *155*
4:33 *154*
5:6 *106*
7:11-18 *155*
11:44 *174*

16   *150*
17:11   *153-54*
19:18   *139*
19:34   *181*
23:5   *148*
23:39-43   *150*
24:22   *181*

Numbers
11:17, 25   *203*
13   *153*
14   *146*
16:22   *203*
19:11-13   *153*
23:19   *44*
24:2, 9, 13   *204*
28:26-31   *149*

Deuteronomy
1:17   *235*
4:8   *133*
5:6-21   *131-32*
5:12-15   *150*
6:4   *49, 93*
6:5   *139, 163*
7:7-9   *164*
11:13, 22   *164*
12—26   *132*
16:9-12   *149*
16:13   *150*
17:8—26:19   *137*
18:9-22   *213-14*
20   *183*
21:1-9   *108*
23:3, 6   *182*
26:5-10   *82*
26:27   *139*
27:11-26   *151*
29:3-4   *91*
30:15-19   *238*
31:24-26   *130*
32:6   *64*
32:39   *238*
32:46-47   *173*
33:27   *48*

Joshua
5:10-12   *148*

6:17   *182*
7:16-18   *82*
8:30-35   *151*
24   *115, 214*
24:15   *82, 139*

1 Samuel
3:10-14   *36*
6:19-20   *52*
7:5-11   *156*
8:5, 7   *57*
10:1, 6   *204, 215*
16:14-16   *204*
17:45   *46*
24:13   *190*

2 Samuel
7:12   *57*
7:12-17   *120-21, 228*
14:2   *190*
22:51   *233*

1 Kings   *120*
8:29   *147*
11:29-39   *214*
12:19   *106*
13:33-34   *120*
18:21   *49*
19:18   *205, 232*
20:11   *190*
22:21-23   *204*

2 Kings
2:9, 15   *205*
17:22-23   *120*
18:1-8   *220*
22—23   *220*
23   *123*

1 Chronicles   *121*
22:9-10   *121*

2 Chronicles
20:14   *216*

Nehemiah
9:20, 30   *208*
9:32-33, 38   *123*

10:29   *137*

Job
7:12   *69*
12:13   *194*
19:23, 25-26   *241*
26:7   *66*
36:6   *106*
40:6-14   *193*

Psalms
1:1-5   *130, 139*
2:7   *122, 233*
8   *83, 234*
13:3   *238*
16:10-11   *239-40*
19:1   *167*
19:2-4   *75*
19:9   *235*
23   *240*
24:7-10   *47*
26:1   *163*
36:9   *240*
37:3-7   *163*
40:6, 8   *93*
45:6   *233*
49:15   *239*
50:2   *168*
51:4   *105*
51:5   *107*
51:7, 10   *153*
51:11   *205*
62   *240*
73:26   *240*
74:13-14   *69-70*
76:10   *57*
79:6   *183*
88   *236*
89:3-4   *120*
94:8-11   *168*
96:10, 12-13   *237*
102:7   *82*
104:31, 35   *68*
110:1   *233*
111:10   *162*
116:12   *156*
119:137   *54*
122:1   *148*

130:7-8   *158*
144:2   *58*
145:10-12   *194*

Proverbs
1:21   *192*
2:1-5   *193-94*
2:6   *195*
3:5-6   *172*
3:19   *194*
8   *198-99*
8:13   *192*
8:34   *192*
9:17-18   *197*
11:30   *241*
13:20   *192*
14:15   *196*
16:33   *194*
22:17-19   *191*
23:10   *191*
26:11   *196*
29:14, 16   *198*
30:24-28   *195*

Ecclesiastes
2:12-19   *198*
3:11   *198*
7:13, 23-25   *193*
9:4   *238*
11:1-9   *193*
12:1   *193*
12:7   *202*

Song of Solomon   *82*

Isaiah
1:4   *218*
1:11-15   *218-19*
2:2-4   *140, 222*
2:11   *234*
4:4   *208*
6:1-5   *36, 217*
6:3   *147, 167*
7:14   *233*
9   *231*
9:7   *55*
10:24-27   *220*
11   *231*

11:1, 10   *233*
11:6-9   *71, 80, 234*
14:12-21   *69*
14:26   *223*
25:8   *242*
26:19   *240*
28:5-6   *206*
28:16   *223*
30:15-18   *224*
31:3   *44, 202*
32:11-12, 15   *208*
40:4-5   *168*
40:6, 8   *88*
42:8   *51*
42:1, 6   *122, 232*
43:19   *228*
43:22-25   *158*
43:27   *106*
45:1   *233*
45:18   *49*
49:1-6   *232*
50:4-9   *232*
51:9   *69*
52:8   *231*
52:13—53:12   *232*
53   *158-59, 174, 185*

Jeremiah
1   *217*
4:8   *220-21*
5:12   *218*
5:13   *206*
6:16-21   *220*
7:4   *147, 218, 230*
7:5, 7   *230*
18:18   *190*
26:16-19   *220*
31:31-34   *122-23, 141,*
  169, 207, 234
33:25-26   *76*

Lamentations
3:21-23   *235*

Ezekiel
1—2   *217*
1:12-14   *202*
7:10   *229*

8—11   *221*
11:19   *207-8*
18:32   *239*
28:11-15   *67*
33:30-33   *137*
36:22   *230*
36:26-27   *208, 234*
37:5-10   *202, 234*
39:29   *207*

Daniel
4:27   *56*
7:13-14   *234*
9:25-26   *233*
12:2   *240, 242*

Hosea
2:19   *234*
6:6   *125*
11:1-3   *59, 219*

Joel
2:28-29   *87, 207*

Amos
3:1-2   *219, 224*
3:12   *232*
5   *228*
5:20   *228*
5:21   *145*
5:21-25   *218-19*
7:10   *217*
7:14-15   *217*

Jonah
1:1-3   *222*
3:3   *222*
4:11   *222*

Micah
3:9-12   *220*
6:8   *125, 185, 236*

Habakkuk   *221*
3:17-18   *221*

Zephaniah
2:3   *232*

3:12-13   *232*

Haggai
2:11-13   *130*

Zechariah
4:6, 10   *208*
8:16   *236*
14:5-9   *234*

Malachi
2:6-7   *130*
3:6   *44*
4:5   *215*

Apocrypha

Ecclesiasticus (Sirach)
51:23   *192*

1 Enoch   *186, 229*

New Testament

Matthew
5—7   *186*
5:17   *140*
5:20   *56*
17:5   *213*
22:37-40   *173*

Mark
7:13   *138*
10:45   *185*

Luke
1:46-55   *231*
23:34   *184*

John
4:24   *47*
4:25   *213*
7:17   *172*
7:40-41   *213*
12:31-32   *237*
14—16   *201*
14:1-3   *241*

Acts
2   *149, 201*
2:16   *87*
2:16-21   *208*

Romans
2:4   *75*
5:12-21   *104*
8:3   *89*
8:16   *87*
8:19-22   *80*
8:28   *68*

1 Corinthians
2:8-9   *57*
10   *18*

Galatians
3:24   *52*
6:7   *241*

Ephesians
5:2   *154*

Colossians
1:15-17   *199*

1 Timothy
4:4   *94*

Hebrews
4:9-10   *74*
10:5   *93*

James
1:15   *107*
2:10   *173*

1 Peter
3:8-10   *184*

2 Peter
3:9   *75*

1 John
1:1-3   *93*

Jude
14   *229*

Revelation
14:8   *55*